LOVE & WAR
IN LONDON

LOVE & WAR
IN LONDON

OLIVIA COCKETT

Edited by Robert Malcolmson

The
History
Press

This edition first published 2008
Published by arrangement with Wilfrid Laurier University Press

The History Press Ltd
The Mill, Brimscombe Port
Stroud, Gloucestershire, GL5 2QG
www.thehistorypress.co.uk

British Library Cataloguing in Publication Data.
A catalogue record for this book is available from the British Library.

ISBN 978 0 7524 4409 3

Typesetting and origination by The History Press Ltd
Printed and bound in Great Britain

Contents

Preface & Introduction

The central source for this book is the World War Two diary of Olivia Cockett, who was born in 1912 and grew up and lived in London. She wrote this diary for the research organization Mass-Observation (M-O)—its work is discussed below, mainly in the introduction and appendix—and the original manuscript is preserved in the Mass-Observation Archive at the University of Sussex. Olivia Cockett started her diary in August 1939, continued with it for much of 1940, wrote only irregularly in 1941 and 1942, and ended it conclusively in October 1942, when she turned thirty. In addition to her diary, she also sent M-O a number of "Directive Replies." These were her responses to M-O's monthly, sometimes open-ended questionnaires to its volunteer participants, which were referred to as "Directives." Her responses to these Directives are linked to her diary at appropriate places.

Olivia Cockett also kept private journals—three in total (one very short)—which are held by her niece, Hilary Munday. Almost all of these writings predate late 1940. Whenever this material is referred to below, it is clearly distinguished from the material in the Mass-Observation Archive.

I have also offered a number of extracts from other diarists who were writing in 1940–41, and whose comments and observations about wartime England can be connected to, and amplify, those of Olivia Cockett. The words of these other diarists, all of them women, are found mainly at two points in the diary: February 1940 and September 1940. Quotations from other contemporary sources, such as newspapers and J.B. Priestley's Postscripts (1940), help on occasion to clarify or enlarge upon matters mentioned by Olivia Cockett herself.

The following text represents a complete and unabridged transcription of Olivia Cockett's diary-writing for Mass-Observation between October 1939 and October 1942. While she sometimes typed her diary, it is mostly handwritten, and her script is not always easy to decipher. Her writing, though, is largely free of errors and obscurities, for she valued highly clear, precise prose. However, almost any personal diary (diaries are often composed in haste) includes a few obvious mistakes, such as a typo or a word missing a letter, and when these occur I have made corrections silently. My main interventions have related to punctuation, paragraphing, capitalization, and consistency in usage. Most personal diaries are, in some respects, punctuated whimsically, and Olivia's diary is no exception. She also capitalized a lot of words that would now not be capitalized (e.g., "News"), and a few words, such as "War," were sometimes capitalized, sometimes not. Small numbers (less than 10) were on some occasions written as words, on other occasions as numerals. My editorial goal on all such matters has been consistency and clarity. Thus, for example, small numbers are consistently presented as words except when they refer to clock time. I have not in any way tampered with the substance of Olivia Cockett's writings or deliberately omitted any words from her M-O diary during these three years. Her "Directive Replies," by contrast, have been used selectively, depending on their relevance to the diary, as have her private diaries and other personal papers not in the Mass-Observation Archive.

England during the Second World War had a pre-decimal currency, of which only the pound sterling (£) still exists. There were twenty shillings in one pound (20s = £1) and twelve pence in one shilling (12d = 1s). In 1939 Olivia Cockett's annual salary was £160—that is, about £3 1s per week—and she seems to have spent almost all of it for basic sustenance. Wages and salaries tended to rise during the war, but so too did taxes and the cost of some goods and services, assuming that they were available, which they often weren't. An expenditure of, say, two shillings represented one-thirtieth of Olivia's pre-tax weekly salary.

I am happy to acknowledge the help I have received from a number of people. One person who has been a major—indeed, vital—source of support for this project is Dorothy Sheridan, head of Special Collections and director of the Mass-Observation Archive at the University of Sussex. Her help was especially important in 1999–2000, when I began and pursued much of my archival research for this book. She offered some good suggestions, led me to related sources, and facilitated my research from abroad in various practical ways. She also contacted Hilary Munday, Olivia Cockett's niece, advising her of my work on her aunt's diary, and thus initiated a very happy relationship that I have enjoyed with the Cockett family. Olivia's brother, Freddie, invited me to lunch in February 2000 at his home in Petts Wood, Kent, where I met some other members of his family and was able to question them about Olivia's life. Since that time the support of Hilary Munday has been especially crucial. She inherited her aunt's personal papers and has given me full access to this material, some of which I have used at key points in this edition. I am deeply indebted to Hilary and her husband, David Munday, for their encouragement, advice, and generosity. Olivia's nephew, Mike Cockett, kindly sent me two photographs of his aunt, including the one on this book's cover, and responded helpfully to a draft of the epilogue. Danielle Bylfield, Mike Cockett's daughter, knew Olivia, her great aunt, from the 1960s and showed a keen interest in some of the literary and psychological dimensions of Olivia's writings. I am grateful to Danielle for her insights and thoughtful reflections.

I wish to acknowledge as well the assistance I received from several other people, notably Joy Eldridge at the Mass-Observation Archive, Jackson Armstrong, John Coulter, Patricia Malcolmson, Jennifer Grek Martin, Debbie Stirton-Massey, and Judy Vanhooser. Cathy Dickison was responsible for producing a final polished typescript, and I thank her warmly for her efficient and friendly support. I am also indebted to the Advisory Research Committee at Queen's University for timely financial support of my research in England.

Robert Malcolmson, Cobourg, Ontario.

"On the whole I prefer life to be bracing rather than relaxing."
—*Olivia Cockett, October 6, 1934*

In the 1930s, Olivia Cockett, a young Londoner, kept a private journal that was intended only for the eyes of her lover. Their love was passionately intense but unfavoured by circumstances, for he was married and a divorce seemed unlikely. They met each other furtively, and these meetings were fleeting. The strains of keeping their relationship alive were sometimes acute and often tested their composure. They succeeded, however; and on September 14, 1935, when Olivia was coming up to her twenty-third birthday and her love affair had already survived for some five years, she wrote of it in the following words. It is, she thought, "a strong growth; a shoot of Romance; a challenge to Hitler. It keeps alive a tradition of Love for love's sake which might otherwise die."

Here, in her mind, was an intersecting of personal and public realities. The private, intimate world of erotic love was set against the brute force of Hitler's aggressions. The "hearts" of two individuals, she thought—her own and her lover's—were kept "green" through love, and this was not a colour much associated with the Nazis. Olivia Cockett was testifying in these reflections to a collision of sensibilities, and to a clash between the external world of coercive politics and the inner world of feeling and fulfillment. Most of the time, for her, the deeper meanings of life were to be found within herself, and they were pursued though reading, listening to music, contemplating the natural world, and being with people she loved. She also loved books, and she was entranced by words and what they could create. She found poetry more appealing than, for example, political journalism. While she followed public events and was committed to social reform, she wrote mainly about her own emotions. The youthful self that she portrays, a self in the making, developing and maturing up to the age of thirty, is the centrepiece of her diaries.

Olivia Cockett's diaries are vibrant and engaging. She discloses a lot about herself, and is candid about her frustrations, pleasures, worries, and self-doubts. She records her mood swings and tries to understand them. And she is often observant about what she sees and hears in her daily life from 1939 to 1941, as she and her lover, family, friends, and fellow workers are swept up by the momentous events of yet another European war. Prior to 1939 almost all her writing is in the form of private diaries. From August 1939 most of her diary-writing was produced for Mass-Observation, the remarkable organization established in 1937 to conduct a sort of anthropology of everyday life in contemporary Britain. Mass-Observation's goal was to create a "social anthropology of ourselves," and Olivia Cockett was one of *hundreds of British citizens who contributed voluntarily—some for only a month or two, others for several months, others for years—to this project of self-study and self-observation. (See the appendix for a brief account of Mass-Observation's early work.)*

People wrote and still write diaries for all sorts of reasons and with many different results. They write because they are lonely and need a "friend" to talk to. They may write as a means of self-exploration, and perhaps to vent feelings that would otherwise be bottled up. Perhaps they write to give some order to their thoughts, or to keep a record of their own experiences. Some diarists are introspective and self-disclosing; others write more as chroniclers of the incidents and events in their lives. While a few diarists may write entirely for themselves, with no expectation that their diaries will ever be read by anyone else—indeed, these diarists usually take pains to ensure secrecy—many (probably most) know or expect or hope that at least one other pair of eyes will someday see what they have written. Diarists may not start writing with others in mind, but they often move in this direction, away from an exclusively private orientation. There is, then, often something of a public dimension even to very personal journals.

Diary-writing was not, of course, for everyone. Many people who started a diary gave up quickly. Others wrote only intermittently. Some 475 wartime diaries are held in the M-O Archive, but many are very brief; only a minority represent sustained, uninterrupted writing over a period of at least two years. Conscientious diary-keeping was demanding, and many well-intentioned people found that as their lives unfolded, with wartime bringing various unexpected challenges, they had neither the time nor the energy for daily writing, and M-O heard from them no more. Or perhaps they got bored with what they came to see as repetitive and banal reporting of everyday events. Some M-O participants warmed readily to their tasks; others did not. One married couple in their mid-twenties, living in Leeds in late 1939, testified to a contrast of just this sort. On November 27, 1939, the husband admitted that "writing a diary does not come at all naturally to me, and it requires an effort akin to work to do it. My wife on the other hand jots down all her thoughts throughout the day in shorthand as easily as you like; and then can type them out as quickly as you can imagine, and I envy her very much."[1]

The blending of the private and the public was a crucial feature of many wartime diaries, including those composed for Mass-Observation. These diaries were designed in part to be public documents, for once or twice a month their authors mailed what they had written to the M-O headquarters, where M-O staff would read and analyze the submissions. While a degree of confidentiality and anonymity was promised, diarists clearly wrote for an audience, and what they said was sometimes cited or quoted (anonymously) in M-O's own publications, such as War Begins at Home *(1940), which documented the public mood in Britain in the last third of 1939. Many M-O diarists felt that they were making their own modest contributions to a much larger project—a project that was intended to help ordinary citizens to better understand themselves and their society. Diarists saw themselves—and were encouraged in this by M-O—as observers both of their own lives and the lives of others. Certainly, Mass-Observation was a project informed by democratic and egalitarian impulses. Moreover, M-O's attentiveness to commonplace events in life appealed particularly to women, many of whom felt intellectually devalued in 1930s England. M-O offered them, as Angus Calder and Dorothy Sheridan have remarked, "a means of self-expression…in keeping with women's traditional skills and inclinations," such as writing letters and social observation. Mass-Observation's "insistence on the importance of the details of everyday life and the value of recording even the mundane and routine activities gave a new status to the daily preoccupations of most women engaged in housework and childcare."²*

Mass-Observation championed openness and inclusiveness. It fostered communication among people who would otherwise have known nothing about each other's feelings and attitudes and thus brought to light commonalties (and some differences) that would previously have remained concealed.³ To write for M-O was to participate in an intellectual community—a sort of open university years before any such formal institution came into existence. The M-O diarists commonly had the feeling that, by portraying their everyday selves, they were producing raw data both for current generalizations about social experience and for posterity's knowledge about the Britain in which they were living. People participating in Mass-Observation were made to feel valued and useful. Frequently they were encouraged by communications from

M-O headquarters to keep up their good work. With another war looming ominously on the horizon in 1939 and then in September breaking out, those who agreed to keep diaries were also aware that they were documenting lives lived in extraordinary times. Every voice, every perception or insight, it was thought, was or might be worth hearing. Each subjective point of view was credited with its own authenticity. Each individual's experiences of the war would help to inform the nation's awareness of its own diverse history as it was actually being made, and not just the history of the governing class. "I feel that I must write in my diary regularly these days," wrote a woman in her mid-thirties, a mother of three children, on May 15, 1940, as German troops were over-running much of Western Europe and Winston Churchill was in his first week as Britain's wartime leader; "things are happening so quickly and one feels that one has a seat in the front row of the stalls at the making of history."[4]

While diarists for Mass-Observation were encouraged to talk about matters that would be amenable (broadly) to sociological generalizations— the blackout, rationing, transport, morale, sources of information, topics of conversation—a few writers who were psychologically inclined also gave a lot of attention to emotions, mainly their own, and to their own reflections and ruminations. These diaries are marked by a good deal of self-disclosure and self-examination. They are the products of introspective personalities; they are the works of people who were moved to probe their own states of mind; and the best of these diaries were produced by people who liked to write and often had some experience with writing.

Olivia Cockett was intellectually inclined from an early age. She received her secondary education at Haberdashers' Aske's, a school for girls in New Cross, southeast London, and passed her General School Examination in June 1929. She then worked briefly at the Times Book Club *and the New Education Fellowship Library—early signs of her intellectual leanings and love of books—before joining the civil service in February 1930 at the age of seventeen.*[5] *As a teenager, she had written for her own satisfaction (including accounts of the books she had read), and from the age of nineteen she produced, in an intermittent fashion, more than 250 handwritten pages of private journals, prior to embarking on a diary for Mass-Observation in*

August 1939, when she was twenty-six. So, in her mid-twenties, she was not new to diary-keeping; and when she had time and solitude she liked to put words to paper. Writing, for her, was not a struggle; words came easily to her and they enhanced her pleasure in living. "To me the apt word adds to any experience," she wrote in her private diary on July 1939. "Adds positively. I mean, it heightens joys and lessens sorrows."

Personal satisfactions were, unsurprisingly, put in jeopardy by war, and while much of Olivia Cockett's diary is concerned with the European crisis and its impact on her own life and the lives of those around her, war was not always at the centre of her consciousness. She had her own life to lead. She had a job to do, friends to see, books to read, parents to share space with, a baby nephew to admire, and a lover to meet. Certain realities of wartime were inescapable, but she was not war-obsessed. Indeed, one of the merits of her writing is that it reminds us that each Englishwoman in wartime had her own personal inclinations and priorities, and that these individual tendencies, preferences, and habits coexisted with and adapted to the abnormalities of living in wartime, especially during the startling dislocations of 1940–41 in greater London. War, for Olivia, was important but not all-consuming, and she responded to it in various ways—with fright, with stoicism, with boredom, with courage. Frequently her main objective in her diary was to portray her own physical, emotional, and attitudinal reactions to the new dangers that she and almost everybody else were suddenly having to face. For while Olivia was interested in the facts of living in wartime, she was interested more in the feelings *of wartime, the feelings of others as well as herself.*

A central merit of Olivia Cockett's personal writings between 1939 and 1941 is that they vividly reveal a multi-layered existence in which private and public experiences were closely entangled; an existence of common threats experienced in individual ways; an existence of pronounced mood swings and vascillating emotions; an existence that embraced both the mundane details of daily routine (including the jolts to these routines) and the prospect of violent death—for many were bound to die prematurely—and the need to take special steps to survive these extraordinary dangers. Olivia Cockett was sensitive to the ordinary as well as the extraordinary. She noticed a lot, she recorded a variety of observations, and she rarely repeated herself. At one moment she was focused on the public world "out there," in the streets or in Waterloo Station, in her place of work, or (when the German bombers attacked) in the sky above London. At another moment she was attending to her baby nephew or to the flowers on her dresser, or she was concerned about the safety of her mother or father or lover. In wartime, and certainly in London in 1940–41, the line between the public and the private blurred somewhat. This was a major feature of total war. It swept people up, often unwillingly, even as it left most of them with enough private space to carry on with many of their pre-war outlooks and relationships.

For Olivia Cockett a major impulse for writing was to record, not life's routines but rather the specialness of wartime existence as she experienced it. She did not like to go over the same ground again and again, ploddingly, repetitiously. Rather, she liked to explore, to be active, to be stimulated. From mid-1939 until late 1941 there was much to say, for there were many novelties, crises, and upheavals. Olivia's writings during these two years are informed by a definite narrative power. There is a dynamic and self-reflective quality to her life story, as it unfolded bumpily and unpredictably. Indeed, it was probably her sensitivity to the twists and turns and tribulations of her life that gave her much of her drive to write, sometimes very revealingly. Then, in 1941–42, when these dislocations were ironed out and a routine of sorts took hold, she did not try to keep on writing. Rather, she signed off—and at a moment of significant self-recognition, on the occasion of her thirtieth birthday. She was then to move on with her life. For her, one chapter of living had drawn to a close.

What is presented here to us is a two-year slice of one sensitive person's life, which coincided with one of the most critical periods of Britain's history, indeed, of modern world history. Olivia Cockett began her diary for Mass-Observation just as war was about to be declared. She was most keenly involved in diary-writing during those critical and momentous months of mid-1940, a period of crisis for which no precedents existed in Britain's past. And she wound her diary down a year or so later, a time that happened to coincide with a new phase of the war (the Eastern front, the active involvement of the United States, and the cessation for a while of intensive bombing of London). What we have in her diary is a vivid rendering of a portion of one woman's experience, addressed, mainly though not entirely, to the here-and-now, and highlighting the sentiments of the moment. Since these experiences were those of a perceptive, energetic, free-thinking personality who read widely and had her own way with words, she was able to construct her "ordinary" life in a manner that is evocative both of her own character and of her times. We, as readers, are allowed to engage and perhaps even identify with her struggles, her satisfactions, her confusions, her self-questionings, and her efforts to find an anchor for her life.

A Note on Sources

All references to sources held in the Mass-Observation Archive at the University of Sussex are presented in brackets within the text. Material from M-O diarists other than Olivia Cockett are identified not by name but rather by the number assigned to the diarist; material generated in response to the monthly "Directives" is identified by the different numbers assigned to these "Directive Respondents" (DR) and the month and year in which the particular Directive, or what we might now call an open-ended questionnaire or prompt, was circulated. Most other references, both to the primary and secondary sources, are presented in the notes at the end of this book.

War in Name Only

October 1939–April 1940

In the late summer of 1939, as political tensions in Europe mounted and war seemed increasingly likely, numerous people began to keep, or resumed keeping, a diary. As alarming events were unfolding, a significant number of people responded to the crisis by writing of their lives and their feelings and describing what was going on around them. Olivia Cockett was one of these people. She started her diary for Mass-Observation in August 1939, when she was twenty-six years old, living in Brockley, southeast London (SE4, in the borough of Deptford), at 33 Breakspears Road, and working as a payroll clerk in New Scotland Yard.

London, then the world's largest city with a population of some eight million people, was already on a war footing, and Londoners were gearing up, psychologically and in all sorts of practical ways, to defend themselves against an enemy attack that seemed more and more inevitable, perhaps even imminent.[1] Olivia Cockett's diary, in late August and early September 1939, recorded many of the sentiments and sudden changes in everyday life that were reported by hundreds of other Englishwomen at that time. There was the heightening sense of anxiety during the last week of August, after the news of the Nazi–Soviet Non-Aggression Pact. There were new intrusions into people's daily routines, such as the requirement to black out windows at night—"having blacked windows with curtains, feel stupid and bewildered," Olivia wrote in late August—and there were plans for the evacuation and relocation of families and offices, with consequent major upheavals in civilian lives. Newscasts were eagerly devoured. Younger men expected to be called up by the Armed Forces any day. Some families prepared air-raid shelters. Private cars displayed "Air Defence Priority" labels on their windscreens, according to Olivia's diary for August 31. The face of London was conspicuously changing: "Walking through Oxford Street to Holborn," on August 30, Olivia "saw many buildings sandbagged and windows shuttered." On September 1 she "Felt weepy at seeing groups of children with their bundles [they were being evacuated to the provinces]. Mothers being very very brave, few breaking down."

Olivia reported (sometimes minutely) on her own feelings and what she saw of the feelings of those with whom she had contact, at work, at home, and while travelling. "Some exaggerated cheerfulness, singing etc., among junior clerks," she noted on Wednesday, August 30. "Few people will talk of the facts in a reasonable, broad-viewed way. They get irritated. But they will swap wild rumours and make spiteful suggestions for as long as you like." As for her own emotions that day, "Found myself 'snapping'—first observed sign of nerves. Have stronger desire for lovemaking—may be full moon. Am eating more than usual—two cream donuts today along with tea; usually nothing." The next day, Thursday, August 31, she noticed a more positive mood in the office. "There's a marked rise in the 'kindness' in the atmosphere. Small jokes and 'Please and Thank You' and mistakes quickly explained away and apologies easily tendered and accepted." Almost everyone wondered at the end of August what would happen in the potentially explosive world of high politics, and speculation was rife. On Thursday, August 31 Olivia felt "quite certain all will blow over after he [Hitler] is given something at someone else's expense." Appeasement, however, was now a discredited policy. Germany's attack on Poland that night brought Britain to the brink of armed conflict, and Olivia spent the next night, Friday, September 1, in a restless state.

Friday, September 1 1939

Mother went to bed and I continued to search the ether [short-wave radio] and picked up various world reactions. Felt very depressed at the war atmosphere. Got some milk to drink and went to bed and read mathematics[2] till I couldn't keep my eyes open. But the minute I tried to sleep I was fully awake again. Lay imagining horrors and noises. Switched light on and realized I had removed blackout curtain. Felt so disgusted with world didn't bother to put it up again. Had diarrhoea most of the night and was glad to get up early and bath.

Sunday, September 3, was, unusually, not a day of rest. Olivia was required to report for work, and to new premises, for her office was being evacuated from central London to a school in Putney, much farther to the west of her home. She offered a detailed account of this day.

Sunday, September 3

3 pm. I wonder how the moths will get on with so few lights to fly to.

Last night the thunderstorm woke us all up and we walked round the house to see if we were all alright. Inevitably we thought of raids, as Dad and Son [her brother Freddie, aged twenty-five] are on duty all night. I slept well till 7:30 after the storm but Mother slept only between 4 and 5. Got up and played with baby Michael [her nephew, born February 1938] over breakfast and left for new HQ at 8:45. Got lift part of the way. My travel time and fares will be doubled. Very annoying. Arrived on time and found place in uproar. Workmen still adapting all over the place. No stuff arrived. Got school desks in position to work at—will be comic to see senior fat men at them. Another girl and I wandered off to try and buy some milk. Got back with some just in time to hear end of PM's speech. WAR. Silence and general air of, "Well, that's that." Then the Warning at once. Vague confusion but no panic as no one knew what or where. Several of us got to the basement, but felt silly standing watching the workmen getting on with the job. So went back upstairs and worked. Was able to shout the All Clear to several who stayed. Felt pleased that I was not frightened, but I probably shall be when there are real bangs. Sweated carrying goods up three flights of stairs from the lorries. Damn mad to hear that one man had borrowed a byke and gone off to his sister who lived near—missed most of the heavy work. Went to the nearest pub at midday and sat in the garden with a shandy and my own sandwiches. Back to more sweat as we made some tea.

Then asked to go as my things were in order. Not very popular but given permission. Tore off to rendezvous with Friend on Common. Not there. Sat and enjoyed the sun and breeze and scribbled some of these notes. Plenty of people in Sunday clothes taking a stroll, many with gas masks in boxes. I am now carrying my service mask all the time.

Still can't take it in as real, this war.

Guess Friend has gone to office. Ring up and get him with difficulty. Arrange he will call. He has tried to ring me but new phones are not in order. Get home and play with baby on lawn. Lovely romp in the sun. Mother was alone with him and was scared at raid. I change into cooler clothes and stick up a few brown strips on Mother's windows—more for something to do, really. Then put up winter curtains at my own. Listen to 6 o'clock news. Am disgusted to hear the Cabinet have several First War ministers. What a waste of time it all is. Same men, same policy, same mistakes.

Friend comes. Tired, fed up, hates being separated from me. Chats to parents over a cup of tea, fairly cheerfully, but is very dismal when we are alone. Goes at 7:30.

I do some more to windows, leaving all the bits about untidily; unusual. Sister-in-law learns that Mother cannot see in gas mask without glasses and decides must stay home with baby. Tells Chief. I get German news in English. Call parents. It is mirror version of ours. Well put over. Probably appeals to Germans as ours to us. Blah but something to listen to. Like King's speech. I say, Last war made people fed up with wars, this one may make them DO something. If so almost worth it. We talk to neighbours over wall. Religious but nice. I rather enjoy shocking them with cynical comments. Get a bit worked up but soon cool down again.

Night falls and we check up on the windows. Spend half an hour more on them. Dad very tired; on from 11 last night till 7 tonight. [He drove a lorry for the local Council.] But keeps cheery in front of Mum. Dims to me and I gloom a bit too. Then we both cheer one another. We eat, talking about last war and the day's incidents. No one seems to like this war at all. We listen nervously to a sound in case it's a warning. It isn't and we grin and hope for a goodnight. I go to bed without bathing and type this in bed. Don't really like being alone. Feel tense but must try and sleep.

During the next few days Olivia and everyone else tried to get used to the fact of war. There was a lot of gloom about. She reported some of her own feelings on Thursday, September 7.

Thursday, September 7

Have been too utterly fed up to bother to write last two nights. And miserable. The whole business seems madder and madder to me, and my Mother feels the same. Other people seem willing to treat it all as slightly out of the ordinary but sufferable. She hates to hear we have bombed Germans as much as to hear they have bombed Poland. (WHY NOT US? Many people begin to suspect some funny business, and would not be surprised by a speedy dirty peace at Poland's expense—and feel so sick at <u>fearing</u> that they would swallow it.) Have been travelling down to new HQ with moderate ease. In the early raid of September 6 I got two lifts, private car and lorry, and arrived at normal time…. Blacking out windows, living in gloom, not sleeping, waiting for the warble, are so far our troubles; and that ever dreadful feeling that so much worse may be to come. Hopefully, one discusses Germany's early collapse, clutches at straws of rumour; even at the straw that M-O suggested a diary for the next three weeks. Perhaps it won't be necessary after that. I have heard from one of my three closest girl friends that she will be Red Cross in Devon. The other two I have not had the heart to write to, nor they to me, though probably they are carrying on normally as far as possible. But we have so often implored that this wouldn't happen, we should probably just weep if we met, at the tremendous pity of it all.

A few days later, responding to M-O's "War Directive No. 1" (which is found among her private papers and apparently was not mailed to M-O's headquarters), she described her evening of Tuesday, September 12. She was driving in a car from Putney to central London.

Tuesday, September 12

Called at Boots for a battery for hand torch—no luck. That's the tenth shop in four days. Struggled on to a tram. Was still aware of everyone's gas mask. Went to a friend at Brixton for the evening. Ate a lot of sausages and mash and talked vaguely about the war and its reactions on us. So far she has felt little change, but may have to evacuate to North of England at any moment. Got fed up with war talk and blackout precautions. Agreed that none of us knew any real facts of the matter and just swap rumours. So played Bach and Beethoven and sang some Schubert songs until 10:30. Early to bed but slept badly, hearing sirens in every passing car. Stayed the night with her. I usually do, but was extra pleased to as the blackout makes travelling so miserable.

A few days earlier, on Saturday, September 9, Olivia had written a few sentences in her diary; she then fell silent for almost all the following four weeks. She was distracted and upset, mainly because of her strained relationship with her lover, Bill Hole. Her one explicit reference to these stressful weeks was written around the end of September and attached to a reply to a Mass-Observation questionnaire.

End of September [approximately]

My personal life has been hurricaned in the last month, not by the war particularly, but by having to decide <u>not</u> to "live in sin" after trying it for a few days. The decision was forced by personal fastidiousness and a longing for my Mother, both unexpected facts.

In early October Olivia resumed her diary, in a new spirit of determination and candid self-exploration. She was finding her voice as a diarist—a voice suitable to representing both her inner self and external events.

Thursday, October 5

I believe I kept a diary and sent a few pages at the beginning of this phony war. I don't think I have sent anything for the last three weeks. I have been too easily fed up. After the few days in Town with a friend had fizzled out from a romantic love affair to a bloody inconvenience, I came home again utterly tired out. Work has been heavy and uncomfortable. I have felt unpopular and out of touch with my colleagues. I have resented the war whenever I have thought about it, after getting over the first few awful days and nights of funk-diarrhoea.

Until October 1st I have sat about once I got home and lazed gloomily until I could decently go to bed. I have written one letter to a friend, putting off a weekend; done a bit of M-O work, answering damn silly leaflet questions; and got really interested in dream reportage. At the weekend I woke up a bit and cleaned the flat, which was very dusty and untidy after several weeks of complete neglect. I have read a book a day—travel, novels, thrillers, poetry, two plays—and only while reading have I really lived.

Today I phoned Tom Harrisson[3] at the Park number as suggested in Wartime Directive no. 1 for London Observers with time to spare. I felt enough energy returning to want to do something and perhaps meet people. But he only suggested as many verbatim conversation reports as possible about the war, and I am fed up with the damn war and don't want to talk, or listen to talk, or write about it. But I did one properly, with a man in the office, just to show [that I'm] willing.

I want to find myself, and more and more it seems an inside job. I have spent a lot of time in the last few years trying to find out objective facts about the universe; and I feel the time has come for more inside knowledge. My emotions have been worked to a standstill and now I must lie back and let life sweep over me, stop making efforts and plans and guessing at the future and just rest in the certainty that life is still worth living. But it's no good struggling. Admit nothing, deny nothing, accept everything, is going to be my motto for the next phase. Even in politics—I am disgusted with arguing and predicting and chewing over these mean events; Lin Yutang[4] shall be my guide, "men are not even clever enough to stop war"—and I shall let all my energy flow into <u>enjoying</u> small beauties and stop struggling to create anything. I am not experienced enough and not disciplined enough to make anything worthwhile yet.

But I will try to help others to create understanding by keeping even a sketchy M-O wartime diary.

Monday, October 9

A wet day, should have been depressing but somehow it wasn't. I sang to myself all the way down to work from Waterloo, having a carriage to myself, which was pleasing to begin with. Then I got a bus up the hill, which was pleasing as it was still raining hard. M (in charge of my room) was in a better temper than last week and the new clerk arrived—turned out to be young and willing and intelligent, thank god. There was a lot of work, but I didn't feel overwhelmed; decided to stay late in the evening. At noon walked down the hill, enjoying the mild clean damp air and the smell of the leaves trodden under foot. Took back two books to the library, got out a new [book by J.B.] Priestley and went into the ABC for a cup of coffee, beginning to read the book, not feeling at all lonely, as I sometimes do when going alone to a teashop. Ate the three lumps of sugar they gave me as I don't take it in drinks, sucking the hot coffee into the hard lump of sugar in my mouth and savouring the changes in texture as it dissolved. Got a bus back up the hill as the rain was again falling, and read for three quarters of an hour whilst eating my cheese and tomato sandwiches. Chatted a while to D, the new clerk, about his difficult journey to the office. Then worked hard till 3; went with Gussie to the canteen for a cup of tea and she wondered if she may be going to have a baby. She was married a week ago, but is staying on as a temporary for the duration. Worked solidly again after tea till 5 and decided I was too tired to stay late, so left a trayfull of work and walked down the road with Gussie. Missed my train connection at Waterloo, but didn't care, just stood and stared at all the wet, tired looking people and wondered about them, as I love doing, vaguely. Walked slowly up from the station, not minding the rain as I wore my rubber cape and hood. Hated the heavy ominous weight of my service gas mask on my left shoulder. Enjoyed the drips of rain from the plane trees.

Came in to find Mother toasting cosily by the kitchen fire. She soon gave me hot eggs on toast and comforted me with kindness. She was pleasantly surprised with the flavour of some margarine she had bought today for the first time in her life, having always been agin it, but feeling now that butter is so dear she ought to try it for cooking anyway. Dad says he can't taste the difference between it and butter, but Mother and I exchange glances meaning "We can!" We listen, while eating, to the BBC <u>Palace of Varieties</u>. Mother and Dad enjoy it and laugh, but I am bored and escape as soon as possible upstairs to my own rooms. I put up the blackout curtains, leaving the staircase one down, deciding not to put on the stairs light out of laziness excused by economy. I type out the rough notes of a dream, having been rather flattered by another thank you note from Tom Harrisson. I would like to go into more detailed surmises about my dreams, which are a good deal more valuable to my own life than people's opinions about the war; but I feel this is selfish perhaps in the circumstances and leave them bald accounts.

Last Friday evening I phoned Joan; hadn't seen her for a fortnight; asked her to come and stay the weekend as parents going to be away. She came on Saturday at 4 o'clock. We made China tea and had chocolate cake with it in my pleasant sitting room, with sunshine. I had made it bright with flowers from the garden, a spray of blood-bright love-lies-bleeding in a blue jug on the dark book case, a tall green glass vase on the light oak book case with clear pale purple Michaelmas daisies and a spray of golden rod, a bright orange splash of nasturtiums with round soft leaves under the shelf of the bureau. And roses, creamy pink, on the cream mantel shelf.

Joan told me of her evacuation adventures, in charge of 400 expectant mothers, with small children too; only two mishaps, all the way to Weymouth, both slight. She was sad in the train when she had time to be, looking at the Dorset fields, where she had planned to spend a few days walking this autumn. She has a woman staying with her who is afraid to remain alone in her own flat. Joan is pleased with company too, for air raid warnings and soothing evening chatter, although normally she likes to be alone after an office day as much as I do. She told me of her troubles with blackout screens on her big windows, so we walked around and put up my curtains to be admired.

Went down to the local Saturday evening market at 5:45 to buy potatoes and Dreft [a laundry detergent]. Got the potatoes alright, but none of the shops had heard of Dreft. We got quite giggly as one after another repeated the rather odd name in puzzled tones; in the end got Lux in a shop that was just closing at 6:30. Couldn't get on a bus or tram, huge queues of people waiting, so went into Lyons and had coffee till the crowds should clear a bit. Discussed the people around and deplored the number of uniforms. We agree that the war is disgusting and unreal and do not talk about it much. We guess at the life stories of some of the tired middle aged women, and hate the hot bright foody air of the big shop. It is dark when we come out. We get a bus home and for an hour Joan washes her undies while I sit around and chat and we stop every now and then to listen to Askey on the air.[5] He really makes us laugh heartily with his earthy spontaneous jokes and such lots of vitality. Then listen sullenly to the news, exchanging snorts. Went early to bed as both tired.

After late Sunday breakfast we walk down to the station, wanting to be in the country for an hour or two. We can't afford to go far out and don't want to wait on the dismal platform. Flummox the ticket man by asking where the next train in goes; he wants to know where we want to go and won't believe that we don't mind where. Get on a train quickly, but at the next station I get Joan to get out, as I dislike the full-up carriage and the way the train will go. As the next station is a junction we cross over and get the next train on the other platform; we don't know where it is going and mildly enjoy guessing what the next station will be. We reach Addiscombe and get out. I have a map with me covering most of the SE of London's suburbs. We find our position and make a beeline for the nearest green patch, which turns out to be a nice tangly unexpected wood. There are a few people about in their Sunday best as we walk by the new-estate-monsters of houses. They all carry gas masks; we don't, having politically decided that Hitler is safe for the few days it will take the Government to answer his Peace Putsch.[6] But we wonder rather brazenly whether any policeman will query our reasoning.

There are a few blackberries in the wood, not very nice. The grass is very green in the cloudy light, and rain drops are dew understudies everywhere. The trees are changing colour under winter's rough approach and polished chestnuts, greeny-buff acorns, [and] three cornered beech mast insist on being collected and carried and admired. For three hours we stroll through six miles of mixed woods and fields and estates and commons, back to the Hayes station. Once indoors, we light the boiler fire and wash in hot water as we are chilled. Quickly sausages and potatoes are cooked and we eat and eat until we are beautifully stuffed, finishing with coffee. We wash up lazily and finish just as Mother and Dad return. We greet them cheerfully and put the roses they bring into vases. Then up to my sitting room to sing in the glow from the electric fire, on and on, songs from our mutual schooldays in duets, solos for those learnt since, until we remember Mozart is on the air for 15 minutes. We tune in at the right moment and absorb the clear fresh shapely music.

Then Joan, curled up and sleepy, says "Read to me" and I browse through book after book, picking out phrases and passages. Then poems; and then a few Thurber burbles. We are thirsty and make a surreptitious expedition to the cellar, steal a jugful of homemade grape wine and sip and sip and admire the clear ruby colour. Soon it is 11:30, and we switch on for more Mozart, but this is dull after the delicate charm of the chamber music and we are rather sorry we listen. Soon after midnight we wander off drowsily and happily to bed, having achieved our aim of creating a few sane hours among the hideous welter of war hours we have both had lately. And yet it hasn't really got going yet! I can't bear to think about what the next months may bring to each of us. We're both 26, both in Government jobs, both in love, both wanting families very much indeed, both enjoying simple pleasures, longing to live simple sane lives and see justice. What is to become of us?

Friday, October 13

Been too lazy to write regularly. Since last time Monday, I have done little that is different. Caught the proper trains, done my work, eaten, enjoyed the weather, read and read. It was my 27th birthday on Wednesday, and a lovely clear bright morning. Had a pile of presents beside my breakfast plate, chocolates, several books, two lampshades to match, big bath bottle of Eau de Cologne, one card, a book token, later in the day five lots of flowers. An unexpected scrummy meal in the evening, duck and green peas and five friends to share it unexpectedly. Then we all listened to Gracie on the air[7] and to the news, with sarcastic commentary and almost an argument. Then all but one went to another room. Eric and I stayed to listen to playing of Beethoven's Eighth, very refreshing and real after the music hall hour. Then birthday cake and milk and chat till 11, then reading in bed till midnight past. I dream every night, always have done. I cannot always be awake enough in the mornings to get much down for [M-O's questionnaire about] Wartime Dreams; now [that] I shall have to be at the office an hour earlier I shall get even less. But I enjoy my dreams thoroughly. Have an odd habit of remembering every detail of last night's dreams in a flash the minute I turn out the light and put my head on the pillow. Am always too sleepy to put them down then though.

Decided today that one of the reasons for my disregard of the war inside is that, travelling on the train now instead of the road, I am not battered for an hour morning and evening by the awful poster placards of the papers; so that it doesn't enter into my consciousness so hard. I don't ever buy papers, rarely read them and don't specially arrange to listen in to the news. We are too busy at work to talk much so the war might as well not be on for all the attention I give it lately. Still, I realise it may get bad soon now that Hitler's plan has not been accepted.

Now, sleepy, at peace in my mind, I shall have a hot bath and go to bed and read. (Funny, because before the war started I worried about it tremendously.)

Monday, October 16

I stayed at home on Saturday morning, did some cleaning and later washed my hair. Went to the library, got two big volumes of

Dorothy Richardson, an [Richard] Aldington poems, and Humbert Wolfe's Winter Miscellany. Wet day, but I didn't get depressed. Had macaroni cheese and tomatoes for supper, and cider to drink. Then chatted to our new house-sharers, old friends of the family, man and wife and Rene (19), and Eric (23), who have come now that my brother and his wife and baby Michael have taken a flat elsewhere. They are much more cheerful people to have in the house, thank goodness.

Sunday, up at 9:30 to breakfast in dressing gown, lengthily. Then dressed in warm housecoat and sewed a new jacket. Grand hot lamb lunch at 2:30 and more sewing. Tea and a romp with Rene at 5 and all looking out of window at barrage balloon drifting in the mist. Sunday evening sewed and listened in to foreign news in English; said some probably true but not apposite things about the situation. Mother and Rene came and sat in my sitting room and sewed too; pleasant. Then Rene went to have a bath and Mother and I looked through the Sackville-West book Some Flowers I had for birthday; lovely photos. Planned to have lots of them in Mother's retirement garden. Went to the kitchen at 10 and had some cider and so to bed to read Wolfe and to dream a lot. Slept early as I have to be in to work at 9 instead of 10 in future and have an hour's travelling.

Monday, in at 9:10, after flood on the electric line and confusion at Waterloo. A foggy damp morning cleared to a heavenly blue sky by noon so I went for a long walk over Putney Heath among the silver birches at lunch time, purposely "forgetting" my gas mask etc. Was aware of guilty feeling when passing two policemen. But the Heath and the free feeling on swinging hands and striding without parcels was worth it. Leaves of gold wet thin leather were very slippery underfoot, bare boughs enticing the eye upward aiding downfall.

Worked hard all day, left sharp at 4. Went to Westminster to book seats for self and four girl friends tomorrow night. Town looks much as it did six weeks ago [at the outbreak or war]. Met Lover for a brief while, decided we mustn't kick too hard against the pricks of separation; but we still try to catch those passing trains! It is difficult not to moan about not seeing one another, we are so fondly used to daily meeting. However, there is a kind of pleasure in the pain, and a self-conscious faithfulness in the face of passing temptations which is amusing, while it lasts.

Now sleepy, for bed, after an evening spent listening to Eric going over Brahms'Third Symphony on my piano, and talking about music rather vaguely.

Thursday, October 19

On Tuesday morning I put a toothbrush and nightgown in my handbag, as I was going to stay the night with Peg, after going to Westminster with her and four other girl friends. We all met there in good time and enjoyed the play very much; original idea well produced. For four out of the five of us it was our first night out since the blackout, and we were pleased to find it less trying than we had expected. We were all in very good spirits and not nervous; ages varied from 26 to 40 (26, 27, 35, 40) but no big difference in reaction discernible on any topic which arose.

Wednesday, cold dull day. Everybody at the office mentioned the raid on Scapa,[8] appreciating the German courage; but when they spoke of the raid on Edinburgh they were annoyed. Except one man who laughed and laughed because the day before a friend of his had gone up there for a holiday and had boasted of getting out of the fuss about air-raids! Had a very hot lazy bath and was in bed by 8; read till 10:30 and slept soundly.

Today, slacked and bored and ate too much.

Verbatim War Conversation: Me with M, male civil servant, 34.

Me: How's your sister?

M: A bit lost without the two children. Says she doesn't know what she'd do without the old dog, though she's going to have him put to sleep if anything happens.

Me: What does she think about the war?

M: Oh she doesn't know what to think. She was telling me she had listened to Churchill's speech over the weekend and then read in the papers (I don't read the papers myself nowadays) that Lloyd George and Chamberlain were saying exactly the opposite. So what are you to believe?

Me: What do you think will happen yourself?

M: I think myself it'll either fizzle out within a month or be real war within a week, you know, raids on both sides. You can't get away from it, we've been more or less mucking about up to now.

Me: What about the Navy?

M: Well only one ship's been involved really; but there's quite a long list of killed in the Air Force now. A lot of our planes must have been shot down over the front line. But I definitely think the time is coming now. We have deliberately refrained from bombing over Germany, though we ran big risks with the leaflets. I think our Government have been sweating on the top line on fostering a revolution in Germany but now they realise they have overestimated the unrest, and anyway the actual people have no means to make a revolution. After all Hitler made all the lively ones into ss or something and the people have no chance to get arms. Suppose there was a lot of unrest over here even, if we'd been on short commons, even we couldn't do much about it, and there's no doubt in my mind they have been ground down under an iron hand. Though mind you I don't fancy his chances when he has to put all his troops on the front line. I reckon the Austrians and the Czechs and the Poles will take a bit of keeping down when they know the soldiers are out of the way, and they'll all feel the pinch when it comes to rations. (Then the boss came in and we had to work. I was able to scribble down the actual words because I had my back to M and he thought I was doing accounts and just listening.)

Monday, October 23

I think I posted the last instalment on Friday night, October 20th. Had a cold in the head, so went to bed on Saturday afternoon, after a very busy morning at the office and a lot of annoyance on the way home through being put on the wrong train by a stupid porter. Went fast through my station, and had to go right back to London Bridge to get another train.

Stayed in bed until 7 on Monday morning, reading Vols. 3 & 4 of Dorothy Richardson's <u>Pilgrimage</u>.[9] Hope the war does not prevent her continuing this unique chronicle of a woman's mental development. Was so immersed in this book that I did not notice the time and my cold passing. Heard afterwards that it was a lovely mild autumn day.

At noon on Monday went with girl from the office over the Heath. Grand hour walking in the sun, staring unbelievingly at the colours on the trees, appreciating the spring of the turf and the soft west wind. On the way home was again misled about the train, again went fast through my station. Very exhausting to one's nervous energy, all the subsequent annoyance, especially as I knew Peg was coming and she might now get home before me. But I need not have worried, as she also had been told the wrong thing about the trains; this is almost too coincidental to be true, but it really is true!

We had a welcome hot meal and took tea up to my sitting room to listen to the German news in English; strongly worded attack on Churchill included. I have listened about a dozen times since the outbreak to this station. They sound mostly quite as reasonable and convincing as the BBC so that I am more than ever wondering where TRUTH lies. From a passionate interest in politics has evolved a steady disgust; the tricky housekeeping catch-as-catch-can side of the world, leading to footling fights, will never again have any glamour for me. After the broadcast, Peg and I talked much in this strain for an hour. Peg is following, with more interest than I can muster, the events as they flow; thinks that unless the profit curbing is stopped the war will stop. Hope she is right. If the last war removed the pomp, and this one removes the profits, perhaps pacifism will have more appeal to everybody.

We sang folk songs to a one finger accompaniment on the piano; listened to a movement of the Fifth in C minor from a foreign station; browsed through excerpts from <u>Pilgrimage</u> aloud; and had hot milk before going to bed at 11. Satisfactory evening.

Tuesday, October 24

Stood awhile and watched a lot of people at Waterloo, as they went through all the preliminaries of entraining for the USA boat train. Lived again through those thrilling moments this spring when Mother and I caught it.[10] But many of these people Jewish and sad; and I was not sorry to be staying in England. The great glass roof of the station was spacious with bright sunshine. Even the sooty horror of the journey to Putney had moments of clean beauty under the soft westerly air and sun. But by the time I was able to get out for a breath on the Heath great angry clouds were bearing down dark from the Northwest, and by 5 the rain was pelting.

My baby nephew was visiting when I got home, so we had a very mutually satisfying romp before our meal, and he was very loth to part when the time came. I had tea with the other six people in the house, laughing and joking and dismissing the war. Then up to listen to Bach flute and piano for fifteen minutes. Then more German news, followed by a talk by an Englishwoman on the women's point of view. She slanged the press for underlining the frivolous side, praised the German women for their mutual helping hands, gave an "atrocity" story of a London woman's evacuation death; had such an unpleasant voice that I disliked her talk, but it probably represents an aspect of the facts. Now shall have a very hot bath, then bed with [Richard] Jefferies' Story of My Heart.

Sorry I don't seem to be giving much help about general points of view. But most of the people I know are bored by the war, glad not to talk about it; and many of them rarely talk about anything unless it is in the papers; and the war isn't. The BBC features it, but makes it as remote as the Manchurian, or Abyssinian, or Chinese, or Spanish. Come to think of it, war is not very "new" news.

On the 24th and 25th [of October] I went to work as usual, to the Heath at lunch times for a few minutes of absolute happiness. Then on the 26th awoke with a dreadful throat. Went to work, was made to see a doctor, sent home and have been in bed till now, November 2, with pharyngitis. Shall get up tomorrow. Have slept most of the time and forgotten the war intentionally. Listened-in a lot (set by the bed) and to foreign news, Moscow, Zeesen [site of a German short-wave station], Rome, America. War, war, war, ships sunk, etc. Feel gratified that the "newses" generally confirm one another, in time. But all of them leave one wondering what is happening <u>behind</u> the scenes. Germans the only personal abusers <u>yet</u>; sounds most undignified on the air.

Have enjoyed schools and children's hour; wish could more often listen in daytime. Appreciate the courage and energy of BBC workers. Resent so much "light" music, so little classic. And lack of poetry.

Mass-Observation had asked its informants to describe the dreams they were having. Olivia had already (in September) reported some of them to M-O and she now took up this project with enthusiasm. In early November she sent in a detailed record of her nightly dreams during the weeks that she was ill and staying at home.

Thank you Tom Harrisson for acknowledgement of last instalment. It undoubtedly spurs me on. Having been in bed for the last week Dad's 7 am reveille has not interrupted thoughts, so the account is rather fuller than before. I don't know whether pharyngitis has had any effect on my subconscious.

October 24

A little grey kitten is lost. I follow it into a cinema, up a lot of stairs, across the seats, and come out in a side street in Deptford where I talk to my Mother's sister Maud.

Walking along in the evening pulling a rope, dragging several soapboxes in which three or four small cousins are sitting, all tired. Am following a route chalked on the street and on walls etc. Come to a corner with railings round a tenement block. The route seems to go outside these railings on to a single steel rod, very rusty, laid along the top of a brick wall. I despair of balancing the convoy of boxes along this and stare round in dismay. Some small children stop and tell me there is a short cut through the yard of the buildings and

I am very relieved. Going past one flat I see my second cousin Ada (haven't seen her for ten years) and say she must let the children and me rest. She refuses to let us into her flat but takes us to a room on the ground floor. There is a sink and some chairs round a table. I set the children up and give them some baked apples. Ada asks for some but I won't let her have them unless she gives the children a pie, which she does, and takes baked apples. I feel very tired and wish I had not got to go on with the journey as the boxes and children are heavy.

October 25

There are some special flowers on a table. An American woman is admiring them. The Prince of Wales walks by. There is a long pink gladiola on a green leaf, tall white lilies, lovely roses, and an air of enthusiasm about. I am not in this dream myself.

October 26

I dream I am playing different hands of cards all night! (Spent the two hours before going to bed playing cards; first time for some years.)

October 27

Walking round a canteen on the top floor of an unknown building looking for a place to sit. I am very unpopular and nobody wants me to sit near them. I decide to go somewhere else and go to the lift. No room for me in it as my department chief and a lot of girls are in it. I walk down many stairs, trying to race the lift. Finish up in an Underground station, at the barrier. A ticket inspector is asking people where they are going and is assessing the fares, very seriously. He says he thinks sixpence would be fair for my journey and I give him a coin and go through. Am worried to realise at once that I have given him not sixpence but a farthing.

October 28

Looking up at a bunch of balloons high in the sky. Their cables are all tied together round some railings near me. One seems loose so I pull it hard to loop it round again. I look up to see how I'm doing to find that this cable is attached to the corner of a very high square brick tower, called the Eiffel (not a bit like it), and that I have pulled so hard that the tower is falling over towards me. It crashes across some houses a few streets away and I run to see it. The whole top floor has slid off and is not broken, though the middle is. I go into the rooms and find a woman and child rather scared. I prepare some food for them and look and view.

I've been working in this solicitor's office for a week. It is musty. The people who employ us are interested in music and we all play. There has been a series of concerts in the last week and in the signing off book all the others claim musical papers for the week, 7 @ a penny. And on Sunday the "Sunday DO'Y." I can't understand this, and I have not claimed the money. My Gran calls at the office with a baby in a pram and we go for a walk along the river. We walk south away from a bridge. It comes on to rain and we wonder whether to cross the river by a stone causeway which is getting covered with water or to run back to the bridge. We run back pushing the pram over a lot of narrow gardens in the front of little cottages. I hope we are not doing much damage as the gardens are wanted for war vegetables. I lean down and pull up roots of small flowering plants, getting a bundle which keeps dropping, thinking "they will all want these flowers again when the war is over so I MUST keep some." We push the pram through some very dark arches and up a little path into the solicitor's office again, very wet from the rain and hot.

October 29

A party of mixed friends, office and school and family, are at the seaside. We have just arrived and the name of the hotel we are to stay at is forgotten. We get on a bus. I get on first and the others aren't coming. Then they jump on at the last moment. We get off at a little Post Office and go in and ask to look at some guides of the town to try and guess the name of the hotel. Someone thinks they have it and we walk up the hill between red brick tall houses. We go to a very smart "Hotel Kern" and wait in the lounge and decide it can't be the right one. On the way out we meet three very handsome men, all in uniform, one army, one navy, one RAF. Then I am crying on Joan's shoulder in a bedroom in the right hotel. We hear a knock and go to the front door in our nightdresses. We open it and a man is there with a letter for Mrs Morgan, the proprietress, who comes up at that moment.

October 30

On a lawn in a lovely garden, my Gran and a family party. A man and his wife and a baby are throwing a big new ball for me to catch, and the man and I exchange very significant glances when the baby keeps throwing it to me.

I am riding a Fairy cycle down a white narrow road between tall white wooden houses in a hot midday sun. The byke gradually gets bigger and bigger until it is a high powered motorbyke roaring along.

In a corner near a sink in a cookery centre I am watching the teacher peel potatoes and we are talking about the laundry and how difficult it will be to get down Tanner's Hill in the dark.

October 31

There is a table in the corner of a very narrow room and I call out "This is much too dark to work at." Someone tells me to switch the light on.

There is a very bright landing, with three bedroom doors opening on to it, and some thick sheepskin rugs. I am lying naked on one in the sunshine and discussing the details of a journey with Joy through her door.

I think "This is a very peculiar shape, this railway carriage" but I can't decide what is wrong with it. There is a man with a lot of luggage and then I am standing waiting on an island in the middle of the road, enjoying the hot bright sunshine.

November 1

Mother and I are in a cafeteria. She wants to sit in a corner but I think it is draughty so I sit in the middle of a long bright empty counter and eat biscuits and butter and ask for more butter. I go through into a big long hall with many windows opening on to a garden. I am interested in some bright red marigolds in a vase on a table. There is a crowd of people from the Dramatic Society rehearsing an inquest. People come and talk to me, but I want to be alone with my man, so I tell them to go out into the garden and choose roses. He helps me to change for the dance and we find I have no dance shoes, only brogues. So he walks across a grassy common to some shoe shops in the distance and I watch him and hope he will bring back the right size. I sit for a long while at the window thinking how much I love him. I am on a bus with a lot of these girls when I see him across the road. I get off, telling them I must go to shop. I buy a bar of soap, and when he comes over to me he laughs very much and says "Now we shall have to carry it round all day."

November 2

I am in a small public garden, with lots of houses all round. I want to go northwards, but there are no roads leading that way. I try to find a short cut through the gardens of the houses. A door opens and some people come out arguing. I say "Good evening" but they take no notice of me, so I walk into the house. It is very dark and smelly and I am just going to go down a few stairs into the kitchen and out that way when a girl comes down and I explain but she makes me go out. Then somehow I <u>am</u> out through the back garden. I have been a long way round on the 47 bus, which is pulled up round the corner. I stand thinking about the bus, how big and red it is, and wanting to get back to the public garden. I can't face that Air Raid girl again so I walk to the corner house, where there are two men talking at the other end of the path. I walk into the yard and out near them and through a gap in the iron railings. They grumble at me but I don't mind as I can see the gardens again.

Olivia resumed her diary in early November. She also recorded details of her dreams for the next ten days, most of which are reported here.

Last instalment took me up to November 2nd in bed with a bad throat. That evening Dad constructed a rough bed table for me, to take the weight of the typewriter off my knees. Next day Mother scrubbed it, and now the old margarine box is doing a good job of work. I shall have a pleasant comfortable winter blackout night office, in bed, with the radio now installed beside the bed too.

Friday, November 3

Dressed, first time for a week, at 9:30. Wandered around with a duster for an hour. Stood around in Mother's way in the kitchen till lunchtime; Dad pleased to see me at table. Rested for an hour after lunch, listened to Schools broadcast. Then answered four letters for Mother and three for myself, took till tea time. Meanwhile Mother went out shopping. Was told by milkman at door this morning that he had no butter and could not supply her regular order this week; so she went to several shops, could get only half a pound. Said that the shops were crowded and people queuing; much grumbling, and the shop assistants wishing rationing would start. Mother says they have put up the prices of everything; many things she can't see are affected by the war.

After a lazy chatty tea we sat (oh so rarely) in the sitting room and listened to Music Hall from the North. All noticed the BBC are allowing much broader humour since the war began.

At 7:45 Mother and Dad went out into the very blackout to buy the usual Friday night quart of cider, and I went to bed. Listened to the Zeesen news in English, still dislike the peevish voice and inane humour of their announcer. Was interested to hear comments on a letter to the Star regarding dachshunds as I had read the letter earlier in the week. It said that that D's should not be considered as German.[11] Their comment was a quotation from a supposed Egyptian script, talking of D's long BC. No actual inference was drawn; I am not quite clear what the implied inference was.

Read [Sir Ronald] Storrs' Orientations till 10, couldn't sleep, so listened in the dark to various bits of sound around the dial, switching off after a particularly pointless story by M. Armstrong; disappointed as I usually enjoy him. Slept badly. Pondered on dream fragments for Tom Harrisson's collection; now [November 4] still in bed 11:15 am; shall write up the week's dreams for him.

Saturday, November 4

Dressed in time for lunch. Listened to Dad and his friend praising the Navy's exploits this week. Went upstairs to the Willmotts for a cup of tea and sat talking to them till 3, hearing all about tennis clubs and last summer's activities. Helped Rene look for a half-made frock, seems to have got lost in the moving. Spent a leisurely afternoon looking at her clothes and some old photographs. Found some stuff like their curtains and decided to make a pelmet [i.e., a valance] for the dining room. Then Eric went out and bought paper and wood to make proper blackout blinds for the big front bedroom windows. All worked busily and finished jobs by 8 before we stopped to eat; had toast and honey and tea while listening to <u>Band Waggon</u>. Then I went to bed. Tried to sleep, but the others were in such a hilarious mood, my Mother and Dad, Mr and Mrs Willmott and the two grown up children, all laughing and tearing about the house, that I couldn't. So chased distant stations on the radio instead. Got the best USA reception I've ever heard. Football matches all over the States, Alabama v. Kentucky Tigers, Yale v. Dartmouth, Notre Dame v. Army, all very excitingly commentated. Filled in the readings on <u>Radio Times American Log</u>. Then thrilled to hear "This is the voice of Manchukuo" giving local news about railway services etc. with a chunk of praise for Japan now and then. Listened to Germany describing the slums of London and the good conditions of the German working classes. Making all allowances for propaganda on both sides, I think we must be aiming at very different ends.

Slept some time after midnight and had unpleasant dreams about bombers and soldiers.

Her dreams that night.

Walking on a wide bright esplanade I suddenly realise that all the other people have disappeared. I look up the streets going northwards and see a train stopped on a railway bridge across the road. Over it three huge bombers are heading towards me. I watch but nothing moves or sounds till a small plane comes fast and a voice booms out of it, very afraid, "They're COMING" and I wonder if he has a loudspeaker up there. I think "It must be gas, they are all so quiet." I look round for somewhere to hide but all the doors are shut so I stand and watch and begin to feel afraid and intensely curious as to what will happen.

In a street of shops, all the shutters up, lot of people about. I walk carefully over a shutter on the ground and hear the glass crackling underneath. I go up two steps to a door which is latched, though I knew it ought to be locked, and go into my office. This has been turned into a restaurant, which makes me cross, and I shout "So this is why all our papers are lost every morning." I sit at my desk and read a good book, philosophy, explaining everything, and I am getting thrilled when a girl comes and reads over my shoulder. Slowly the book becomes a cheap exciting love story and the girl says "Oh, that's the one about the Swiss maid." I look at a clock and it says 5:30 so I decide to go and meet my man. The girl and I walk upstairs and out at the front of the shop into a big formal park. We are walking very happily towards the river when a lot of soldiers appear, in gay red uniforms with bands. They appear from an arch, half left of us, and as they reach the wide path we are walking on they split up, half marching in each direction. They do this every time they come to a path till they are all over the park. At every place where a path meets another they put a barrier and men to stop you passing. We want to turn right to the river at one barrier. There is a carriage without a horse standing there with a big notice "THESE WE HAVE REJECTED" and a dark-haired boy and two women are sitting in it taking no notice of anyone. The soldiers are very excited and pleased with themselves. As we get to the barrier a short red-faced Sergeant pushes forward and tries to stop us. I say in a very important tone "We have our orders" and he apologises and makes way for us. We walk on a bit. I am very trembly because we have no orders but I was determined to get through to meet my man. But then we see more and more soldiers and barriers in front of us and I think "Oh what's the use of anything, they are all so silly, it's not worth trying to get anywhere." Then I woke up, sobbing.

Sunday, November 5

Mother kindly brought me coffee and baked apples in bed. When I took my tray down to the kitchen at 11 she and Dad were ready to go off to the bungalow for the day; and soon after all the Willmotts went off to relations at Maidstone for the day. I return to bed, read <u>Radio Times</u> for twenty minutes; then sit up and till 12:40 type out dreams. Then this, while listening to the BBC students' songs—very jolly and impromptu effects and lots of chuckles. There's a lovely clear pale blue November sky now, the trees warmly coloured in the sun, leaves floating in the air all the time. A perfect day for walking. But I don't really want to be out, still feeling without energy. Shall see the doctor again tomorrow.

Her dreams that night.

A lot of girls from various schools are going through a classroom door into the tram tunnel under Kingsway. They are all laughing and talking.

The office keeps being moved from one place to another. We have just arrived at a new room where a very elaborate plan of where everything is to go has been drawn on the walls, showing even the position of every book.

We are sitting in rows as though at a concert in the Park, in front of an empty shop window. One young man is sitting just inside the door, eating sandwiches. He has two friends just outside, near me, and they are laughing and chatting. I look at them when they aren't looking and then they invite me to join them. I feel very shy and don't say much, just smile. I take out a cigarette stub and begin to smoke it as they are all smoking. The shop window gradually fills with baby clothes and I am inside listening to a woman saying angrily "We always do keep it dry" and her husband says "We even get up in the middle of the night to change it." He is holding baby.

Tuesday, November 7

Didn't see the doctor on Monday. Watched the unexpected storm instead, while dusting my rooms. After lunch slept awhile, then moved the wireless back to the sitting room. Dressed in outdoor clothes (retaining comfy trousers though) and ambled to the library and back. Telephoned from a box to my bloke, but was only rewarded for my attempt to show off about being "up" by his absence on business. Bought a <u>Radio Times</u> to replace my borrowed copy; had to go to three shops before getting one. Was disgusted at the wobbliness of my legs when I got back home. Sat and read <u>Finnegan's Wake</u> (lucky to spot it at the Public Library) without any comprehension at first; and then with a growing enjoyment which makes me anxious to get back to it. Any extra bad typing is now partly due to [James] Joyce's phonetic influence. My baby nephew came for a brief while at tea time. Mother went part of the way home with them, leaving me by the kitchen fire. I sat there sleepily and began to feel very depressed; but just sat and sat, more and more depressed, until Dad came home to find me in the dark and dumps. Soon came back to life when Mother and Peg came and we had toast for tea. Then an old schoolfriend of Mother's came, to tell her the news; her daughter has become a war bride, much to the father's anger.

Peg and I came up to my sitting room, blacking out the house on the way; and then went all the way downstairs again to borrow some music from David; to such good effect that it took the three of us to carry it all up the stairs. He has a solid pile four feet high. We picked out all the classics and spent two hours meandering happily, finishing up with half an hour singing. Then David returned to his somewhat neglected parents and Peg and I talked satisfyingly of human bondage and Joyce and the weather. We have been friends now for 13 years and like one another more each year, especially since we stopped living together. She could not stay the night for once and went happily at 11, into the pitch black night.

Mother and I arranged to get up at 8 this morning, in an effort to get back to normal by next week. But we didn't meet till 8:45, with lamentations. I reached the Doctor's by 11 and was told to take it easy. He seems very interested in my blood pressure all at once; keeps taking it; probably has some new text book and likes to test out his theories. Went by train to town; rang my bloke and arranged to meet at National Gallery at 12:45 to hear Myra Hess.

Meanwhile I bought some rubber overshoes—annoyed the girl at the first shop because I wouldn't take her next best. "They are out of stock all over the country"; but I got what I wanted 50 yards away.

Then to the CSSA; had eye lotion made up while visiting Ladies Room. At 12:30 into Lyons by Gallery for a bowl of soup; [it] hadn't come by 12:45 so I apologetically cancelled the order. Waited three minutes in drizzle for Bloke; arrived in time for Standing Room only; last straw; my legs regretfully refused to stand. So B [her lover, Bill Hole] took me back to the Lyons and revived me with coffee, being unable for soup by then. Escorted me to collect Readers Union for the month, bought a pound of chocolates for Mother, and a pound for me as an afterthought, and saw me on the 1:33, rather sadly. Felt very weak on finding an empty house; but soon got some beef tea hot and potatoes and found some pears and custard. Then up to my own room and wrote to a girlfriend not seen for three weeks. Listened to a good Dvorak variations and thought how pleasant it is to lead an unofficed life for a while. If I could have my £3 a week without the tyranny of office hours I'd very soon play with more than one finger. And I'd try oil instead of watercolour; and I'd make that rock garden really bright; and I'd read <u>everything</u> aloud instead of only having time for bits here and there; and I'd visit all my friends and some of my relations and make up that stuff I bought in the sales and clean the windows. I might even possibly ARP [Air Raid Precautions]. But now I must go and get the tea, before going on with <u>Finnegan's Wake</u>.

After family tea helped Rene cut out her frock on my pattern. Then to bed by 8, reading Joyce. Listened in to [Lord] Halifax [Secretary of State for Foreign Affairs], blah. Slept lightly, many dreams, tossing and turning.

A dream that night.

(This next is an odd dream because all through I felt as if I was part of everybody and everything in the scene and yet I wasn't there.) There is a big white concrete building, built on a lovely curving shape with a dwelling tower at the right hand end. The top floor has huge letters DENTIST, but the lower part is a garage, with equally big letters OUT on the left and IN on the right. A young newly married couple are going past it. It belongs to the boy's Mother and he doesn't like it. They walk on up the hill and come to _____ Mansions, an old fashioned expensive block of flats, and he says shyly "You're back now darling." She says "Yes, the one on the first floor is ours." They go in and ring for the lift. (I hear the lift man's footsteps and for the moment I am he, hurrying, just as I am each person and thing, even the lift and the carpet; I feel them tread on me.) The lift stops and they get out. Then the young man is lying back on a bed. "Now we'll be happy, I've told several people about the car. Now I must be going." But the girl puts her hand on him and says "It's no good, you must love me" and he says "But you know we said we couldn't afford that and a car" and they argue. The girl is very smartly dressed and should have no cares but she is in despair. And she can feel that he wants to take her but won't.

Wednesday, November 8

Up 8:30; breakfast and housework till 10. Typed dreams till 11 when baby Michael arrived. From then till 5:30, when he went, was fully occupied amusing him. Played a game for over an hour, I lying on settee and he emptying the six bits of sago [a starchy foodstuff] out of a small aspirin bottle into my hand, over and over and over again. Then my brother (his father) collected him. Mother and Dad went to the pictures. I had a cup of tea with the Willmotts. Read Dorothy Sayers' <u>The Devil to Pay</u> with some food. Now in my sitting room, ruminating on the comfort of an electric fire and a pleasant room. Shall listen to the symphony concert soon; blisses. Ought my conscience be more disturbed at all this selfish serenity in wartime? I comfort myself that the doctor told me to look after myself; and I don't feel that I'm imposing on any fellow men. But having just read Sayers' dictum that inertia and escapism are the modern selling of the soul, I have an uneasy feeling. How fares my soul? Is there a task lying to my hand, unnoticed? Oh dear, I really <u>don't</u> want to go all political again, especially in wartime! And I do so feel convinced that reform <u>is</u> necessary. Still, I'd better make up my mind in what direction first—so here's to the pursuit of knowledge, through literature. Escapism again!

I sit musing, hearing the November gale rattle the window and door, and it seems to me that this warm bright room is a bubble over the European caldron. Escapism, indeed!

Dream fragments.

(Had no pencil and paper by bed; only these fragments remain.) On top of an open bus in a green leafy lane. Two girl friends and I crouch in a row at the back and make water without any embarrassment. A tumult in a marble room, women shouting and crying, bright sunshine through tall marble openings gleaming on a square pool.

Olivia recounted several more dreams from the following few nights.

November 9

In a chemist's, a woman is receiving tablets, six at a time. I am trying to decide where to go for a short holiday. Want to go North. I am listening-in [to the radio]; there is a map of Germany painted across the front of the set, with a light behind it. There are two main tracts of hills marked, and the one across the south is called "THE WRATH OF GOD" and I think that a funny name.

I am cooking bacon in a basement for my brother. A puppy is running round and I try to shoo him out. He won't go and I pick him up and carry him out into Lincoln's Inn Fields garden. He bites my wrists. I stare a long time at the crinkly white skin mark and the little line of red blood.

November 10

On holiday in a big house with numbered rooms and dark passages. A lot of young people are there and dogs. I have a bath and am disgusted at the dirty edge to the bath. I go along a corridor and meet a girl who says she has borrowed my vest and knickers and I am annoyed and think I shan't like to wear them again.

I get on a tram and the conductor takes my fare and then tells me it is the wrong tram. I ask for my fare back and an Inspector comes and there is a lot of talk but no decision is reached. I go to a shop to get some stuff—can't get it right. Look at some with tiny patterns all over.

November 11

At school a man is teaching and Joan is there too. A wireless set balanced on a chair falls over. A big procession is coming by. I am on a balcony very squashed up. Can only see the people behind me. There are some very nice profiles there and I look at them with pleasure for a long time. Everyone else begins to sing, but I am much too squashed to be able to stretch my chest. The balcony changes to a theatre balcony.

November 12

I am in bed with a man, leaning back on pillows, talking happily. His wife comes in and says "I suppose this happens every two or three days." I say, very earnestly, "Oh no, this is the first time for a month." She sits by him and laughs and talks about paraffin while I dress. I lean over the foot of the bed and say "I can see you two belong to one another." They go into the next room and chink coins while I pack a small case with chocolates, fitting in a bit of crystallized pineapple very carefully. There is a doctor waiting patiently behind a screen in the room and when I have picked up a lot of untidy £1 notes from the floor he sees me and says "I suppose you are the young woman I've come to see." I am surprised and say "Yes, I suppose I must be." (Mother came up and woke me then; and I felt vaguely annoyed because I wanted to know what would happen next.)

At this time, Olivia temporarily abandoned her writing for Mass-Observation. Her personal journal of "General Thoughts" included an entry for "Old Year's Day" that looked back on 1939. "In bed, sore throat. Snow outside. And war." After these initial words, she declared that "This has been a stormy year, of unexpected changes." She mentioned the trip she had taken with her mother to the United States, the changing positions of three of her friends, and, of course, the war. Thinking back, she remembered that "At first we were all very afraid of air raids. Had three warnings in three days. As no more in three months we forget and just grumble at blackout and rationing and call it a funny war." She also chastised herself: "Feel selfish. Am selfish."

In this private journal and in other personal papers from the 1930s it was her relationship with Bill Hole that was pivotal to Olivia's sense of herself. By 1939 this love affair was already a decade old. Olivia first met Bill—William Henry Hole—in early 1930, when she got a job as a junior clerk with the Metropolitan Police, where he was employed in a civilian capacity. She was seventeen years of age and he was thirty-four. He was also married. Their mutual attraction was instant and intense. In July 1939 she claimed that "There were no stages to our friendship, as we fell in love at first sight" (Directive Reply). Sexual intercourse probably began when Olivia was seventeen, or eighteen at most. There is no evidence that she had any other lovers during the 1930s. Since she and Bill were unable to arrange many intimate moments together—he continued to live with his wife and his affair with Olivia was (apparently) a secret to most third parties—she sometimes addressed her thoughts to him in the form of "Letters to a Friend," a journal she began in July 1931 and that he was intended to read. This and two other private journals between 1934 and 1940 afford the reader some insight into a love affair that held together, despite severely inhospitable circumstances and some major differences between them.

Olivia and Bill were drawn together, first and foremost, by passion. Theirs was a highly eroticized relationship, and Olivia testified time and time again to the power of sexual attachment and to her own robust sexuality. As an eighteen year old, she acknowledged "that definite appetite" in herself, which she had only recently discovered. "You can't guess how strange and terrible these new thoughts and feelings are to me. I had always hoped and hoped that music or writing would be the outlet for any such tremendous enthusiasm—never dreamt that it would be a person—and someone else's husband at that" (August 20, 1931). Two weeks later she was telling him, "Bill, I'm only beginning to realise how utterly I love you, and how utterly inexperienced I am, and how utterly wrong all the circumstances are. And I'm just beginning to realise what it must mean to you" (September 5, 1931). The language of erotic attraction did not fade away, even as time passed and they got to know one another better. Three years later, on September 18, 1934, Olivia told Bill, in her journal, that "often I have a swift deep rush of uncontrollable longing for you in my arms and breasts and lips. Oh again and again."

Olivia thought a lot about her own character, and her needs, and what she was looking for, and how—understandably, given her age—she was still learning about herself. "I need a special particular way of living," she wrote on July 5, 1932. "I want a lot, and not a bit straightforwardly. I mean, I can imagine now that some men would be too—what? Spiritual? Anyway, not equally lustful with me." Even when she tried to put him out of mind, "I'm still left," she confessed, "with that ghastly insatiable new appetite for pleasure that I knew nothing of before you taught me: pleasure that won't be forgotten because there are so many things every day to remind me of it—every book or picture or pair of lovers give it a new urgency" (August 17, 1932). She was, she said, "hungry for you."

Later that day—she was in a reflective mood and wrote ten pages in her diary—she was still pondering her sexual character. Might she be "over-sexed?" Olivia offered Bill a self-commentary, her own interpretation of how she had changed during her eighteenth and nineteenth years.

You see—dismissing the last two years—I have been singularly free from any contact with or knowledge of—what shall we say?—carnal appetite. No, just sexual inexperience. I was chivvied at school for being very down on "that sort" of joke, and for refusing to discuss "that sort" of thing with anyone. I didn't refuse it very self-consciously. I was just too interested in other things. And I had read so deeply and satisfiedly of Love—like that without any detail—and felt so certain that it would be my portion, in that land of "after school," that I didn't worry. What little I gathered of the other girls' views I dismissed as rot, and nasty rot. I was content to keep poetry as my guide to Love, not pimply boys and sticky sniggers.

So that I was, I see now, extraordinarily ignorant when I first met you and became really interested in the subject. And you know how much I know now because you've told me. Mother never has, or anyone. Except I've read some Marie Stopes.[13]

She then spoke of her own intensity, and of her strong urges and powerful emotions.

Perhaps if I had joined in with the ordinary vaguely beastly mouthings of the other girls I'd have used up energy that way instead of bottling it all up all unknown until You came. That's what it is you see—the accumulation of all my life till now—the love of every-thing and anything pure and sweet and beautiful expressing itself in my love of you who are so—loveable. And it's still a wonder to me that you should love me. Every time I see myself in a mirror I love you more for loving <u>me</u>, even me as I am.

In discovering the young, naive Olivia, Bill Hole had, it seems, caused Olivia to discover herself, and she had trouble imagining a parting of the ways or that any man might replace Bill in her affections. On April 22, 1933, they were discussing some of their "intellectual divergences" and what these might mean for their continuing relationship.

And then you said you were sorry you'd made love to me, three years ago, because it has made me unhappy; that I ought and could find somebody else. And for the first time I <u>felt</u> you meant it. And I compared a young man—any young clever man—with you and honestly thought I might like one, <u>if</u> one ever liked me; and <u>that</u> I believe impossible. I'm plain and cleverish and it's an unattract-ive mixture. Why darling You should ever have liked me I literally can't imagine. I love you, Bill, though I do recognise your limitations now—ones I never dreamed existed. But I love you more fiercely because of them, because they make loving you unreasonable, which it is. And the more unreasonable the stronger must needs be the pas-sionate affection.

This theme of "unreasonable passion" persisted in Olivia's writings, even as she matured, gained in confidence, and became more vocal and sometimes blunt in her criticisms of Bill's deficiencies. By 1934 she was asserting herself and found that she was (in words she addressed to him) "not so consciously bound by the ever-present desire to be like—appear like—my idea of your idea of me." She was aware of a growing strength and independence in her-self, and of moving into full adulthood (she was now twenty-one). "I think that in fact I am tougher and brighter and more sarcastic than you imagine me. And as I become older, and more established in the mould of my character, these traits are stronger and less hidden in any sweet girlishness. They will probably develop until you dislike them and me too." That same day, August

17, 1934, she had played a little game with herself, rating Bill according to various criteria of her own.

I began then, jokingly in my mind, to classify your different qualities and give them percentages. A rough and ready but interesting guide to my thoughts about you, if not to you. Today they ran thus (another time they may be quite different):

As a lover, 99, most decidedly.

As an economist, 33, if that.

As a manager, 60, a little vague.

As a walk and talk companion, 79 in town, 69 in country.

As an intellectual stimulant, 20, only in opposition.

As an actor, 70, too serious—no, solemn [Olivia and Bill were in amateur dramatics].

As an office associate, 100 in the past, 10 now.

As a listener to music, 60, varying.

As a looker at pictures, 60, varying.

As a looker at maps, 50, disappointing.

As a shopping companion, 85, very good.

As a provider of "treats," 40, unavoidably low.

As a judge of clothes, men 80, women 70, Me 65 (too Turk).

As a reader of books, 50, pity.

As a reader of plays, 60, better.

Intellectually, Olivia and Bill were cut from different cloth, and both were aware of their differences. She was a freethinker, poetic in her sensibilities, impatient with conventional wisdom, and possessed of a restless and inquiring mind. She loved words, and was absorbed by the power of good books, was quick to probe beneath the surface, and blessed with a vivid imagination. Bill, by contrast, was no intellectual and did not pretend to be one. "I can't imagine you being intellectual," Olivia wrote on September 5, 1931, the day after his thirty-sixth birthday—she was not quite nineteen. "You don't like logical and thorough discussions, do you dear?" she asked on January 9, 1932. She spoke that same day of his "sturdy British sense"; on January 3, 1933, of his devotion to "Duty" ("to you a natural law") which differed from the strength of her "Inclination"; on May 8, 1934, of his "hidebound prejudices";

and some years later she described him as "Ultra-Conservative" (September 1, 1939). Given his "domination" of her life, she complained, in December 1934, "I must refuse to be interested in politics, in serious thinking." On August 21, 1934, she responded in her journal to a remark that he had made. "And then you said that were you my husband I wouldn't be allowed to be interested in abstract ideas, new education, or working for them. That's stupid. I would never marry you until you retracted on that point as well as on twin beds!" He, for his part, spoke of her "pursuit of 'isms'" and reminded her, at a moment when there was tension between them, "I never professed to be intellectual, merely 'plain'" (around December 11, 1934).

Bill, then, shone primarily as a lover— "Oh my darling, do always remember you're 99 as my lover! Always and always" (August 17, 1934)—but he also had at least one other merit. He was considerate. "You seem so gentle and good and courteous and a perfect lover" (August 17, 1932). He seemed to her a gentleman, though she never actually uses this word, who embraced both civility and passion. On July 3, 1932, she commended his "blend of living. Your fine appreciation of subtle distinctions. Your ability to be always expressive and never coarse; to be always passionate and never sated; to be always delicately dreadful, and never dreadfully delicate; to love and be loved; and to keep the balance so beautifully always."

Olivia wrote not only about the depth of her feelings for Bill but also about her sense of the fragility of their relationship. Their intellectual differences, and the big difference in their ages, caused her concern, sometimes acute concern, if not always, then at least intermittently. These, however, were not the main obstacles to Olivia's happiness. The central problem was that Bill was already married and seemed likely to stay married. This was the dreadful constraint that weighed so heavily on Olivia's life for many years, through adolescence and into her twenties.

One source of stress was that her affair with Bill necessitated deceit and duplicity. It wasn't long before her parents knew of the affair (after some initial disapproval, they put up no resistance), and two or three of her best friends probably knew as well. But since most of the rest of the world did not know and could not be told—Olivia and Bill might both have been fired from their jobs had word got out—the clandestine lovers constantly had to evade, conceal, and mislead in order to protect themselves from discovery and what they feared would be the consequent social retribution. Olivia complained of these strains as early as December 20, 1931. "Oh cuss all plotting and planning; I do hate it and all the excited worriedness that comes with it. Bill, I shall be a nervous wreck if this goes on much longer. I'm not built to enjoy intrigues and suchlike." Enjoy them or not, they were socially essential, but they were stressful. "I can feel that the strain of 'keeping up appearances' at the office is telling on him," she said of Bill on June 27, 1932; "it is on me." She also spoke of the "continual worry" of bumping into people they knew "when we're out together." Their public roles must have often been painful to perform. "Damn and blast social conveniences," Olivia exclaimed on August 17, 1932. "Two years of hiding round the corner have sapped my nerve. I can scarcely think straightforwardly now." She was also deprived of any sort of recognizable social/sexual identity. "I feel nor maid nor wife nor widow," she lamented, "dirtied and sullied and still refusing to be so natural as to be your mistress." She wondered at this time (August 1932) if their days together were numbered: "we can't go on much longer without a dreadful crash, either outside us among people and events, or between us."

An even more important frustration emerged at this time and would become increasingly distressing for Olivia as the years passed. This was her desire for children. To deliberately have a child out of wedlock was unthinkable, given her social and financial constraints. And yet Olivia's desire for babies was strong and deep-rooted—as early as August 17, 1932, she was hoping for "a father to the child I must have"—and this desire intensified as she entered her twenties. But how could she become a mother and still "stay" with Bill, in this secretive, we-are-not-a-couple way? Was it possible that he could ever become her husband and thus father to her children as well as her lover, or would she have to look elsewhere? Given that a family assumed marriage, would Bill have to be sacrificed? These were vital questions. Olivia, who was deeply in love, was in a serious quandary. "I've always rather despised people who wanted to 'settle down,'" she remarked on December 9, 1934, shortly after the start of her twenty-third year. "Sounds so vegetable and dull and unadventurous. But now I'd give anything to be able to feel vegetable for a few hours."

She thought about other men. In November 1934 she met a man "who made me realise with a shock that it would be very easy to get married and have babies and do all the things I'm longing to do if I could consent to marry some one other than you." Then she "spent a miserable week while you slowly grasped the full meaning of this." They were talking about splitting up at this time, in later 1934, a time that Olivia later recalled as "ghastly." By the next year their love was renewed. "You are so much more important than anything else in life to me," she wrote on September 14, 1935, "that it is worth learning how to adjust to you." She felt that their love was "timeless and expansive" (July 15, 1936) and that "our physical knots were becoming even more intricate" (July 24, 1937). "The Years! How they thicken and mount," she wrote that Saturday evening, "and every day and night of them, every hour, most minutes, I long for you in vain. No wonder a sore heaviness has settled about my heart. No wonder I cry 'hopeless.' No wonder I am depressed. But every conceivable wonder at our blind grim obstinate passion for one another."

She was torn, as she acknowledged, between her heart and her head. A year later, on August 19, 1938, she was delivering a lecture to herself. "I am all sorts of fool to stick to this man. Nearly nine years now and no more chance of settling down, or of him really trying to, than the first day we met." Her youth was fading—she would soon be twenty-six—so "why do I go on? Habit. Cowardice. Affection. He is clean and kind—according to his lights. But after all his lights are not stars, or even moons, just nice ordinary respectable electrodes, a little twisted by me. He 'doesn't pretend' to be anything but ordinary. So why do I go on embittering 9/10ths of my time for the 1/10th sweetness he gives—gives so secretly and, I think, semi-grudgingly?" She concluded angrily, "I'm doomed for a dreamy fool, waking too late." However, in line with the seesawing emotions she so often struggled with, two days later (August 21) she was in an entirely different mood. "Miserable devil to write like that! But it was true for the time being....And this last 24 hours he's had such a rotten time with her [his wife], after talking in his sleep! And I'm comparatively cheerful again, sewing and gardening and went to the pictures with Dad and reading French history."

We arrive, then, via Olivia's private writings, in the year 1939, and we reach that moment, just before the outbreak of war, when she began to write for Mass-Observation. Her sole personal comment for the first half of that year was recorded on June 11, 1939, and it is noteworthy.

On April 22 I went with Mother to America. Met several men who were mutually interested. Thought I would like to marry one, to get a home and children and order in my life. Found out yesterday that he's married.

Olivia spent most if not all of her time in New York City: "I had such a good time in New York!" she told M-O in October 1940. "Wish I had been born in America—of English stock." While we do not know much about what happened during these six weeks away from home, and away from Bill, it is clear that she had romantic opportunities. "I was once in love with a Czech lawyer, for a few days while crossing the Atlantic," she recalled over a year after the fact (October 1940 Directive Reply). Moreover, there was probably at least one other man to whom she was attracted to during these weeks, for on September 9, 1939, she wrote in her M-O diary, "Have had three phone calls, missed me each time, from America. Over on business, met last April in New York. Almost would marry him and flee to New York."

In fact, it was Bill who fled from his wife, at least temporarily. Olivia referred to her as "GM"—her name was Gertude—and she exists in Olivia's diaries mostly in the background. Two or three of Olivia's references to her in the earlier 1930s were in no way unkind; indeed, they tended to be compassionate. By the end of the decade her tone was changing. "GM becomes more and more a neurotic stranger in the house," she remarked on July 7, 1939. "A bothersome burden on conscience, she is weak and so pathetic. We dilly and dally and all the years go by." But then, twelve days later, on Wednesday, July 19, Olivia reported:

Last weekend Bill told her that he had decided to leave her. I think I was as surprised as she was, and as he was. I didn't press for details, but it appears to have been during a row that she at last believed him.

One can assume that Bill's wife's new set of beliefs concerned the true state of his affections, her own inability to hold him any more, or the certainty of the breakdown of their marriage. Surely she must have felt these or some combination of such painful acknowledgements. For Olivia, this was a breakthrough. "I feel amazed and happy about Bill's decision. And I hope and trust that we shall be doing the right thing at last. Thank you, America." This last sentence suggests that Olivia's experiences overseas had in some way jolted Bill into action. The prospect that she might, perhaps, end her relationship with him may have induced Bill to choose at last between the two women in his life. A week later, on July 26, 1939, Olivia was once again enthusing about her lover. "We made love for half an hour to our mutual joy, and you said 'We must neither of us get a bit older than we are.' Dear silly. I love you more and more, and understand it less and less."

Bill's separation from Gertrude was short-lived. In fact, according to Olivia, he left home for only two weeks or so. He slept for two nights at Olivia's home and then they moved to their own flat in London where they spent a tearful and difficult fortnight in September. Then Bill went back to his wife. They moved to Sheen, near Richmond, and Olivia returned to 33 Breakspears, from where she relaunched her diary for Mass-Observation in early October. On the last day of December, now in her twenty-eighth year, she pondered the direction of her tumultuous love life.

Bill is very kind and thoughtful and loving to me. But it isn't enough of course. I'm too old to be living at home still being looked after by my Mother. And I want babies. But I love him, so I go on.

London in early 1940—the place where Olivia was to spend an extraordinary year—was already feeling like a different city. One diarist for Mass-Observation, a twenty-five-year-old married woman who had been living in Leeds, spent a month in the capital in January/February and was shocked by what she saw. "London I found a terrible place, although I always loved going back to it before the war. . . . The blackout and wartime conditions generally struck me as being much, much worse than in a provincial town. I felt unsafe from the moment I put my foot outside the station, and was astonished at the lack of shelters such as we have in Leeds. . . . In crowded districts like Brixton there did not appear to be any shelters, or if there were any, no big yellow notices pointing the way, as in other towns." She also felt insecure for other reasons. "In London I found that girls were very afraid of 'meeting horrid men' in the blackout. My sisters have both had one or two nasty experiences in that direction. I hated going out after dark there, as there were always several shifty looking men lounging about. I've never been particularly afraid of it up here, although I scarcely ever go out after dark alone. But London struck me altogether as having the air of a 'depressed area,' and no doubt this sort of thing goes on more in such places." (Diarist no. 5406, February 1940)

In the winter of 1939–40, enthusiasm for the war in England was lukewarm, especially among women. This was a matter that Mass-Observation was looking into, and its findings were based in part on the testimonies that Olivia Cockett and dozens of other people, men and women, were sending each month to M-O. A twenty-two-year-old woman who was temporarily living in the Highgate area of London conveyed a sense of this reserve in her diary entry for February 10. She spent the evening talking with her cousin, "Ronnie," and reported some of their conversation.

Talked with him till nearly 1 a.m. and found that our views coincided to a remarkable extent. Both feel that this war is so futile and swear at the amount of money that can be raised for it, when any effort in peacetime for social or medical purposes never succeeds as it ought. Feel that so long as people think in terms of nations and territorial barriers there will be no real settlement. Remarked on the supreme irony of the fact that in spite of about one person in a hundred only really supporting war, yet we were compelled to go on with it. Suppose that German people feel the same. Their mistake was to be lazy and to allow a party of gangsters to rule them, to save them from political thought. British fault as usual is negligence. People not interested in using their rights and providing informed public opinion with result that we just drifted into this mess, under incompetent guidance. Wonder whether deliberate brutality or neglect is the worse crime?

A week later, on February 17, she continued with her negative thoughts about the war (her fiancé was about to enter the Army and their marriage was on hold):

This whole damned war is so futile. We have all of us, individuals and nations, got so much to lose and nothing to gain. And soon hates will breed hates. Know so many people who said last September that they wished we were not fighting the Germans, and now they express such hatred. I don't hate them, but I hate war, and I hate the conditions that allow it to happen. Suppose the Nazis must be vandals though, to judge from their behaviour in Poland not only towards the population but towards the beautiful things, the manuscripts etc. What will happen if the Poles have a chance to revenge themselves? Europe seems likely to be tortured by one long vendetta. (Diarist no. 5421)

Bitterness, apathy, indifference, confusion, fatalism, a deep mistrust of the nation's leaders (Neville Chamberlain was still prime minister): these were prevalent sentiments among women in the early months of 1940. A forty-nine-year-old woman in Sevenoaks, Kent, reported that she had not been a pacifist in the Great War, but "now as an adult I feel that war being such a contradiction of man's gregarious instincts, there must *be a better way out of difficulties of conflicting interests, though I confess I don't see how to get to it at the present time!" (DR no. 1583, February 1940). A London housewife, aged forty-two, reported a conversation she had had with another married woman, "who said the present war left her completely indifferent, although she had been keen on the last one, and had made shells because she wanted to kill Germans. We regretted she had not killed more when she had the chance, but agreed that we also felt lack of enthusiasm owing to mistrust of present government and because we had been through it all before" (DR no. 1060, January 1940). Another woman, a twenty-five-year-old teacher in Brighton, conveyed her sense of disgust: "it is the absolute waste and misdirection of energies that sickens me. To think what constructive work could be done for man's benefit with the money and manpower now being thrown away"(DR no. 2047, February 1940). Fervour for the war at this time, in early 1940, was hard to find.*

A woman who was living in Oxfordshire at this time spoke of the feeling of dreary ennui that affected many people. She wrote in February: "I wish I knew whether the average German is as bored as the average Englishman.

If he was, then (taking a very long view indeed) there would be reasons for hopefulness. An enormous advance would have been made if the world were steadily learning to look upon war, not as exciting or glorious or cathartic in any way, but as poisonously boring. *I am certain that this long view is not in the mind of any European government, but it seems to me the only optimistic point of view in the present gloomy circumstances. In war the word 'sacrifice' is always dinned into the ears of the people. My view at present is that* our boredom is our sacrifice—*and in the end it might turn out to be a much more useful one than anyone at present believes" (DR no. 1030, February 1940). Six or eight months after these words were written it was not possible to be bored—certainly not in London. However, in the early months of 1940 people's backs were not yet to the wall and their minds were rarely as resolute and concentrated on survival as they would later be under direct attack.*

At the beginning of February, the first issue of the magazine US: Mass-Observation's Weekly Intelligence Service *was sent to subscribers and M-O's volunteers, and its main mission was to inform readers about the current state of public opinion and provide digests and interpretations of the substantial testimony concerning the Home Front that M-O was receiving from its respondents, observers, and diarists. Olivia refers to this periodical from time to time in her diary for 1940. The second issue of* US, *dated February 10, 1940, remarked on feelings and attitudes shared by many women, that were often evident in early 1940 in Olivia's comments and reflections. "From all our evidence," concluded the editor of* US, *"the dissatisfaction of women appears to be increasing more rapidly than that of men. The war is being run by men and the female point of view has so far been inadequately represented both in policy and publicity. Women's feelings and interests are at all times more opposed to war than those of men. Practically nothing," it was thought, "has been done to deal specifically with female situations and neurosis."*

One woman, a widow of fifty who ran her own business and lived in Maida Vale, London, offered a thoughtful perspective on women's sentiments. According to her diary for February 14, "So many women lately are saying to me how deadly sick they are of life. What with the blackout (that seems to get them down worse than anything), the cold, frozen and burst pipes,"—that winter was exceptionally cold—"nothing happening in the war, a terrible apathy is setting in. And the Government has entirely the wrong orientation in dealing with the Nation," she thought. "If it turned round and said, 'look here, we'll work together,' instead of, 'look here, you damned well do as you're told and ask no questions,' they'd be amazed at the response" (Diarist no. 5356).

The writer and editor Diana Athill, born in 1917, recalled in the 1960s her painfully mixed feelings as war again descended on Britain.

I was no longer pacifist in any formal sense. To make gestures against the war once it had come seemed as absurd as to make gestures against an earthquake or a hurricane. The horror had materialized and it must be endured, but to participate in it any further than I was compelled to do by *force majeure* did not occur to me. A mute, mulish loathing of the whole monstrous lunacy was what I felt; almost an indifference to how it ended, for no matter who won the war, it had happened; human beings—and I did not recognize much difference between German human beings and English ones—had proven capable of making it happen, and that fact could never be undone.[14]

Such stoical reticence was commonplace during this depressing winter. (The next winter's mood would be much different.)

Evidence from early 1940 testifies to a conflicted public mood. One young married woman who had just moved from Leeds to Birmingham confessed to the sort of anxiety and malaise that were widely in evidence. She reported in late February or early March 1940 that "Most people I know would welcome peace at practically any price." She thought that her childhood memories of the sorrows of the Great War (she was born in February 1914) had "a lot to do with the fact that I hated, and still do hate, war, and always dreaded it more than anything as soon as I realised it was possible there would be another. I always thought of war in terms of 'death,' and when this one began I took it almost for granted that my two brothers would eventually be killed, and possibly, even, my husband. The fact that it has not turned out yet as violently as that has given me a tremendous relief" (DR no. 2048, February 1940). A thirty-four-year-old journalist who lived in southeast London recalled that, with the outbreak of war in September, some young women had become very agitated and gone "off the deep end." By contrast, "the older people," she thought, "are certainly tougher about the war: at the moment it is just a tragic drag on the heart, and nothing private matters." But any such generalization was bound to be suspect, and she thought of a friend who took "the opposite view. She says that public affairs are such a mess that the only thing to do is to retreat into one's private life. The war merely disgusts her as a whole, being insane and purely foul. But to me, under the blah of whipping up public enthusiasm for the war, there is the nobility of the eternal struggle of human beings to rise to effort" (Diarist no. 5349, February 27, 1940). Many felt ambivalent, yet heartsick, and were concerned about the manipulation of the news. One twenty-four-year-old single woman, a civil servant who worked in London and lived in Croydon, regarded the news as highly propagandistic, "to keep us optimistic. I believe at the moment that we must go on with the war, but do not like looking into the future with its possible appalling loss of young lives" (DR no. 1047, January 1940).

Olivia's diary resumed after an extended silence.

February 1940

Have not made any notes for diary for two months; indeed, not since I was at home on sick leave, with time on my hands to be spent pleasantly. Since returning to work, life seems to be all travel, work, food and blessed sleep. The war has been only the cause of slight discomforts, blackout, extra work, talk about food. It has not been the ever-present horror which in the past I dreaded having to face: dreaded it so much that I spent a lot of time talking, reading, thinking POLITICS. Now that the war has come I feel that politics are an utter waste of time, a wangle, a racket, and of no real value to us as individuals. I have become an "elementalist," clinging to the simple basic values of the present moment, with mystical values for a measuring rod, instead of materialist social welfare ideals. And I have been happier—oh <u>lots</u> happier—since deciding to make my own "mental weather" and to think only on whatsoever things are pure, lovely and of good report. I never have bought newspapers; now I dislike listening to wireless news even. I rarely discuss the war, or public affairs. [At the end of 1939 she had written in her private diary, "My interest in politics has died of disgust, it seems."]

This sounds, so far, like an "escape" but I don't feel like that. Indeed I feel that I have at last plunged into <u>real</u> life, away from the flickering surface of events, of troubles which are there in some form for every generation back and down into an eternal "present moment," which is also there for every generation, and always will be, even if a generation ever arrives to solve the surface difficulties. After all, one strives to solve those social material problems in order to live the good life, to become a more complete restful balanced soul, seeing life steadily and whole, rounded by eternity. So one must practise the arts of that life, to be prepared for it. And one finds in preparing that it has come.

Pictures, plays, music, books, poetry, all the joys of personal friendship and of love: [these] seem and ARE of far greater value now than ever they were.

Well, that's about enough vague philosophy! I'll now try for a few days to keep a daily diary.

Monday, February 19

Woke late (7:30 instead of 7) after a wakeful night mixed with violent and melancholy dreams—fighting lions in a jungle with my bare hands; seeing a sad woman and children in slums; watching a baby playing with its soldier father; sleeping in a dangerous place. Hurried through toast and coffee and marmalade which Mother got ready, although she should have stayed in bed, being plagued with the change of life and much pain lately. Found the snow had gone and the rain come, with thick cold mist as well. So stopped hurrying quite so much, as the trains would be late anyway.

Got a seat in a 1st compartment (3rd ticket) along with a dozen other sinners. Looked at their tired miserable pale faces and then shut my eyes instead and concentrated on pleasant thoughts. Changed at Waterloo and felt the usual pathetic disgust at the youngsters in uniform who are always sadly lost there, trying to look cocky. Got a compartment to myself and knitted and sang all the way to Putney, keeping my eyes off the dismal sooty chimneys.

Met the girl I work with and walked up the hill together, cursing the weather and laughingly praising the cheek of the Navy regarding Altmark.[15] Monday being a very busy day there was no general discussion among the five males and two females in my room about this incident. Spoke of the Registration on Saturday and I said "Under 2% Conscientious Objectors" and a temporary clerk (50), undersized, smarmy, said "Lot of damned rot, these conchies" with astonishing emphasis, and went on mumbling for a while. Nobody took him up, as we were busy, though some of us appreciate the Conscientious Objector point of view.

I had sandwiches at my desk and read a book about the country. The Chief came in and chatted for ten minutes about the wonderful comfort of his house. Then the others drifted back from the canteen, grumbling about the small size of the portions as usual. Went for a cup of tea at 3, discussed cake baking with Mrs Smith (21), and how she will manage if her husband is killed in the war. She said "It sounds a bit callous, but I shan't mind a lot when he goes. It will give me a rest and do him good—he's so fussy."

Caught the 4:22 in fog and rain and was home by 6. Peg (old school friend) came for the evening. Had a pleasant meal of soup and currant pudding with Mother listening to the radio serial thriller. Dad at a Masonic dinner, so a small gaiety of women. Then Mother bolted and Peg and I went to my sitting room: chilly. Talked of M-O and she answered the Public Opinion questionnaire for me. Listened to Hodge on BBC Art and the Newton smugness.[16] Pleasant to hear an intelligent Cockney accent on the air. Switched round the dial a bit, heard a few American amateurs—twice as human as the cold voiced pros. Heard a scrap of Gigli but didn't like the opera. Showed Peg the woolly hedgehog I've made for my nephew's birthday present, together with four pairs of bought sox and two pairs I've knitted. Read some modern poetry, from the Public Library, Auden and

Waller. Liked Waller; uses modern allegories well, and realises there is a life of the spirit as well as the lovely flesh.

Went down to the kitchen for hot milk about 10. Felt sleepy and a bit cross. Disliked the way Peg sticks her arms out and stands about looking lost and awkward. Felt sorry for that unkindness and told her she could sleep with me instead of in the spare room. I know she likes that, though I don't. Talked [Bertrand] Russell's philosophy for a bit in bed and then settled to muse on my lover till sleep.

Tuesday, February 20

Woke 6:45 to another cold damp foggy February dawn. Hot coffee and porridge and Mother's kind face. Then standing in a stuffy cold carriage for half an hour; five minutes with my man, and into another train; always get a seat on the second train as it goes away from London.[17] Leaned in the corner with warm back and seat, and cold knees and face, planning vague dressmaking and mending, of music and holidays; rehearsing a coming interview with the doctor; re-living love-makings; switching my thoughts violently whenever they ran near the war.

Arrived at the office on time; everyone grumbling at the weather. Still no "news" discussion. Stared hungrily at my four jonquils in a white vase, longing for spring and the country and walks. Lunchtime; walked down to the High Street to change my book at Smith's library. Was surprised to see a big new flower shop opened—expensive. Felt a thrill of spring in the air for the first time. Walked back again, watching people's faces; still mostly look worried, rarely see a contented face. Sat and ate sandwiches and read well past my proper time. Chief came and chatted about work. A giggly afternoon with silly jokes and a good deal of singing.

Caught an early train home, stopped halfway and had an unfortunate social incident which stuck like a fishbone in my mind all evening and reappeared in my dreams. Was pleased, for once, to play cards for a couple of hours as it takes one's mind off other things so completely. Bath and bed by 10:30 and read philosophy for an hour.

Wednesday, February 21

Woke to a warmer grey morning, a bit less wet. Saw a tram run down a hill and smash into the back of another. Was on a bus so don't know if anyone was hurt. I wondered whether to ring the local paper, as it was a spectacular bit of damage. After getting into a phone box I saw my train come in, so pressed B and got my money back instead.

As the indicator was wrong regarding trains I was late into the office, but no fuss was made. Lunchtime, sat and read and ate sandwiches at my desk. Then rang various offices for a solid hour, getting an abstract of expenses completed; my elbow and ear ached. Tea at 3 was welcome; had to wait ten minutes as all cups were in use. Very cheery feeling in the office again; was relieved, as had feared repercussions of last night's incident.

Caught the 5:32 by running very hard and fast. Was home in daylight, for once. Bought Mother a copy of new sixpence magazine <u>Housewife</u> and as everyone was out sat and read it with my meal.[18] Then wrote for all the free samples in it!! First time I've done this. It suddenly appealed to me and I shall look forward to the post for a few days. Finished knitting nephew's socks while listening to Rhythm, then to Walton's Symphony; not exactly lovable music, but sharpening and interesting in a cross-word-puzzle way. Switched off as the news came on and went downstairs to find Mother and Dad and hear all the news of their visit to cousin Eve and her two small children. Her husband (accountant 26) and brother (grocer 26) have both volunteered for the regiment they want to join as they expect to get better treatment that way than by waiting for their call-up.

Mother, Dad, Bert (50, radio-dealer) sat in the kitchen from 9 till 10 chatting about call-ups, reserved occupations. Bert [Willmott] couldn't find Structural Engineer (his son) in the booklet at the Labour Exchange. Spoke of the worry caused by the constant changing of the reserved ages.[19] Talked of the Navy and the probable surprise of the public if a full casualty list was published. Bert retailed two or three strange accidents and adventures at sea, read in the papers. We told one or two jokes, about children. Had a mug of cider (bottled) and went up to bed at 10. Lovely warm bed from electric blanket. Read B. Russell's Sensual Perception of the External World until 11.

Thursday, February 22

Slept soundly till 3:15. Then woke and was restless till got up at 7. Can't remember any dreams. Had a look round garden; apricot sun-rise, snowdrops, mild air, thrush singing. Caught early train and sat for ten minutes in station with W, still telling one another how much we are in love and how much we like it in spite of hellish difficulties. Got to office on time and slacked about chatting for nearly an hour. Not much work in; big job arranged for today had to be put off, as nobody had the details of an area reorganisation which happened in January. Am now writing this diary in work-time; have had one or two funny looks from people with work. Shall now offer to help someone else for an hour.

Lunchtime, went down to the Library, walked a roundabout way back, enjoying the mild air and breeze. Spoke for ten minutes to girl friend on phone, ate sandwiches, spoke ten minutes to boy friend. Read thriller to the end! But still got all my work and some of the others' done. Caught 4:16 and saw a crowd waiting at Waterloo. Enquired of a police constable and it was the arrival of Ajax and Exeter men. Waited myself, but they turned away to the left; a cheer was raised by the people near them; we jumped on a seat and could see they were mostly young, very sunburnt. Sat with my man talk-ing for a while and then walked over Vauxhall Bridge to see a sick girl friend. Took flowers and cake. Stayed till 10:30, talking office shop, war gossip, love gossip, Christian Science (I believed in it ten years ago, not now) and philosophy of sorts. Went out into glori-ous silver of full moon on roofs and pavements and river. Home by 11:35 and got into bed by moonlight, slept well. Moment my head touched the pillow, all last night's dreams came rushing back—a lovely walled secluded shady garden, and I went walking round it in new dreams.

Moonlit nights were greatly appreciated during the war, for they freed Londoners from the oppressive effects of the blackout. The blackout not only tended to discourage mobility and keep people at home at night, but it was also a major cause of road and pedestrian accidents, some of them fatal.

Friday, February 23

Mother came up and called me at 7:30!! Lazed and chatted of small nephew's birthday party and then had to rush and tear and caught the later train. Stayed half-an-hour watching the Ajax-Exeter men assembling before their parade and the King. A few wives and mothers standing about looking excited and pleased. Office not very interested in details.

General discussion of marriage going on while I'm scribbling. Youngsters full of levity. Old S (45) says the dog comes easily first in his wife's feelings.

Monday, February 26

Had a perfectly lovely weekend—SPRING and energy in the air after all this freezing weather.

On the way up to Town on Saturday I felt desperately (although living on ten borrowed bobs) that I <u>must</u> have some flowers; and my Dear Love met me with a great shear of freesia!! Sat and talked to him for twenty minutes and then happily home to eat and stare round the garden before three hours of strenuous cleaning—the first thorough clean since the week before Xmas. All doors and windows open to the mild air.

At 6 Pat came with her baby and at 7 I went home with her, carrying Clive. Stayed and saw him to bed and then home by 9 to bath and sleep soundly. Woke at 11 (Summer Time) and was soon digging manure into the garden, washing off last year's dirt from glass tents and putting in lettuce seed. Sweated happily in the cool pleasant air and crumbled the warm grainy soil joyfully with my fingers. Bath and lunch and then heard Solomon playing B's 4th Concerto.[20] Washed my hair and welcomed Joan to tea. Spent a cheerful evening chatting and looking at books. Cuss that nib won't come clear. [Her pen was behaving erratically.] At 10 we had a glass of sherry and I took Joan to the bus. Back to bed and read poetry by Robert Waller—very good "contemplative imagination"—must get more of it.

Woke late, but made up for it by brief washing. Lots of heavy damp grey mist about; winter back it seems. Spent seven minutes gabbing joyfully to W at station and in to work by 9:10. Knitted by wide-open window at lunch time—the sun is through again and the birds singing. Everyone has spent a happy weekend, most of them in the garden. Taking <u>Dig for Victory</u> seriously? Or just responding to the Ancient Urge.

Must just remember to say Thank You for <u>US 4</u> [Mass-Observation magazine]. It is a pleasure to get these brief reminders of the outside world. The illusion of contact with events satisfies a social hunger. And I am gratified to find my own isolationist attitude reflected so widely at Southwark poll.

At the by-election on February 10 in Central Southwark—an overwhelmingly working-class constituency—the official, pro-war (Labour) candidate won easily. However, only about 24 percent of the theoretically eligible electors took the trouble to vote. (The actual electorate was reduced by evacuation and conscription.) It was this lack of interest in the war—even apathy—that probably attracted Olivia's attention. At the same time, it was clear that explicit anti-war opinion was weak. The "Stop the War" candidate fared badly in the poll, despite vigorous organizational support from members of the Communist Party. (Pamphlets and other material related to this by-election may be found in the M-O Archive, TC46/3/G.)

Olivia mentions "Dig for Victory," the slogan that was designed to encourage people to produce more of their own food supplies, thereby reducing the demands on retailers and commercial providers of agricultural produce, much of which was imported from abroad. The slogan, according to an article in Mass-Observation's US (nos. 16–17 for May 17, 1940), "has caught on, and apart from its immediate purpose of helping out the supplies of green vegetables, it has given many a new feeling (or revived an old one) about the soil and working outdoors." Cultivating the soil was, for many city people, an agreeable, meaningful, and personally satisfying activity. "The big appeal of the campaign to the townsman," claimed Mass-Observation, "is the appeal of the outdoor hobby. Compared with this, the idea of helping in the national war effort is far less often explicitly stated. But all the same, the proportion of those who have this idea, and the way in which they express it, is quite impressive compared with, for example, the amount of patriotism in people's reasons for saving in war time. Digging is an active occupation, more easily connected in people's minds with war and victory than is the apparently self-interested process of putting pennies in a home safe." Olivia, as her diary attests, took gardening very seriously. And, happily for her and the other residents at 33 Breakspears, their back garden was exceptionally large.

Tuesday, February 27

Spent a busy afternoon, had a pleasant calm feeling [during] journey to Town, and then a regrettable small quarrel with W—moody and unexplainable until during the night I was periodically unwell. I had forgotten the date, otherwise I should have been expecting "moods" and set my will a guard upon my tongue. Oh poor women! Pity poor women!

Spent the evening at Peg's. After eating tinned soup and tinned fruit we played some Bach. Listened to mealy-mouthed Newton summing up the <u>Artist in the Witness Box</u> very unsatisfactorily. Talked of the war, apathetically; and then of poetry enthusiastically. Peg read aloud [A.E.] Housman's <u>Name and Nature of Poetry</u>. We dug out Keats and Wordsworth and read lovely bits and both their prose remarks on poetry, and wondered a lot about this magic. While we talked I knitted. And at 10:30 we had cocoa and biscuits. Talked till 11:30 and then bed and talked about pictures and the nature of colour. Peg had been reading that animals see no colour and we speculated on the differences. Slept well, considering I hate <u>not</u> sleeping alone.

Wednesday, February 28

Arose at 7 and left the house, after a leisurely breakfast of coffee and bran and brown bread and marmalade, at 8:15. Walked through the little park, dismayed at the sight of three great pits where there had been trenches. Enjoyed the melancholy humid absence-of-cold and met W for a few satisfying kisses and remarks and his ever-fresh loving-kindness.

Knitted in the empty-but-for-me Ladies Only compartment and walked up the hill with a young man in my room. Not a lot of work in at the moment, although Mrs S is away and I am doing her work as well as my own. At lunchtime I went down to feed in town with Anne, used to be in her branch. She is in love with a man who is getting tired of her and is very unhappy; has been ill; will be again if she can't clear this up. Came back to have ten minute phone call from my man and to rejoice again in his tenderness.

Busy afternoon—now waiting a re-call. No discussion of a general nature today—a few remarks about not standing up for <u>God Save the King</u>. Some comic allusions to spies because M's girl has German measles. One man got a Savings Certificate and was bitter about it becoming £1.0.6 in 10 years. "Lot can happen in 10 years." Man in charge has rented a cottage at Lewes to evacuate his wife and mother-in-law, but we believe it's more for his convenience than theirs. (Gossip)

Mrs L (was Miss B, came back to work at our request on the outbreak) had a telegram last week that her husband was posted "Missing" in merchant navy. And yesterday she had to go to Ministry and get her pension papers. She says she can't believe it—all seems unreal. She's very glad she's got her baby.

Thursday, February 29

Still enjoying a happy mood. Lasted for longer than I can remember before. Perhaps "age" brings it.

Caught train comfortably last night; knitted. Sat and talked to W at station, very lovingly; home by 6 to sultana pudding and pre-war knob of butter and sugar. Mother out at pictures, Dad fussing around on odd jobs. Self spent an hour typing out a long poem by Waller, interrupted by half hour knitting and listening to <u>Music Makers</u> (Strings) on BBC. Then spent half-hour looking through M-O [diary] for February and putting it in envelope; half hour rambling through old letters and remembering hectic trip to New York last year. Then some time cutting holes in middle pages of an old book, imitating one seen in friend's house, to make a hiding hole for money; not much chance of having any to hide! But the idea amused me. Downstairs at 9 to chat to Mother and hear her version of the film seen—don't know what it can have been, except that the singing was bad. Her remarks were quite incoherent, though made in all seriousness. About 9:45 to bed with mug of warm milk. Read B. Russell till 11 and slept well.

Up today at 7:10, comfy breakfast, Mother happy. Came up in 1st class again; no conscience on this as it was (almost literally) impossible to get in 3rd. Met W for six minutes. He went to Doc's last night and told him he was much better—as he <u>hadn't</u> followed Doc's advice. Doc laughed, said "All right, I'll follow yours" and gave him different treatment for small skin trouble. Got compartment to myself again and knitted and met Anne, so bus up hill. She has had letter from her cooling lover, felt a bit more cheerful. But when I read it I thought it sounded like a preliminary to a farewell. Didn't say so though.

Friday, March 1

Was much too busy yesterday for a line. Little to report—office so quiet without Mrs Smith's flirtatious gaiety. Went to news film in evening and later played cards. Heard with much lightening of the heart that AFS [Auxiliary Fire Service] over 25 will be kept AFS—Mother and Dad showed a huge delight—I suddenly realised how much they had been worrying about my brother [Freddie, born on February 20, 1914, who was in the AFS and had just turned 26].

Had awful realistic air raid dreams—noise and bombs and injuries all complete. And dreamed of babies too. But the underlying mood of happiness is still holding firm, with scarcely even a suggestion of peevishness, let alone lost tempers etc. How long? Oh Lord how long…?

Afternoon. Now I shall go round the Department collecting for our men with HM Forces: one shilling a month each sends our own blokes fags and woollies. And shall do the National Savings too—giving out a notice of Annual General Meeting at the same time. (Only one person turned up, out of 300 members!!) Wonderfully bright clear day today, but very cold strong east wind.

Monday, March 4

Had a pleasant weekend, cleaning and eating and reading and walking in the fields getting fresh air. Interested to get Conscientious Objector in <u>US</u> 5,21 and have got book today from Library, <u>We Did Not Fight</u>. Am recurrently glad not to be a man, especially now.

Mrs S has returned; her sister has had a baby. She has been making allusive jokes all day. The men adore it and she plays up to them with naive art and lots of giggles and noise. Actually, she is so kindhearted and full of life that her presence is pleasant and cheerful, though to be sure I could never make her sound attractive on paper—a running fire of idiotic chatter and reminiscence and giggle, interspersed with huggings and pettings and whistling and cooing. "No harm at all in her" but such overflow of sheer sex that I often get hot round the collar and pretend not to hear. And funnily enough our old 58 year-old bachelor (once Cavalry, then 30 years with spinster sister and Civil Service and Sunday School, doesn't drink or go to theatres) enjoys her more than anyone else!! She teases him and tickles him and he blushes and chuckles and gets more and more excited until we all feel amazed that he doesn't bust—or stop her. Never met anyone else at all like her!

Tuesday, March 5

Another very crammed busy day. Pleasant evening yesterday, three lovely bunches of flowers from W because he was going to a stag party. And then to the Library, seven books. Ate and chatted and to bed by 8:30. Read a dressmaking book and ate sweets till 10:30, then read a thriller till 12:20 and slept well.

To office, same few minutes late, after hearing W's scrappy account of his party. He got slightly drunk and was sick out of the train because he had a coffee on top of beer, whisky, and sherry! Sandwich lunch, work, work, work.

Wednesday, March 6

"Only way to cure Germans is to kill 'em all. Do as the Aussies did in the last war—cut their throats on the way to internment. Lot of rats all of 'em. You won't do no good with them unless you exterminate the lot of 'em." Thus the ex-Service carpenter, while mending the office door. "Yes, that's right" from the ex-Service temporary clerk. And chuckles from the 35-year-old clerk. GOD! When <u>will</u> men learn sense?

Just a few days before reporting this exchange, Olivia had responded to a M-O questionnaire asking how childhood memories affected her attitudes to the present war. She replied with the following remarks.

Up to the age of six (1918) I was aware of war as a horrible background to life. Anything and everything nice was to happen "after the war." I can just remember the tremendous excitement of peace. Then from six to eighteen I was taught, and believed, that wars were now done with, out-of-date barbarisms which the League of Nations would forever prevent.

So that I had two strong childhood impressions about war, that it was very horrible, that it was gone forever.

These affect my present opinion in this way. This horrible thing is not done with. I have been ruthlessly deceived by those whose words I valued. Therefore they had little grasp of events, little influence, too much wish fulfillment dreaming. So my present opinions are based on the determination not to be taken in by idle hopes, to find out the real causes, to believe few official theories, to detach myself inwardly from this reeking whirl of events which I hate and despise and am bored by.

Regarding the news in the press and on radio that was available to her and her fellow citizens, Olivia was a skeptic.

I believe the news we are getting nowadays is "cooked" by the authorities to their erroneous recipe as to what will best preserve the morale of the public. News has always been a mixture of facts and opinions served up with a journalese sauce of spicy language, with little indication as to which parts were fact and which fiction or opinion. BBC news reflects most faithfully the "best" views to hold as to the news nowadays. They are so "correct" that no-one can believe they are anything but Gospel truth. But I have a very strong personal disbelief in the accuracy of, for instance, the Finnish news;[22] and a great longing to know what the news in the Chancelleries of the world is, as compared with the loudspeaker version from each country.

Her diary continued for Wednesday, March 6.

Pleasant hour's chat with W on the way home last night, reminiscences and dreams and incidents. I think we love one another so much because we just "think aloud" instead of making conversation—fancies and doodles and dreams instead of logic and argument—generally.

Peg came for the evening. We ate soup and suet pud and apples and cream and coffee. Then she tried on some of my frocks before borrowing one for a Savoy Chapel wedding—is borrowing one that is 12 years old, has come back in fashion again. Listened to [Dorothy] Sayers' Peter Wimsey thriller a half hour and then knitted. She read <u>US</u> 5 and we discussed Conscientious Objectors and were again glad not to be men. Talked of her next week's holiday walking in the country with her man. Discussed my typewriter—a cheap portable in which the paper slips. Can't decide whether to keep it or post exchange for better model. Said might as well spend the money nowadays—still see no point in saving. After all, typewriter makers and sellers must live!

Tuesday, March 12

Can't remember when I last wrote. Have taken previous sheets home, as I had an idea someone was reading this diary after I left the office. Obviously wouldn't matter much—but not desirable.

Weekend was pleasant. Cleaning and shopping on Saturday, up early on Sunday, did some exercises (!) and a lot of sewing and mending. Mother and Dad went to bungalow for the day, so I got my own meals. Two girl friends came for tea, stayed 5 till 9, chatting cheerfully. Very little mention of the war. Mostly clothes, gossip, furniture, men and some philosophy.

Worked hard on Monday, but there is not much in today so there has been a lot of talking: about the office social next Friday; about Mar's sister-in-law who has been living with them and being a nuisance and is now going; about food; about relations. Much good humour and chuckling to give a pleasant atmosphere to very trite sayings.

Wednesday, March 13

Pleasant evening, took two girl friends along the see my brother at his AFS sub station: a huge empty factory, with two taxis and some pumps and 24 men. They have iron beds and blankets along the sides of the room they "live" in: 48 hours on, 24 hours off. A tiny billiard-table, a table tennis outfit, a dart board, a wireless set, no equipment for personal use beyond what they've made or brought from home. But a cheerful lot, with beer and sandwiches and coffee. A sudden tense silence when the phone bell rang; personal call though.

Saturday, March 30

Seventeen days since I last recorded! I've been moody and depressed, felt things were not worth while, and it has been cold in my sitting room. That's just a little excusiveness because I felt guilty when I read the analysis of answers in US 9 to the questions in US 6, which I intended to answer too.[23] I feel that it is too late now, but I will do the March list, even if it is on the last day of the month. I know I do things by fits and starts, but so far I have not missed a month of M-O and I've set myself the goal of at least one year of regular answers. But I can't hope to promise the same in diaries. Up to two years ago I kept a daily regular brief, and an occasional book for passionate overflows. I felt weary and adult when I decided not to go on with it; and now here I am at it again, but now with an adult motive, as well as pleasure.

Well, what has there been since March 13? Easter, spent quietly at the family bungalow in Essex, with Mother and Dad and a convalescent office-girl-friend. She has anemia and is also trying to shake off a love affair with a married man. I am the blind leading [the blind] in that respect, being hopelessly in love with the appallingly wrong person myself. However, we both enjoyed our chats and a couple of days away from troublesome men. We looked over a couple of old churches, admired the Easter flowers and wondered whether there is any real satisfaction in Churches.[24]

Planted 300 bulbs which have been lost since last September; pruned the rose bushes; planted a few lettuce and onion seeds, in the rose bed, as it was the only dryish soil. There is a real satisfaction in the soil; anyway, for me.

Visited a friend in a new flat. Have promised to go next weekend and help make pelmets. All my four—five—close girlfriends share my passion for home making. I am still enjoying the luxury and war-wicked-waste of £6 for a Spencer reproduction (with frame) a few weeks back. I don't really care who wins this war if it does not interfere with my rare moments of ecstasy in the country. This <u>Bridle Path near Cookham</u> recalls these moments, as van Gogh does.[25] And so I go on paying 5s a week to Phoenix with real gratitude to HP. On the other wall of my bedroom I have a copy of the rooks nests poster of the WTPB, for the same reason. I've only recently noticed that all my pictures are of the country!

Oh, a lovely thing happened last week. There has been a lot of fuss in the office about leave. Some senior officers have tried to go all patriotic and deprive the juniors of the remnants of their leave because of the war. I was very much agin this. I do so savour every precious minute to myself. All the same I've had to lose 2½ of my lovely 24 days. But last week there <u>was</u> one possible morning, the last but two of the leave year, when they couldn't find an objection (though I had to come in in the afternoon) so I stayed in bed five heavenly minutes longer than usual, dallied with Mother at breakfast, dusted my bedroom in the sunshine, did my nails and small-tooth-combed my hair, made up my face (rare) and caught a train to Kew. It was a blowy morning, bright sky with white clouds flying, cold, clear English spring. I wanted to shout for joy as I sailed on past my office station! Going over Kew Bridge I did shout, and the wind collected it to help the spring. The man at the gate did not like changing my florin [two-shilling piece] for a penny. Ordinarily I would have been hot and embarrassed at giving trouble, but I just slipped in through the gate and waited impatiently while he surlily counted out 1s 6d. I walked on the first available grass, and felt so excited that I had to find a lavatory before anything else.

Came to the palm house and found it "Closed till 1 o'clock." Stared in at the great tented leaves all dewy with watering, and was for a bit in the jungle lush. Then on again over grass and reminded of the war by ploughed land, like settled sea waves. Came to a gardener and asked the way to the rockery. Passed some more greenhouses, one crammed with flowers; couldn't bear not smelling them so turned the handle in vexation and found the door opened, in spite of the notice! Trespassed gleefully, with great deep breaths of hyacinth and jonquil and unknown beauties, glowing banks of petunias and cyclamen and rhododendron dwarfs. Was spoken to by a kind young country voiced gardener, not turned out!

On through a warm sheltered glade over grass; almond and prunus blossoming; a thrush waiting boldly as I walked slowly closer and closer. I stared as hard as he, at three feet range; I got tired first and turned to go, to find a robin in the way! "This is a racket" I thought, and remembered sandwiches in my bag! Knelt down and rustled paper and fed them. And then held out my hand with crumbs on the grass; three separate robins! And some tits!! Right on to my hand, with their tiny claws and literal featherweight. So heartfilled that when I moved away I found I was breathless, and then wanted to sing as hard as the blackbirds and chaffinches around.

Meandered in a happy daze through the rockery, fed more birds. Then followed a path marked Dell, under trees and on to grass again. Saw few other people. A solitary soldier followed me a couple of hundred yards, needed encouragement, but I wanted to be alone. Stroked the tight opening buds of the bent sprays, broke through a bank of bushes to investigate a rosy cloud, found early tiny rhodes covering a great bush with open pink faces, fresh and warm to touch. Then three children asked me the time and I asked them the nearest way out on realising the hour. Finished my enchanted morning with twenty minutes suburban-neat bus ride. Late in to work, but so happy that none were peevish.

Well, that morning will live as long as my memory, but I don't suppose M-O means that by "Diary."

The war is more and more ridiculous. Sylt sickened me,[26] Finland is neatly forgotten again, uniforms are everywhere, unremarked. I speak little of the war, as little as my acquaintance. Some few office people are making a hobby of it, with all the old jingoism dug up. They are not regarded with favour, and I am lucky not to work in rooms with them, because I could not possibly keep out of arguments.

Rationing gets sillier every day. All the shopkeepers offer rationed foods without coupons being taken. <u>Everyone I know</u> has had more than their ration of something or other. We have enough of everything, although we use rationing as an excuse for thriftiness now, instead of saying we ought not to afford things.

Sunday, March 31

Sunday, bless it. Stayed dreaming in bed till 9. Breakfast alone, Ryvita, apples and coffee. Gardened till noon, lunched alone on steak pudding steamed all morning. Invited by Willmotts for a car ride. Went out via Bromley to Otford, Shoreham and home by Dartford. Saw a field of lambs. It was cold, grey and windy, so spring didn't shew up very much. Nice to get fresh air again though, in their open sports Morris 8.

Olivia had also written in her private journal for this, the last day of March, and her words disclosed some of the stress she was feeling as a result of her affair with Bill Hole.

Curious mood. Lamplight on my new desk and on many spring flowers from Bill. Warm. Well fed. Have today gardened and been for three hours run in Kent. Lambs and streams and new young green. Am in very good health. Yet think quite seriously of what life would be like without Bill. I'm getting so fed up with seeing him for ten minutes night and morning at Waterloo. So fed up with continual conversational evasions everywhere. We are planning a week's walk together in May. And I dread the possible external complications. Is it worth it?

The strain of this longstanding affair sometimes wore Olivia down. She often wondered whether their relationship would ever become a normal one, domestically and otherwise. She mulled over her dilemma in her personal journal for April 2, 1940, during a time when she was feeling that her relationship with Bill might be ending. Ten years was a big chunk of one's life, especially so for a woman still only twenty-seven years of age. "Wish I could just part and be cheerful. If all my memory would die." *Later she looked at the beauty of the flowers Bill had given her three days before, and remarked,* "I hate this half-life, but I hate the alternative even more, what I can guess of it." *She ended that day by chastising herself for being depressed.* "Wallow not in the muddy lurking glooms of self pity. Wallow not in past or future. Dance and sing in the Present, the going coming Present. And let your old age do the same."

The issue of US for April 5, 1940 commented on the current attitudes to the war—seven months after it had started. "Because policies seem so indefinite and because official forecasts of intensified war have so often fallen flat, little short of bombs on London is likely to penetrate public inertia. Indeed, there are many signs that people are gradually getting well adjusted to the war, and almost forgetting that it is one, in so far as that is possible in daily habits and domestic economy. Now, early in April, life is more nearly 'normal' than it has been since September 3rd." *Talk about the war had become much less prominent in daily conversations, though there were lots of complaints about the rising cost of living.* "People have almost given up thinking about air raids. This is reflected in a further loosening-up of the black-out. And a further decline in gas-mask carrying."

From the public's point of view, this was a peculiar war. According to M-O, "People are longing for war to begin. They are beginning to doubt whether this is a war at all. They want it to be a war, and the great majority have it firmly fixed in their minds that, once war is declared, you cannot stop it until it has been 'fought.'" *Public opinion tended to respond favourably to any signs of movement—that is, movement toward the goal of satisfactorily concluding the current conflict. Mass-Observation was in the business of trying to understand these public sentiments and in late March 1940 the following interpretation was included in one of its internal reports.* "Events like the Sylt raid and the Altmark incident"*—both of which Olivia mentioned,* *one approvingly, one disapprovingly—"are 'satisfactory' because they imply that the war is moving, and therefore that the state of war is that much nearer being at an end. For while people are mainly in favour of carrying on the war, it hardly needs pointing out that they are not in favour of carrying on the war indefinitely. Increasingly they are in favour of getting on with it at once. Their patience is exhausted" (M-O Archive, FR63, pp. 7–8).*

There were no entries in Olivia's diary for the first eight days of April. The launching of a new German offensive in the West appears to have stimulated her to return to her writing. "Real" war was soon to begin.

Tuesday, April 9

These Denmark and Norway rumours on the BBC early morning news made me feel quite alarmed. But other people—office and train—seem to be taking it very calmly. Seems to me that the food supply aspect is important.

The most strongly-expressed remark came from temporary clerk S (45). "Why do we get it from America—we're on the phone to Denmark—anyone'd think it was happening in Japan or somewhere." Others expressed surprise that (a) Norway had not declared war on Germany, (b) Norway had not declared war on <u>Us</u>. So I don't think the people I know have got any clear ideas on the situation as a whole. They all dismiss it after a few remarks, quite apathetically, as "Oh, well, they expected something in the spring" and "Things are beginning to look up." Personally, I took the trouble to tell the ticket boy at the station that it was on the 8 o'clock news, and he said "Oh have they?" quite calmly.

Later, A (temporary 67), "There'll be no bacon and eggs and butter for your breakfast now you'll find—with these blessed Germans in Denmark." "Won't worry me" says M (19). General discussion for a few minutes on who likes bacon for breakfast. A says he had five rashers this morning and eats two pounds a week! Still no vivid interest about.

S (Male 45) to A (Male 67), "I expect almost hourly there'll be sensational news coming through now." A (who has borrowed S's <u>Telegraph</u> after being unable to borrow a "picture" paper), "Eh?

H'm, h'm" apathy grunts. Later: Several minutes of really animated and informed talk on dogs—bull terriers and ancestry and types.

10:10 am. Someone has come in and said "It's official that Copenhagen's taken." Noises of surprise and burst of discussion, mostly "Golly, things are moving." Then "You'd better put on your best make-up to welcome the Germans, Gussie." And from her (21) "Oh well, it'll make a change." S (45 male) "There's a lot of English people would like to see the Germans. I was only talking about that on Sunday—some of my neighbours admire the Germans." Nobody likes S much so the subject was not pursued. A car made a noise like an aeroplane and someone said "May be a German—then we'd all run like hell!" I begin to wonder whether I'll get my holiday in May, now.

New discussion arises. Why didn't we stick to League of Nations—no! self-self-self, always leave it till too late and then moans. It's human nature. It's always the same. M (34) "Well, they'll soon issue the proclamation for the 35's–40's now."

10:30. I try to concentrate on work (got plenty) but I begin to feel uneasy. Same kind of feeling as in September '39, but much less strong.

2:15 pm. M (male 34) brought in a lunch time paper with huge headlines on Norway. Provoked half an hour's discussion on the Situation. A good deal of adverse comment on the Way We Run the War. All topped up with "Well it'll be all right tonight—the Prime Minister's going to speak" with much derision. I didn't join in, as I wanted to finish the thriller I was reading.

Wednesday, April 10

Dad says everyone's bewildered and didn't expect this Scandinavian business. Mother says she was polishing the furniture and suddenly thought to herself, What's the good of doing this, it may all be broken up next week. Overheard on the way to the station—Youth: "This'll bring America in, all right." Older Man: "All the better." Everyone in the office is short-tempered and glum for the first half-hour.

10 am. A memo has just been round from the Secretary stating the summer leave conditions. They are generous to the juniors and not oppressive to the seniors, so we are all pleased. But will we take it—"providing the state of public business permits."

1 pm. Lunch hour discussion has been male and technical, about airplanes and bullets and possible blockades of Norway. General opinion that Germany has bitten off more than can be chewed: qualified with "Mind you, they're jolly clever." Then some remarks about America and the last war, derogatory. One lad, who thought that Russia fought as Germany's ally in the last war, was very annoyed because I told him to read a bit more before he slanged America. I was mostly silent while they aired unsound technical knowledge and when I joined in over plain historical error (as above) the discussion became acrimonious. A telephone call put a stop to it, luckily.

"News hunger" is evident again. Our senior bloke even rang up a pal to hear what was on the BBC 1 o'clock. He then walked round all the rooms passing it on.

Thursday, April 11

9:15 am. First question on <u>everybody's</u> lips today: "Well what-d'ye think of the news?" The 8 o'clock BBC remark "England had a good day yesterday" was widely quoted, and pessimists of yesterday are optimists today. Much variation on what has actually been done, on the lines of "My paper says 19 ships sink," "Mine says 9." But definitely a "good" feeling today—it's lovely bright sunshine and that helps optimism.

1:30 pm. More lunch hour news-hunger: one clerk has brought a portable radio. The report about 1,000 v. 600 planes in battle is received with lick-lipping "That's the Stuff." (God! They make me sick!) And many conflicting reports are bandied about in all seriousness.

Friday, April 12

1:30 pm. No talk of war at all today from 9 am until 11:30, when the lack of late news was hailed as sensible on part of our Government because the Germans might make use of it. But two blokes went to listen to the 1 o'clock BBC and grumbled at "No news." Followed a discussion as to Russia's attitude in the next few days and what has happened to the Petsamo Russians.[27] Then queries as to the small amount of damage done to the Navy in the last few days. Mostly believe we've suffered much more than has been reported. Technical discussions (soi-disant) about planes and ships and armour. M (35 male) thinks we ought to land a big BEF [British Expeditionary Force] in Norway. Has been listening to Haw Haw [nickname given to William Joyce, the English-language propagandist who broadcast from Germany], and quotes him with relish. Mrs S (21) says "Honestly, it does look as if it's coming to H.G. Wells' Things to Come!" And that led to horrific descriptions of possible post warfare.

Monday, April 15

9:45 am. The Saturday night BBC effort at tension was briefly commented on, no interest shown. "Jolly good sending five—no, seven—of 'em to the bottom," says the senior bloke, and two of the other five grunted "yes." No discussion ensued.

Spent yesterday evening with three friends. All were interested—very—in "politics" previously. All said they had lost interest since the war began. Said weren't interested in the news most of the time, but got excited again over Norway, partly because they have holidayed there and have acquaintances in Oslo.

Talked for three hours about the mess the world's in and argued all the time about solutions. Agreed eventually that "politics" will not be the method, and also agreed that "Education" is the key word. But how to get the educators? And what to teach? Decided we want to eliminate Fear first, fear of poverty and lack and war. But that all sounds like Heaven.

Wednesday, April 17

Very little comment these last two days—possibly because so busy. A few remarks that "we don't seem to be doing so well."

2

Real War

June–August 1940

In May, Germany invaded the Netherlands, Belgium, and France. By early June, both of the former had been conquered and France was in serious danger of falling. Winston Churchill was now prime minister in a coalition government. There was an air of gloom about—but also a determination to press on and not to give in. On May 14, the day the Dutch conceded defeat, one woman in her early thirties, a shorthand typist who lived in Putney, wrote in her diary:

The weary reiteration that we will do our utmost to crush the invader, the warning that we must be prepared for the most horrible forms of warfare very soon now, that air-raids of such ferocity will begin any time, that all manner of new and undreamed of horrors will be ours almost at once. All these things are slowly getting a lot of us down into despondence and hopelessness. I know we shouldn't take these things this way, that the British are never down and that our "old school tie" would curl up in agony at our lack of spirit, but this long waiting for these things is very trying and eight months of slowly accumulating nervous tension are not calculated to make us the jolly-hearty-carefree people we should be. If we could see any hope of this beastly war finishing soon we should perhaps buck up, but the stations crowded with young men, bewildered but determined to be jolly, all being sent off somewhere to fight in one of the many countries attacked, the enrolment of the older men to act as watchers for parachutists, the dozens of search lights which illuminate our skies at night, the hundreds of balloons which litter the spring sky, all these things speak of long, weary months of horror yet to come. All our statesmen din into us by the papers and by the wireless that we must expect this, and that even when we get peace living will still be hard until the world is readjusted. I know I'm a coward but it fills me with immense sadness to think of all these things happening everywhere—what has gone wrong with us, and what can we do to get back some happiness?[1]

Olivia Cockett heard the news of Germany's new offensive while she and her friend Joan were walking in the countryside west of Oxford. On May 10 she was in Chedworth, Gloucestershire. "Felt utterly miserable and numb. Went to the pub for 9 o'clock news and heard Neville abdicate for Winston. Couldn't enjoy cider. Went back to brief wash and shiversome bed." The next morning she called Bill. They had planned to walk together during the coming week and he was to join her in the Cotswolds that very day (Saturday, May 11). But his leave was cancelled. "Dearest, you can't imagine what this means to me," he had written her on the 10th, "but I know you also will be terribly disappointed. Damn Hitler! He might have waited for another week." Olivia returned to London on the afternoon of May 11. "Crowded trains back. Tea with Gay and Joan. Home to empty 33 [Breakspears]. Got meal. Bill CAME, the dear darling, for half-an-hour and turned the grey to gold again. Now love and ever-renewed and we're determined to look forward to a week later in the year" (private journal and papers).

Olivia resumed her diary for Mass-Observation after a silence of seven weeks.

Thursday, June 6

Having dropped my attempts at a diary I have been spurred to fresh enthusiasm by the circular letter from M-O, dated 1st June. It was very disappointing to hear that <u>US</u> would not arrive for a time, but we had already discussed the possible value to the enemy of its objective picture,[2] and were not surprised that "High authority" had blocked it.

Cannot remember the last record I forwarded. Don't think I said much about a week's holiday I had in May, walking in the Cotswolds.

It was heavenly and should have gone on for a fortnight, but the wireless news on the Friday night before Whitsun was so alarming that, both being Government servants, we came back to work voluntarily on the Saturday. We didn't feel specially noble or patriotic, because the holiday mood vanished when the Low Countries were invaded.

Once back, office work continued much as usual. One or two minor changes in staff, middle-aged women taking the places of young men. On May 30th told to do a 48 hour week instead of 39. A little good-natured grousing, because it's not as bad as it might be, after that Decree. I'm still breathless about the speed and scope of that Bill, and surprised at how little grasp is shown of its implications, historically, by most people. [She is presumably referring to the Emergency Powers (Defence) Act, passed by Parliament in a single day, May 22, which gave the government unlimited power "for requiring persons to place themselves, their services and their property at the disposal of His Majesty."] And anyway, our lives have so far been tranquil compared with the conscripts.

As the Flanders battle grew, faces lengthened, tempers shortened. A radio appeared in the office, and now the 1 o'clock news is a daily feature I can't escape. I had been trying to ignore the daily details of news in papers and on the air. A remark in <u>US</u> that this might lead to nervous-breakdown-types made me think. Now I listen and read and ponder, but talk as little as possible, and try never to pass on horrors. I have found I don't dream so violently since trying this, so Thank You, US.

Gardening has been my chief recreation for the last few months. In addition to the one at home I have permission to use a piece of ground at the office, about 6' x 20', and a square yard of shelf in a greenhouse there. (Our office is evacuated from SW1 to a school at SW15.)[3] Lunch time and a few minutes at the end of the day are pleasantly occupied with attending to a few rows of peas and beans, lettuces and radishes, beetroots, turnips, cabbages and carrots. With a dozen small tomatoes in the greenhouse and a few inches of cress.

The family. Mother and Dad had a holiday, the last two weeks in May, spent at the bungalow in Essex, gardening between thunderstorms and air raids. They went and inspected the nearest bomb craters, quite small ones about six miles away: counted nine windows broken. Mother was remarkably calm about it, considering how very upset she gets when the BBC talk of casualties. That's mostly because she is so sympathetic and can't bear hearing of people hurt. We (Mother and I) talk about affairs at breakfast, when Dad has gone. There is a noticeable absence of general talk about the war in the house. The Willmotts, who live with us since the war began, talk to us separately about the war, but all together we keep cheerful and have jokes and gardening talk.

My brother and his wife and two-year-old baby are still managing on AFS [Auxiliary Fire Service]. He doesn't yet know if he personally is exempt from military service. (10 June '40: He is now.) One cousin (24) is in the Military Police; no news for six weeks since he sailed from a Northern port. Another (26) is on a destroyer in the North Sea. Another is an Air Raid Warden (24, deformed). Another (16½) has applied to join RAF several times, trying to falsify his age. Cousin's husband and brother in RAF. Five boys on Dad's side all in the Army.

Friends. Two girls in Government service, carrying on, longer hours, plenty of work, see them rarely, expecting evacuation. Another (35) was Red Cross trainee, gone over to CRN on request [she may have meant Civil Nursing Reserve] and sent last week to a hospital 20 miles from London. Boy (22) was Terrier; went to Flanders in February, Artillery; no news since then. Cousin (36) in Gas Company; has been working seven days a week since September, guarding works when not "fitting." Boy (24) registered; no medical yet, doesn't know if his job is on the exempt list, as he is doing Government building contracts.

Can't think of any more general details. If I don't begin daily diary soon, it will never happen!

Friday, June 7

Caught the right trains and arrived on time, 9 am, having been told off last week for being a regular five minutes late. At lunchtime watered tomatoes in greenhouse, hoed the allotment (20' x 6') and sighed for rain but enjoyed the sun. Back at my desk by 1 pm, forcibly BBC'd by the senior clerk's portable radio. The other seniors make a point now of meeting in our room at 1 for the news, behaving as though in church and making correct comments. I feel shy of eating my hefty sandwiches in this atmosphere, so leave them till later, and so overstep my lunchtime regularly. But I keep up with the work, which is the main thing, while grumbling occasionally at slack times. It's maddening to have empty hours in this place, with the garden so invitingly out of bounds. Now that I've begun this diary again it fills in odd moments, which partly accounts for the disjointed effect.

The afternoon was enlivened by an ice-cream treat from Mrs S, on a bonus. And I got very thirsty explaining a complicated job to Mrs Mc' S, a newcomer (45, was in a bank). Intelligent, but quite unused to our work. I was surprised at the number of technical details I had acquired and taken for granted, when it came to passing them on. They seem like common knowledge and common sense until a fresh eye queries them. At 5:10 walked down the hill [Putney Hill] chattering with Mrs S (21) and Mitch (19); very happy mood. Bought a pair of shoes on my bonus. Caught 5:40 to Kew, where my man was waiting with impatience and two ice creams. We sat and ate and saw a blackbird's nest with four eggs. W was in a jealous mood; I was late and when I came wearing a rose from another man's garden, he sulked. I told him so, he denied it, and we both chatted artificially brightly about the birds and trees in the gardens. Then at 7:15 we caught a bus and had to sit facing one another. We grinned and stared and fell in love again and his mood had quite changed by the time we were on the train, for five minutes blissful kissing.

When I got to Waterloo at 8, found the Junction closed. Some mysterious breakdown. Advised to go by road and show rail tickets.

Joined two last-war soldiers not sure of their way. As it was my way we caught the same train; they accepted fags and chatted shyly—the weather, holidays, bombs on London, their leave. Took hour extra getting home. Went straight out into the garden. Dad and three Willmotts doing odd jobs and watering. Chatted. Persuaded (I hope) Dad not to wait for me on Saturday afternoon to go to the bungalow, as W may get off and come down for a couple of hours. Dug out my 12 year old racket with a view to cheap re-stringing on my bonus. Had a knock about on the grass with Eric. Lousy; and light bad. So he demonstrated shots instead.

Had tea and bread and jam with Dad (Mother gone to Essex bungalow this afternoon with brother and family), talking desultorily until 11 pm. Tried one of his handmade herbal fags: no good. But he was smoking an ounce a day at 1s 5½d; now a 3d ounce lasts two days, so he's persevering with a pipe. To bed and read till 11:45, [Peter] Fleming's Brazilian Adventure. Slept better than usual, no nightgown.

Saturday, June 8

Woke at 6:30. Up soon and dusted and mopped and tidied two rooms. Waved goodbye to Dad at 7, down to bathe and breakfast and clean, quick look at garden, and caught the 8:10. Bought Postal Order for friend's birthday at Waterloo. Had eight minutes with Man. Made arrangements for this afternoon. Office punctually; not too busy. Treated seven to tea and buns and fetched it from Cartier. Wrote to friend. Lovely heat and sun again.

At 1 o'clock watered the greenhouse plants and caught the 1:22 to Waterloo. Home by 2 and W waiting for me. But as Dad had not gone we sat on the settee instead of going to bed. I had been arranging to go by train, but Dad stayed so long that W went in time for me to go in the car with Dad. Were stopped by the police and showed our identity cards, and Dad cursed having no insurance certificate with him. Arrived about 6 and had tea on the grass. Played with baby nephew, watered garden, chatted vaguely. Bed after bread and cheese and cider at 10.

Sunday, June 9

Up 8:30 and gave baby breakfast. Wandered round in pyjamas all day in the terrific sun. Played ball and lounged in deck chair and read a spare magazine. Salad for lunch. Read again while baby slept in the afternoon. Then watered the garden laboriously, watching clouds pile into a black storm in the West, wondering. But no rain reached us, though when Mother and Dad and I reached home at 9:30 we found everything drenched from a big storm.

Felt horribly depressed for an hour, seeing Willmott's boy with girl friend and girl with boy friend, everyone in couples but me. So I went off to bed and read. Had beastly thoughts in my head and when I tried to sleep was haunted with wounded people and abandoned babies starving. Made a big mental effort and eventually slept.

Monday, June 10

Up 6:45 to a dull heavy world. Mood a bit better, but worsened again when reached office ten minutes late. W had missed his train and I missed mine while waiting for him; but the five minutes with him is always worth it. However, I am so unpleasantly arrogant-minded that I can't bear being told by the man in charge of the room that the Head of the Department saw me coming in late and would like to remind me that my time is 9. Half of me quite saw the point, but the behaviour-half reacted sulkily. Worked half-heartedly, felt better after lunch. Shopped unsuccessfully in the High Street. Watered greenhouse, sorrowed over storm-beaten lettuces and peas and the rocket weeds.

Idled after my lunch hour, annoyed by the wireless being on for the senior clerk's amusement. All rather startled at the Norway news [Norway was falling to the Nazis]. Privately I'm alarmed. Publicly much more reaction from all about the death of "Cobber Kain," though honestly it was the first I'd heard of him.[4] The black heavy clouds continue all day, though no rain falls, and they are the chief subject of conversation. Rather touchy moods all round.

Most cheerful news over weekend. Cousin in Military Police wrote, is safe in Scotland. And the boy-next-door (years ago!) wrote, safe home from Dunkirk! Mother chirruped and wrote long chatty screeds to them. She writes lovely letters, horrible spelling and no punctuation, but her loving-kindness shines through every word. When I am away from her and get letters I immediately feel home-sick, however much I'm enjoying myself.

The trouble about this "unpunctual" business is that the seniors concerned treat one as a pariah or a naughty two-year-old for at least a week after any rebuke, which is trying for my sense of humour, because they get extremely offended if I show any amusement at their attitude. And with the war about it really is funny that they bother! If my work was "behind" I could understand it. At the moment I'm quite up-to-date. The punctual percies are all chatterers once they get here (I believe they come to talk) and so I have to help them. Odd pin-pricks for one who yearns to be a philosopher! Blasted awful self-esteem and vanity wounded, I suppose. Writing like this has practically removed the sense of grievance, though; another point to M-O.

4:30. That bloody wireless on again—comedian, just inaudible from here.

Left at 5:05, missed a train. No Man at Waterloo so went on shopping in the Cut. He discovered me there later. Spent 15 shillings on belt, stockings, health salts, soap, calamine lotion and sunburn stuff; saved about 3 shillings. Walked back together in happy mood in spite of heavy black weather, but in the station he put his hand on my knee and realised I had no petticoat under my dark brown silk frock and proceeded to be "heavy" about it. I resented this, not being a "come-hither-I've-no-undies" type and we parted more in anger than in sorrow. All the way home in the crowded train I thought—Oh how I hate the human race, I hate its bloody silly face. Which was funny, as Peg spent the evening with me, and last week she had been thinking hard thoughts of the human race and I had been defending it. With her usual beneficence she smoothed away my wrinkles and we laughed together over the absurdities of life. Sobered a bit by the Italian news [Italy declared war on Britain and France that day], and laughed again at Duff Cooper's all-is-better-than-ever speech [he was the new Minister of Information].

Several people yesterday [i.e., June 10] connected the unusually dark day with world events and bad omens. "A lovely day for a murder." "Well, all the Allies want now is all England flooded; they said they wanted something to fight up to." "The day Christ was crucified it came dark like this, something terrible will happen." "Looks like the end of the world's here."

We had a salad meal, Mother got it ready, and bread and dripping. Sat and chatted and then walked round the rain-battered garden, smelled pinks and honeysuckle and roses and admired archuse-blue. Decided to stay up and listen to the President's speech at 12:15. Peg did my hair-massage-for-stuff-with-lotion while I read G's hospital nurse letter to her. We wondered whether G would like to do the job for life. Thought probably not, although she is very enthusiastic for it during the war, being quite determined to do nothing to help the war. As she realises, this is not all logical, but that's how she feels.

We discussed Russell's recantation of Pacificism.[5] Not altogether surprised. "Power" showed the tendency to reconsider the matter. Agreed again that we would hate to be men and have to decide on action at the moment. Fell asleep on the settee between 11 and 12 but woke in time for the speech. Didn't listen to the end, the "sympathy" trend being clear enough after ten minutes. Stumbled into bed and slept till 6:30 am.

President Roosevelt's speech was delivered at the University of Virginia and focused in its second half on Italy's declaration of war earlier that day. Before becoming specific he spoke of "the boast of those who say that a belief in force—force directed by self-chosen leaders—is the new and vigorous system which will overrun the earth" and "the ascendancy of this philosophy of force in nation after nation where free institutions and individual liberties were once maintained." He went on to link this philosophy of force with industrial power. In "this new system of force the mastery of the machine is not in the hands of mankind. It is in the control of infinitely small groups of individuals who rule without a single one of the democratic sanctions that we have known. The machine in hands of irresponsible conquerors becomes the master; mankind is not only the servant; it is the victim, too. Such mastery abandons with deliberate contempt all the moral values to which even this young country for more than three hundred years has been accustomed and dedicated." He concluded his assertion of general propositions by criticizing those Americans who persisted in their isolationist attitudes. "Overwhelmingly we, as a nation—and this applies to all the other American nations—are convinced that military and naval victory for the gods of force and hate would endanger the institutions of democracy in the western world, and that equally, therefore, the whole of our sympathies lies with those nations that are giving their life blood in combat against those forces."[6]

Tuesday, June 11

Caught the right train. Met Man, very pleading-eyed to be forgiven last night's "words" but I couldn't feel altogether happy with him. Had a cigarette on the second train and felt better. In punctually. Suddenly remembered the probable reason for the boss's fault finding lately. I told him off for getting "fresh" with his hands—foolish of me not to have realised before the obvious cold reaction. As the other female allows "liberties" and enjoys them I suppose he thinks me unreasonable; and unflattering to five foot nothing, fat, bald, Cockney and sixty.

Spent an hour learning more of the National Savings job. I'm Hon. Ass. Sec.—entirely sinecure till now. "Drive" on and I'm being roped in whether I like it or not. As it's run outside my Department in office hours my seniors frown, but unavailingly. The distant Powers-That-Be override their local frowns, but [this] adds to my present unpopularity.

The 1 o'clock news (after lunch hour hair cut) called forth fresh storms of invective from the men, for the Enemy and (!) for the Americans. Can't understand their continued dislike of USA. This unpleasant boasting and name-calling is childish and does <u>not</u> induce strong patriotism in me. It certainly relieves their feelings though. The worried serious frowns of 1:10 are boyish giggles by 1:30 after a lot of back slang name-calling.

From 3 to 3:30 a social half-hour. Cake and tea by Mrs Mc'S and light comedy by all. KM (35) and JM (19), male clerks, enlarged on a Lottery by the Nation for £1 million, prizes to be collected after the war. Embroidery; sell tickets to Enemy, but don't put their counterfoils in; sell to America; run a penny one in office; and then ten minutes badinage on personal appearances. Much giggling, a few witty remarks which I can't remember.

Did 25 minutes gardening after office hours. Met Man at Waterloo; me still in a bad mood. He thrust a basket of strawberries on me just as we parted. Home, hot meal ready, took it upstairs on a tray, then couldn't eat a mouthful. Mother chagrined. Sorry, but couldn't change that blasted black mood. Sewed for half-an-hour. Planted out onions. Then 9 onwards read The Yearling [by Marjorie Kinnan Rawlings], American backwoods boy country story. Chatted for ten minutes to Rene, her young man went off to the Army that morning. I know she had been crying, so I tried to cheer her up. She's very brave, really.

Wednesday, June 12

Continued in a black curse-the-universe mood. Slept badly, didn't want to get up. Was bright to Mother at breakfast, gave her some shoes. Listened to 7 o'clock news—bombs on Malta. Damn this beastly stupid destruction, whoever does it.

Met Man at Waterloo. Was unpardonably rude to him. Avoided other office people on train; smoked gratefully alone. Had a busy morning and rang up Man and apologised. Felt better after work and a gardening lunch hour.

G rang during the afternoon, having time off from the hospital, and we spent the evening racing from place to place collecting things she had found necessary. I won't go into details as she hopes to find time to keep up her M-O Diary, so we should only duplicate [no diary by "G" seems to exist in the M-O Archive].

Eventually walked home over the local park, admired the allotments, the balloon, the soldiers. Had a pleasant heart-to-heart with Mother and took my supper up to bed with me. Glad to find that, in action, my mood had completely recovered; bile gone and the sun come out again. Read <u>The Yearling</u> until finished, past midnight. Got quite lost in it; so different from war, and so real.

Thursday, June 13

Wake to misty morning, cheerful breakfast (fruit, bread and butter, coffee) and caught trains easily. Happy five minutes with Man. Carriage alone and fag to office. Pleasant people, plenty of work, talk of Zoo, where Mrs Mc'S is frequent visitor, behind the bars too.

Watched one set of tennis at lunch time, acting ball boy. Then gardened until 1. Everyone cheered by the five miles push from Paris on 1 o'clock news. Glossed over the unpleasantness of 6,000 English captured as if they hadn't heard it. At tea Gus talked of her schooldays and said "Isn't it amazing how much you remember when it's so long ago." Actually, five years!

Caught early train home. Went to CSSA and bought overall 65 [shillings?] (!!) and to bookshop and paid £1 off debt. Collected Readers Union book for June. Man met me but in a hurry, so I went down on his train and came all the way back alone; useful season ticket!

Found young HP (21) visitor at home; came out of Dunkirk last week, after giving up hope. He told us an awful tale; biggest emphasis on the fact that we could have held the Albert Canal if the Belgians had blown up their schedule of bridges; and on the la-dy-da British officers compared with the French. A parachute German pilot was seen to be dropping; two officers resting; the French one ran two miles over the fields in his socks, the English one stopped to put on all his equipment, including binoculars. As neither got him, the point of the story is not quite so emphatic, but it's there; and it annoys the men. The full details are too long to scribble. Retreat and hide, watch pals shot, retreat, see 'em coming, retreat, dodge, get by in the dark, hungry. Watch the Canadians go over and smite the Boche on Vimy Ridge when the Memorial was shelled.

Listened a lot, doing odd jobs of gardening. Washed my hair. All had supper together and watched him eat with gusto. It is a shame, he has come back to find his stepfather dying of cancer in the bowel.

He hopes to get his leave extended, as Sid cannot live long.

Slept well. Dreamt a lot, about women on a corridor, or verandah, talking about prostitution. One old charwoman turned and smiled softly at me as she went saying "I'm one of them, you know."

Friday, June 14

Caught early train today, five minutes with Man, all compliments. Met girl friend on second train and talked of the war. Hoped Paris wouldn't fall. Came back from weeding at 1 o'clock to hear it had. All very silent for a bit. Then four different expressions of the "We've let the French down" idea. Plenty of work about; so must do some.

Caught the early train home. Met Man at Waterloo and he came home for an hour on his way to a relation. I found two visitors, Aunt and Grandmother, having tea in the garden. We all chatted a bit, false-bright about the war, truly cheerful about the (up-to-date) lack of casualties in our own group. Gardened till dark and then ate—new dish, cooked radish tops and poached egg; tasted like turnip tops. Gran staying the night and going (she hopes) to Essex bungalow with Mother tomorrow, staying for week's holiday. But the BBC warning [against travel] to the coast-strip troubles us.

Slept very badly, dreaming gardening—having cabbages planted all over me at very irregular intervals.

Saturday, June 15

Up early and saw Man at Waterloo. Got in punctually. A senior officer from another room came and had a violent argument more or less to himself, to our bewilderment. Complained of being "mis-understood," so I suppose it's nerves.

When M (35 male) came in, he was very concerned about commercial advertisements in today's <u>Daily Telegraph</u> asking for Government work, uniforms and metal. We all agreed <u>we</u> should have expected it to be the other way round. Grave doubts are being half-ashamedly put forward as to the Government's genuine concern; especially as there have been so many flowery speeches lately—always taken as a bad sign.

Was very pleased to get Diarist letter from M-O—feel kept in touch. So will forward this instalment accordingly.

Monday, June 17

Last instalment finished on Saturday last. When I read it over on Sunday before posting, I could see it suffered badly from being written in the office; very one-sided picture of my life and reactions. If I could make an analysis of my thoughts at the moment it might be true to say: Myself, 75% (watching my own reactions and attempting a philosophy); My man, 10% (dreaming and analysing); Gardens, 5% (planning); Family—mother, 5% (fearing future); War, 3%; Office, 2% (apart from "attention" while working). I am still so immature in my attempted "philosophy" that I find it difficult to put into words how and why it is so very important to me. But over and over again I am trying to "see life steadily and see it whole" through the midge-cloud of war and work and social surface. I shan't mention this again; it's too vague, however huge it is to me. And I guess that M-O finds quotidian reaction to events more easily classifiable, though I know they're not more important. My whole conviction shouts passionately that if everyone would concentrate more on contemplation, synthesis, contentment, more actual results would be achieved which are in line with a deeper desire than—warfare.

3:40 pm. Poor France! The 1 o'clock news was a bomb to me. I'd said over and over again that I didn't believe France was ever going to give in to Germany. We all fell very silent. I couldn't speak, couldn't eat my lunch. Lucky didn't get noticed by the others, so busy talking. Gradually their talk became more and more facetious, till M brought the tea up. I was grateful for a cup, for once.

But—What next? Tremendous query. What will happen to our men over there? Everyone's agog for more news, news. I've got a terrific headache now; was quivering and with tears for an hour after that awful news. Worked, but hazily, making the accounts a bit damp! Nobody noticed, I think. It's just come over me, that I still don't hate Germany. I supposed I shall before it's all over, but, thank God, I don't yet.

Tuesday, June 18

10:10 am. Marvellous blue-gold day again, roses on my desk breathing scent and colour.

Felt very numb the rest of yesterday. Met Man and was glad he was calm, even if in despair. He felt we should give in, which had not occurred to me but which seemed reasonable at the time. Went part way on <u>his</u> train and we gazed and gazed at one another in a genuine love-wonder, as if we hadn't been in love 11 years already! I went in to Zeeta's for bread and suddenly felt empty so had a coffee-ice. Home by 8. Gardened; made a scarecrow, sowed seeds.

Young HP came again, in uniform now. He came last Thursday, returned from Dunkirk. When he got home that evening he found his stepfather had died.

I still couldn't eat. Had a cup of tea and fag. Then at 10 a hot bath; and a couple of bits of lunchtime sandwich in bed, and some chocolates, lime juice. Read J.C. Powys[7] till midnight. Took blackout down and was thrilled by the full silver moonlight on the garden. Slept much better than I expected to. Put siren-suit out ready to jump. (Just been listening to 20 minute argument that our Government have/ haven't done their best for France. That "somebody at the head of affairs is to blame." That our BEF should have been two million strong.)

4:25 pm. Went to the allotment at 12 and killed a lot of cabbage caterpillars. Watered greenhouse. Felt like <u>the</u> hottest day of the year. Am wearing three-year-old linen frock instead of usual drab pinny and blouse. Still very hot. Ate my lunch before the 1 o'clock news today, just in case! Spent an hour being Hon. Ass. Sec. again, issuing National Savings Certificates: 250 members collected £62 this week. Supposed to be a Special Effort; not very wonderful, but there was not much advertisement or appeal.

Thank goodness—or mental exercises—that I am happy again. That black-devil mood last week was horrible. It seems to me the most important truth that the <u>one thing</u> we have any control over, short of actual pain, is our own mental weather. The most awful outside events must and can be forgotten; and a strong effort made towards individual control of our minds, discounting propaganda.

Thursday, June 20

11:30 am. Didn't write yesterday—spent half the day at County Hall LCC working on regular job. Walked in and out without pass, in spite of five blokes on door!! Good job I'm not enemy. I didn't do anything special either. And the man I went to see has to show his pass and wouldn't believe me. So he came and watched me walk out!

Nothing unusual happened to me these last 48 hours. The news at 8 o'clock this morning of South Wales bombed really shocked me inside. Had a great struggle not to tell the people in the train, who couldn't have heard. Then in the office the Guv walked in laughing at a "silly rumour" about bombs on Wales and my feelings were greatly relieved by saying violently "Well, it's TRUE."

Mother and Aunt went down to Essex yesterday to see if Gran wanted to come home from her week's holiday. Although she had been up from 11:30 to 4 all night, with the bungalow "rocking," she wouldn't come back! Said she'd rather die in the country anyway. No windows broken, surprisingly. We wondered at breakfast how many more times we'll be allowed to go there, now it's a "Defence Area."[8] They gave a lift to a sailor on the road, who told them he'd been sunk or blown-up five times, and was the only one, of 28 who blew up petrol at Dunkirk, to get back. His Mother doesn't worry any more about him as she knows now that he's "lucky." In peace he's a Holborn dustman.

We all watched the glorious sunset from my top window last night—best for years. In bed I read the last few of Keats' Letters, when he knew he was going to die, and was comforted by them. Am now reading Havelock Ellis' Autobiography. Lousy.

Think as little as I can, forget as soon as I can, about the physical effects of air raids. Found myself "worrying" on the way today. Then told myself sternly that I was only being theatrical and dramatic and unreal; that "sympathetic worry" at the present time is a patent foolishness; that energy must be conserved; that nothing had yet happened to me and that I couldn't do anything for anyone else, so I try to keep cheerful.

Friday, June 21

10:40 am. No air raid news today. Can't decide if this is Government secrecy or there were really none. Can't help thinking it would be wiser not to tell everybody every day; really is disproportionate, 50 million worries over 50 deaths in the circumstances.

Have been sneezing this morning and got a slight temperature; makes me feel a bit heavy and tired. Had a "deep depression" yesterday evening—may have been due to approaching cold—and fought back at it with mental weapons and determination. First really conscious struggle against "mood"; not very successful, but it helped. Played for half-an-hour with 5½-year-old girl visitor, then went up alone to my sitting room and ate and read and stared at the clouding sky. To bed at 10 and read till 11. Slept well. (As I write an office discussion "Rats I have known and their Habits" is raging. Unusual natural history.)

Saturday, June 22

Had a dull-feeling day yesterday, menstruation began. Spent a pleasant evening at home; an hour's play with Micky (2½) and then Peg came. Sat at window and talked and watched sunset. Undercurrent of disappointment as I had expected Man to come for an hour. At 9:30 walked round the garden and picked a lot of flowers for her. Then talked and talked again of Powys and life and the war. We feel very cynical about most public pronouncements on the Cause. The only genuine feeling reaction I can achieve in the patriotic line is that less cruelty appears to be imposed by the English than by the Germans. Most of the other "freedoms" are either shams or undesirables. We spoke vaguely of the "tactical" aspects of France's loss; precisely of our own reactions to air raids news, which we try to forget as soon as possible, knowing, or believing, that our own turn for reality will come all too soon. Had both found the war heightened our appreciation of the things we loved.

Watched the light fade on the longest day, felt poetic about the stars appearing. Saw the moonlight silver the near roofs. Heard the church clock strike and expected 11; were very surprised when it was 12. Peg decided to stay. Walked round the black and silver garden, stared at the moon, felt the cool grass, smelt fragrances. Then the boom-thud of the guns in the distance sobered our delight, and we drank some water and went to bed.

Was cheered to get another Diarist letter [from M-O] last night—the reassurance about officialdom one. Do send further little notes as often as funds allow. They spur one on and make one feel in touch. US leaves a great gap, emotionally! And I find my convictions and arguments relying on previous US facts, feel the lack of topical facts very much. However, it's understandable.

Have knitted an inch of khaki sock in the last hour, in office time as I have no work in. Queerly, this is resented by the men (who'll later wear them!) who have not much work either. It seems they would rather have me lazing and pretending to have work to do than obviously knitting. That's the kind of hypocrisy which is specially galling to a woman.

Monday, June 24

11 am. At 1 pm on Saturday went and watered greenhouse. Caught the 1:22 to Waterloo and met Man, who came home with me and stayed till 4. We were in a heavenly accord, two perfect hours of mingled personalities, completely satisfied to be together. We talked of the war, of course, but it didn't feel real.

Then I packed a weekend bag and went as far as Barking with Dad, who was on his way to the bungalow to fetch Mother and the grandparents. I spent the weekend with an old school friend. Went to the pictures on Saturday evening, first time since the war began (except news films) and saw Boris Karloff in Enemy Agent!! All air raids and bombs!!! Made me giggle, it was so idiotic to go and see films of coming horrors. The audience reaction was slight. A laugh at Prussian officer who waggled his behind (but it was the movement that they laughed at); no reaction to a long "Fatherland" speech as a medal was given to the female spy; no reaction to pictures of London being bombed; a gasp at a grand (obviously faked) picture of Zeps against a moon-lit cloud-patched sky. About a fifth of the audience clapped [at] a speech at the end by the British Secret Service bloke, about England only fighting wars to keep the peace.

Spent a lazy Sunday, did a little cleaning and cooking and knitting. Admired the rain, for the garden's sake. Listened to the 9 o'clock [news] giving the Terms to the French and was secretly horrified, but none of the four of us (all women) said much. Heard J.B. Priestley's postscript and was emotionally moved, but not intellectually convinced.[9] Joan took me to the bus and we gazed hard at one another, just <u>not</u> saying how much we liked one another and hated the war. I went by various buses from Barking to St. Johns, through Blackwall Tunnel. A soldier boarded us there, inspected Registration Cards. Was a long time on top and eventually a man about 30 came down and got off quietly with him. Everybody inside turned round and looked, but nobody said anything, which was unusual for an East London crowd, and made me think of Gestapo stories.

Got home by 11 and heard Mother's account of the raids near Southend on Friday, and a daylight one on Saturday morning. She saw the German planes. Several people were killed within half-a-mile of the bungalow, and much damage done. Many people were leaving hurriedly, taking all they could on horses and carts. Shops on the main road were deserted, with windows still full of goods. She wept as she told me she doesn't expect to go much more, if at all, and described the perfect state of the crops, and the awful waste of digging up fields of growing things into trenches to stop planes landing. It really is heart rending for her. She began to work in 1915, worked till 1938 and saved money and put all her thought into this plot and house in the country to retire to. Expected to go in May 1940. Poor dear, I <u>am</u> sorry for her. Yet I have to try and cheer her up and not show too much sympathy, as she weeps then.

In September 1939 Olivia had remarked on her mother's reactions to the outbreak of war. "The war has shocked her; she never really believed it could come again. She has been twice to the bungalow and is grieving bitterly that she may not enjoy it after working a lifetime for it" (September 9). A week before, on September 2, the day before war was declared, mother and daughter had listened to the evening news and, in common with millions of others, were suitably gloomy. "We discussed the last war and her despair at this possible repetition. She felt that the only thing which had helped her last time was the feeling that her children at least would be free for ever of the horrors. Irony."

Olivia's mother, Elsie May Cockett, was born in 1893. She married in 1911, the year before Olivia's birth. Freddie, her only other child, was born in 1914. Olivia's father, Frederick, born in 1891, was posted to France for much of the Great War and after 1918 drove a lorry for the local Council. A household with two steady incomes was unusual at this time, for a married woman with children did not usually pursue a career. Olivia's mother worked in the insurance industry as a collecting agent. Because of her job she had lots of contacts with doctors, at least one of whom had advised the young Olivia on contraceptive devices. Olivia, in her early twenties, produced a 1,500 word typescript entitled "My Job: By a Woman Insurance Agent," a descriptive account that was based (one presumes) on her mother's experiences as a collector in poor neighbourhoods of southeast London, where she was known as "the insurance lady." This full-time employment would have contributed significantly to the material well-being of the Cockett family, including their acquisition of a retirement home.

Her mother "never acted over 30," Olivia recalled in 1992, when she herself was eighty (DR for Winter 1992). By all accounts, her mother was sweet-tempered, generous, and tolerant. In July 1939, Olivia portrayed her as the "dominant partner" in the marriage and "unusually progressively minded" and thus not at all typical. The bond of affection between Olivia and her mother was exceptionally strong.

3:10 pm. [Monday] Was very annoyed with the "Englishwoman from Paris" who spoke after the 1 o'clock news today. All power to her (and the Authorities') elbow for wanting to keep rumours down, even if they have let the cat out now that it's her morale and not for anti-spy. But I am sorry to hear an official "hate" on the Germans and a phrase "if there is anyone left who thinks there are 'nice' Germans." OF COURSE there are nice Germans; and how-ever many times I get called names over the air for thinking that, I still shall think it. Gosh! It's self evident: 80 million people <u>must</u> be mixed. Don't know why I even bother to write this thought down for [Tom] Harrisson, except that it got me so hot to hear the BBC allowing such idiocy. Suppose it will get worse though. Obviously, from the official point of view, there's not enough hate about yet. And this from one who was a member of the Left Book Club from the start, with the avowed object of opposing Fascism and War! I felt <u>so</u> strongly, tried <u>so</u> hard to persuade others, and was laughed at for prophesying war with Nazis. No wonder I'm disgusted with politics, or the little man's efforts at intervention in these affairs.

Then, from 1:30 to 2:05 pm, H (19) and M (34), male clerks, discussed the situation. Agreed that the French people had been let down, or perhaps betrayed, by Nazi-minded leaders, and that it was still possible <u>we</u> should be. Otherwise why are so many things still left undone—deep shelters, more shadow factories, more munitions, more fighter planes, Nuffield's mass plane offer, more trained shooters? And why are luxury goods still being made and advertised in national papers? Why are Putney rich women still shopping in big cars? Why are some people working seven days a week, some not at all? Why are rich cakes and rich meals in hotels still available (for the rich)? Why aren't more men <u>and</u> women being taught shooting? Why isn't the coast <u>all round</u> manned? Why isn't more food being grown? Why aren't soldiers with little to do kept fit by land work on local farms? Why aren't parks growing more? Why isn't <u>all</u> food rationed—<u>if</u> the danger of invasion and blockade is as bad as they say? Why why why?

And why worry all us little people with news and decisions that cabinet ministers must tackle? There's too much repetition of the news. It beats on people. They listen every time in case there's something fresh. Twice a day would be plenty for BBC news. Especially as the Home Front news is beginning to be doubted.

Reading that paragraph over, it seems very muddled. What do I want? Honestly, I'm damned if I know! I'd like to know the whole truth, but I don't want my Mother worried with it. So what [do I want]?

The following day's account was composed specifically in response to a M-O request for detailed experiences of an air raid.

Tuesday, June 25

Heard siren in sleep, 12:45. Called to Mother, heard her moving in room below. Got up quickly, put up blackout, put on light. Put on normal suit (trousers and coat) and scarf and raincoat. Picked up watch and glasses and handbag. Went downstairs. Sirens now loud and near. Heard all others moving, was first down. Went and opened back door, saw pails there all right. Stayed in passage. Others dressing and speaking. Dad stayed in bed. Mother put on dressing gown, socks and slippers. Mrs Willmott dressed in jersey and skirt and stockings and coat, Mr Willmott [in] trousers and coat over pyjamas. Eric (24) the same, Rene (19) trousers over pyjamas and top coat on. I left my gas mask upstairs. None of us went into the cellar which the men have been getting ready tonight and the last few evenings.

We chatted, fatuously, cynically describing the bombs dropping on some other fools, or us, who hadn't gone into the proper shelter. I went to the garden door several times and looked at the moon. No search lights after the first ten minutes. Several trains still going, steam ones with sparks. Made a good many sarcastic humorous remarks about Eric playing with a pack of cards. Sat in Mother's sitting room; nearest one to cellar door and had the light on. All yawning and laughing, no-one at all scared. Listened now and then and grumbled at the nuisance.

At 1:45 began to be really sleepy. I got up and switched off the light and then sat on the floor with my head on Mum's lap. Chatted a bit. Then Mrs Willmott decided to "lay on the bed" (downstairs room) and after a few minutes her two children decided to go back to bed (1st floor) and so did Mother. She and I went and looked at the garden in the moonlight. Both went to the lavatory. Drank a little cold water and I suddenly remembered M-O. So I've sat on in the room downstairs for 20 minutes scribbling. Shall now go up to bed again, on the 2nd floor, although the All Clear has not yet sounded.

The night is very still. The clock ticks loudly. Four bowls of roses and one of tall white lilies scent the air deliciously. (I lay on the rug and put the lilies on my chest and told the others I would die decently. All laughed, but not very uproariously.)

I fancy I hear planes in the distance. There was one <u>with</u> the sirens (which didn't sound so loud to me as last September) but none really near for the last hour. Feel very heavy with sleep so shall now go up, 2:15 am.

She concluded her account with a report on what her fellow office-workers had said about their air-raid reactions.

Mrs——— (45). "It was the first night I was <u>sure</u> they wouldn't come." Went into the basement. Had to move an invalid there. Went back before All Clear.

JM (19½). Didn't hear a thing. Stayed asleep.

JAM (46). Put shirt on back to front in blackout. Played shuvapenny and went to the door and talked to the lady warden. Stayed up till All Clear.

JF (39). "Brought down several planes myself."

AS (50). Lazed about in armchairs and went to sleep. Stayed up till All Clear.

AM (35). Stood at the front door all the time. Wife saw "parachutist." <u>He</u> saw an owl. Baby didn't wake till they fetched her down.

XL (40). Little girl (7) heard the Wibble Wobbles and was first downstairs in her dressing gown. Was found in dining room with a ton of sweets.

Mrs S (21). Not in today. Rang up at 10 and said she had slept all through the air raid noises, but went to Doc's this morning with a stye on eye.

Wednesday, June 26

Posted last instalment Tuesday morning, after air raid warning. Felt a bit sleepy, yawned several times. Gardening lunch time. Caught early train to Waterloo. Met Man. He later came to my home for a couple of hours. Played and ate bread and cheese and cider. Both felt rested and refreshed at being together. Slept well last night.

At breakfast Mother decided to try and fetch more linen up from Essex today. Still feeling very weepy about bungalow. AG across the road there is trying to sell 20 budgerigars—can't even get 1 shilling a pair. Intends to leave the place; would sell, but what hopes!

Office, cheerful and quiet—lively Mrs S still away with her stye-eye. AM (35) at Woking had another night awake [from] air raid—no guns though. He was mad because he had expected to be "safer" living out of London, yet he gets far more warnings than we do!

Set fair in my happy mood still. Am curious as to the effect of actual danger and pain on this mood business. Don't expect I've anything like enough control over my mind yet; but until it's tested can't tell. After all, I've spent the last ten years doing without my dearest wish, for home and children and Man. So that's some discipline. And I don't feel soured—yet.

Thursday, June 27

11:15 am. Thank you for the letter, Tom Harrisson. Hope you're right about the material being of some use. Haven't got a very strong missionising impulse, but should be heartened to think that someone, somewhere, would someday be helped somehow by something I've done. Some sentence! Funny that we've become so brightly cynical that any mildly idealistic or helpful remark usually sounds priggish! I am returning the envelope as it arrived, to show an example of some GPO humour. And by the way, it's BREAKSPEARS Road; sorry about my writing!

Yesterday lunchtime, weeded and caterpillared; sowed spinach. Occupied (scarcely "busy") afternoon seeking through old files for information, back to 1906. Found some genuine red (or pink) tape! At 5 again gardened, planting out about 60 carrots, grown in the greenhouse in a pot. Caught the 6:03 to Richmond, met Man, had tea in Kew Gardens. Marvellous odours and freshness after the heavy showers today, and very few people. Overheard an odd telephone conversation in the tea house, wondered if it was a spy, decided not. But felt quite dramatic for a few minutes. Had a "mood" test, quite severe. We had arranged to spend Sunday walking together, first time since war began. Man told in the afternoon he's got to work on Sunday. Felt utterly mad for a split second, and then brought the focus down and said "Oh well, we ought to be used to disappointments by now" and we sought some way of spending a <u>little</u> while together. But the heavenly green clear peace of the Gardens was the best soother of our ruffled feathers.

Man offered to show me the Canal. I, knowing Kew from childhood, asked if he meant the river. He thought not; but when we got there it was the river, and he was quite put out. He'd always thought of it as the Canal, without any reason that he could think of!!

As it was nearly closing time we turned left and walked along the tow-path to Richmond, with the sun behind us. Lovely bright light reflected up on the undersides of the many chestnuts along there, and quivering on the faces of girls we passed. Seemed to have no effect on male faces; wonder if powder has anything to do with that. Sails and sunny ripples and ducks and a breeze and clear air—entirely forgot the war. Wandered through Old Palace Yard. Coveted an empty cottage near the Swan. Crossed the airy Green. Man said the Theatre is to be closed. Commented on the scratching-out of all place-names. He was amused to have seen "_____ Hotel _____ Bournemouth" left up very prominently in Basingstoke. Saw a gang of Boy Scouts enjoying a clue paper chase. I longed, for a minute, to join in; and remembered with a palpable shock that they would think me a "grown-up."

Had to wait 15 minutes on the platform for a train. Made an "I Love You" plate on the one penny metal machine. Then a fast Waterloo train came and, although it meant leaving Man to the slow one for his station, I couldn't resist going on it. I've often watched them whizz by, and enjoyed being in it and passing the slow train. Stared at the flaming calm of the sunset and admired the springing of the carriage.

Ran and just caught my connection. It was still clear daylight but the blinds were drawn over the open windows, as the train lights were on; and the people by the windows peeked cautiously round and under the blinds at stations, and fixed them carefully when a babe released one accidentally. I giggled to myself and thought of the reputed "verboten obedience" of the Germans. As I got out I glanced at the 1st Class; of course, they had all the blinds up, common sense. Don't really draw any conclusions as to class from that![10]

Rang up the Man to show him what a quick journey I'd had. He was surprised—at my ringing and at the speed. He didn't react with quite the enthusiasm he usually does—or I thought so. And as I had been reading Antony and Cleopatra on the train—"Say that he weeps, report me merry"—I quite deliberately put a break in my voice as I said Goodbye. He said in alarm "You're not crying are you?" and I rang off without relieving his feelings. There was someone waiting to go in the box, anyway. On the way up the road I reproached my coquetry, mildly. He knows me so well that he probably guessed, anyway.

I took bread and cheese up to bed with me, had cider with it, in bed. Read [Osbert] Sitwell's Those were the Days [1938] till 11:15 and slept well. Lots of dreams, jumping out of windows, but not alarmingly, only adventurously.

When we met at Waterloo this morning he tried to be serious about the phone incident, but we were both in cheerful spirit and parted in laughter.

Gardened. Then listened to 1 o'clock news; descriptions of single combats in the air. Felt all my muscles tighten and set, leaden face and quivering nerves; horrible. These "glow inside the enemy aeroplane," "rear gunner silenced," make me squirm in disgusted horror. Can't see it as anything but tortured flesh, singed hair, screaming agony of a person—not an "enemy." HATE this inflicting of pain—pain is the one enemy of us all. To purposely cause it is fearful, the worst last sin.

From the morale point of view it's a stupid thing to broadcast these descriptions. All women (I don't often generalise, but this is intentional) all women leap in their minds to their man suffering. When it's just "five enemy planes brought down" even I sometimes think

"Good!"—my imagination just sees danger destroyed—vaguely. But descriptions like today's 1 o'clock news are <u>bad</u> for me—make me want "Peace at any price" even when my head says "But this 'price' would lead to more pain, torture in concentration camps and Gestapo-fear." My privatest self hates the war anyway. My Social self hates the Nazis and wants England to win. My Socialist self says "What next though?" But all my selves are outraged by the ether, "the casing air," [<u>Macbeth</u>, III, 4, l.22] the children's ears, my mother's ears, being filled with this evil pain-record.

A record of Cortot playing <u>Flaxen Haired Maiden</u> of Debussy followed. And immediately my muscles relaxed and I breathed properly and my face felt pleasant again. But the others in the room said "Switch that muck off." Two of us protested and it was kept on.

3 pm. Our Mrs S (21) is back today, stye better after two days off. My head quite aches with her constant good-natured chatter, hum and whistle. She is lively and pleasant, but the last two days were more restful. The end-of-the-month atmosphere is on the office again. Most work cleared, no pressure. Ball games are popular, tennis and stump cricket in lunch hour. Saw some staid elderly gents in a quiet corner today, playing a variety of cricket with a black round ruler and a tennis ball and much concentration.

Several planes gone over today. A sudden tense silence falls as we all listen, broken for the first time or two by some facetiousness, later no remarks, just waited till noise died away.

At tea in the canteen today remarks were passed about the Coming Famine. "Better eat now and get ready for it—have some butter on your scone while you can—no blasted sugar in them even now—I'll be able to live on my fat for a couple of years—I do hate being hungry." I suppose we shall be pinched, but my imagination doesn't respond yet.

Mother got to the bungalow quite easily yesterday. Brought back a lot of linen and some food stores, also 20 budgerigars from Goom. RJW is keeping them for him, in his disused pigeon-house at Rotherhithe. She said it was pathetic to see the people on the road, all from the coast, with old cars and carts and home-made trailers behind, one with three stories, goats below and chickens above. Reminded her of the descriptions of refugees in Belgium. But of course they are not machine-gunned—yet.

There's been a competition in memory here this afternoon. Songs of the last war. Several sung right through, and now a residue of hums and whistles and "How did that one go?" Alec said he made up a song a couple of months ago, but it would be no good now because we aren't doing so well. Nobody thinks the songs of this war are any good. Again remarked the lapsing of "Siegfried Line" and "Rabbit Run." "There's a pot of money in a war song, too."

For the last few evenings Dad and Eric and Bert have been very busy clearing out the cellar—a job Mother has been pressing for years—to make it safe for shelter. Looks quite good now, one end clear, two very strong wooden uprights in (Eric the engineer says they would take 56 tons) and lots of whitewash. Some lime on the floor, an electric light. A curtain to keep out of view the coal and workbench end is coming, from the old linen, and folding wooden chairs from the bungalow, also deck chairs if there's room. A hurricane lamp for when electric light's switched off. Shall probably put food [in] soon. The males' work is much admired by the females. The garden has been neglected, but the rain has made up for that.

4:30. Just been to the lavatory. Usually evacuate only in the early morning; feel pleasantly virtuous if my bowels move again later in the day. Reminded me of an overheard air-raid remark yesterday. "The people downstairs in our house said they took no notice of the warning. But I heard the cistern go four times and drew my own conclusions." (Discussion of jumping technique proceeding now.)

Friday, June 28

11 am. Went over to the greenhouse for 15 minutes at 5. Watched a little bit of the departmental tennis tournament (the big one has been frowned on—a very minor affair now progressing). Caught the 5:33. Travelled with AM (35) who was very emphatically puzzled—

"Just can't understand it"—that London has not yet been bombed. Met JK (old school friend, 27, girl) and her first remarks over a cup of tea were to the same effect. Her young sister joined us at 7 and we went to Snow's for steak and kidney pudding and apple tart and bitter. Very filling and good; but cream was "off," and mushrooms were "off," indicating supplies limited, the only noticeable war effect. Laughed a good deal. Heard the story of their air raid Tuesday. They went to the public trench 20 yards away from their back door on a football ground. Main memory seemed to be of "noises from behind the curtain." They felt they had to stay there till the All Clear went, though they wanted to go back to bed. As Snow's hasn't a Ladies Room I marched across the road and into Regent Palace [Hotel], boldly and coldly ignoring the commissionaire's stare. As I paid tuppence for one pennyworth value in their cloak room I didn't feel embarrassed.

At 8 we walked up Shaftesbury Avenue to the Cameo for cartoons. Was surprised at the number of shops shut. Few people about, mostly ANZACS with street women. Laughed a lot at Mickey Mouse in <u>Clock Cleaners</u>. Rest dull. And the Paramount News maddening—guns and soldiers and facetious comments on bombed civilian houses that "no military damage was done." Not much consolation to a civil audience. We didn't stay to see all the news film. All three groaned aloud to see the pictures of French Army and Navy "now to be used against us." Audience reaction slight; some clapping at a boastful "we'll show 'em" statement. Hoots of laughter everywhere when request for scrap metal finished up with a reference to Italian Navy.

1 o'clock news stirs up interest in the Balkans again, very little discussion ensued—I feel it's important myself [the Soviet Union was demanding territorial concessions from Rumania; these demands were successful].

Had some excitement in the office this afternoon—a promotion for a senior clerk. Congratulations and cigarettes all round and a general air of "Well, that's good" although he's not a popular man.

Saturday, June 29

9:45 am. Another wonderful June morning—never been such weather. Clear starred-sky sunset last night. Man and I lay entwined watching it fade.

Last night spent 6 to 7 picking peas and carrots and cooking him a meal. 7 to 8 Peg came and talked. She was at home in the air raid (at her Mother's) and they all slept in the dining room after the first half hour in the cellar. 8 to 9 we ate and talked of the office and the war—hoping Russia would turn on Germany (wish-fulfillment). 9 to 10 enjoyed one another's body. 10 to 10:30 walked in the cool twilight and parted regretfully. Then till 12 read Sitwell in bed. Slept well, dreaming of much action and shouting, satisfactory activity of some sort, pleasantly.

Mother got to the bungalow again yesterday. Brought back chairs for cellar, more linen. Saw many more moving vans and evacuees.

Peg was very sad about the philosophical collapse of the man she's fond of. She's respected his intellect and character for some years, and had tears in her eyes as she said "He's the living example of a newspaper 'defeatist' now; and the worst of it is his prophecies are always right!" But, we agreed, <u>that's</u> the real test, to be mentally right and aware of the situation, <u>not</u> to pull comfortable wool over your own eyes and <u>yet</u> to remember that life is more important than war and death, and that while there's life there's a sensible duty in forcing yourself to be happy. Philosophy's no good at all unless it can induce the feeling that life and happy soul-weather are the most important things under any circumstances. But he's gone to pieces—is dull and miserable and won't exert his mind to think of anything but the war. He's a civil servant of importance, too. The worst case among my acquaintance. Pity, because he was one of the most respected.

Brought photos and letters from our American friends today to show H in another office, who may send his young son out to them under the Government scheme. We know they would be ideal people to take him and would be fond of him and glad to do something. But it's a big step for parents to decide on, and a few letters and photos of the people the child may go to would be a great help. Mother asked me to go the other day—really seemed to think I would! Apart from the fact of work I'd hate to run away from history-in-the-making and the opportunity of seeing life under extraordinary conditions.

Monday, July 1

4:10 pm. Just been laughing heartily at the horseplay in this room today. All spirits very high and cheerful, seem quite genuine too. Lots of jokes and japes. The 1 o'clock news was passed off with a pun on Rumania. I feel that we seven in this room would find a laugh in any situation, together. Though separately we are as concerned and puzzled and afraid as anybody else.

On Saturday Man and I spent the afternoon lounging in the sun in Regent's Park, in one of the quiet side gardens. Had tea there. Lots of people, no specially sad or worried ones; a few uniforms, plenty of children. We looked around and indulged in a few horrid prognostications; the scene would have supported "decadent" description as supplied by Goebbels. Had a domestic evening sewing, and washing hair, and garden. Bed late. Didn't listen to any news. Had bad dreams.

Rose at 8 on Sunday. Didn't look at the papers. Met Man at 9:30 at Waterloo and went walking in Hertfordshire till 6. Hot and lovely and very much in love. Felt very pleased with immediate life and our bodies. Gardened in the evening, transplanting lettuces. Read in bed after my bath. Heard running water about midnight. On investigation found our tank was overflowing. Damned awful job, lavatory on 1st floor and pantry and hall all swimming with water.

Talked during the day about the war and agreed, quite cheerfully, that we expected an awful time and couldn't see how we could possibly win; but that we must keep cheerful.

Mother told me she went to C's, the market gardener, at the bungalow. He said nobody seemed to come and buy his tomatoes this year and he had a lot going to waste. She said they couldn't get there to buy them, and as he didn't seem to understand she said "You know they're stopping cars and people coming here." He did not know and was very surprised when she told him about the Defence Area and

20 mile limit and possible (!) evacuation. He said he'd got "fed up" with the wireless and rarely listened now, and he hadn't got time for papers. He can't afford beer and pubs, so I think he was certainly telling the truth. Mother was very indignant and said the Government ought to let people know they may have to go and the soldiers are about. I said they let people know by BBC. But that <u>would</u> miss a lot. She said the police ought to go round and tell.

Tuesday, July 2

1:20. 1 o'clock news again—only reaction from six adult men, a hearty laugh at Italy described as a small tail to a German dog. No comment at all at the end. BBC obviously working up the wish-hope of a German-Russian fight. More raid descriptions. I don't believe the very low casualties reported. Silly, every time <u>our</u> raiders cause great damage, <u>theirs</u> cause slight or nil. Why does the war go on if we're so jolly good? And they're so jolly bad?

Last night, caught 5:22. Called on brother at AFS station, told him his budgies were ready. Gave him some six inch radishes from my office garden. He was very fit and well, been to three fires over the weekend and got one arm burnt. Met Man for ten minutes chatter. Both very sleepy. Home by 7, wandered round the garden, ate a little. Shouted Yes and No and On and Off for Dad while he mended the water tank. Then felt suddenly tremendously sleepy, struggled out of my clothes and dropped straight off to sleep in bed before 8!! Was awakened just after 9 by deputation of family, inviting me to join stirrup-pump squad being got up among neighbours. I grunted sleepily and understand this morning that I'm counted in. Hope I'm brave enough when and if the need arises.

Mother went <u>again</u> to the bungalow yesterday. More blankets up and offered to take in a couple of families if they come to London. Don't know where she'll put them, but expect we should manage. Only saw one policeman on the way down. Not stopped by any military this time, either.

Man said he'll never vote Conservative again, after the way "they've let us down." And he was an officer 1914–1918, always a

<u>very</u> Conservative person too. Says he won't vote Labour either; so either there'll have to be a new party or he'll be a-social.

Mother said today "Our Government's all right at dishing it out, but now they can't take it." AM (35) said "This blasted Government can't see past its nose." But it's traditional in England to blame the Government.

Monday, July 15

At work on 3 July I banged my head on a marble mantelshelf and was taken home with concussion. Hence the gap in my diary. I spent some days in bed; the rest lazing and resting. Went for an eight mile walk yesterday, back in the office today, feeling a bit achy.

Haven't bothered much about the war. Listened to Churchill's speech last night and that <u>terrible</u> commentary on an air battle off the coast. It <u>shouldn't be allowed</u>. It makes play and sport of agonies, not to help people bear them, but to pander to the basest, crudest, most-to-be-wiped-out feelings of cruel violence. I can't bear not to protest as <u>strongly as possible</u>. And then to <u>repeat it</u> on Monday's news. Gosh! It's <u>bad</u>. It's Germanism of the kind we <u>ought</u> to be fighting against. Four other people have been revolted as much as I have. Two people I hate have said they liked it.

I will try to write some more diary, but this had better come to you.

Churchill's "The War of the Unknown Warriors" was broadcast on France's national holiday. He spoke of Britain's relations with France and celebrated Britain's continuing resolve to withstand Nazi aggression. The nation, he said, was preparing for its own defence—and also for the defence of other people's freedoms. "We are fighting by ourselves alone; but we are not fighting for ourselves alone. Here in this strong City of Refuge which enshrines the title deeds of human progress and is of deep consequence to Christian civilisation; here, girt about by the seas and oceans where the Navy reigns; shielded from above by the prowess and devotion of our airmen—we await undismayed the impending assault. Perhaps it will come to-night. Perhaps it will come next week. Perhaps it will never come. We must show ourselves equally capable of meeting a sudden violent shock, or what is perhaps a harder test, a prolonged *vigil. But be the ordeal sharp or long, or both, we shall seek no terms, we shall tolerate no parley; we may show mercy—we shall ask for none" (*Into Battle [1941], 248–49). As for the air-battle commentary that Olivia condemned, it was sufficiently remarkable that it elicited newspaper attention the following day. According to a report in the* Manchester Guardian *for July 15 (p. 5), "The BBC last night astonished listeners by broadcasting a running commentary on the air battle in the Channel. The commentator, Mr. Charles Gardiner, and his colleagues watched the fight from the top of the cliffs from a BBC recording car." Had it not been for the gunfire in the background, "the commentary might well have been one of a boxing or football match. The commentator became almost deleriously excited, and the broadcast was punctuated with loud cheering from spectators on the cliffs whenever one of the raiders was brought down."*

Two or three days after sending off the above portion her diary, Olivia got a message, probably of encouragement, from Mass-Observation, and on July 18th she wrote the following letter to its leading figure, Tom Harrisson.

Thursday, July 18

Dear Mr. Harrisson,

Thanks for the acknowledgement of the last bit of diary. You say you are interested in the points regarding morale and Government. The one thing that worried me while I was away sick was that my senior would snaffle that packet of diary, which was among work on my desk (I went off unexpectedly) and have me sacked on the strength of it! That worry arose from half-hearing next door wireless talk on civil servants and morale, and that those in authority were instructed to dismiss any staff whose views had a bad effect on their colleagues.

When I went back to work (without Doc's consent and I think too soon—got a horrid headache still) I was relieved to find the pages apparently undisturbed—along with the rest of my work (piles of it waiting)—and no remarks were made about it. After a few hours I realised that there was no difference in the tone of the conversation. In fact there was a good deal more argument as a new scheme for armed volunteers to guard the office at night was being criticised; and later in the day we had instructions to consider the possible effects of bombing on our punctual attendance; and a few details of a billeting scheme were given. Great wrath among the staff at the unfair conditions and the inadequate data on which we had to give a definite reply in three days. Later enquiry of the chief elicited only grunts of annoyance at "a lot of damn-fool questions" so we still don't know all we want to. We've since discussed the "no naughty talk" order, and my joke is the girl who got dismissed for keeping on saying "OF COURSE we'll win" and disturbing people enjoying a moan! Opinion unanimous that it was much better to let people talk as they thought, instead of bottling up worries and grievances; and that anyway surely one of the things we're fighting to restore to Europe is FREE SPEECH. Agreed that we'd never really had that in England, but that it looks as though we'll lose the little we have. A general moan ensued, that the Government is being too damned military in its methods and orders; that a great deal of quite unnecessary inconvenience was being put on people, apparently just to make sure nobody forgets there's a war on; that anyway we shouldn't notice the war half so much if it weren't for the wireless; that several were giving up listening in to so much tripe; and that the Government would have to <u>arrange</u> a spectacle soon, to keep people up to the mark! A continual spiel too is that it's only those with plenty of money who can really enjoy this war; but, by God, they DO. Difficult to avoid this last thought, surrounded [in Putney] by luxury flats whose advertised rents are double our average salary, constantly seeing huge cars with one person in, and watching the lovely clothes of the local lovelies.

Her diary continued.

Sunday, July 21

Sunny settee in the evening. Have not written daily at the office this week for two reasons: (a) been in charge of the room, so felt conscientious; (b) had a lot of work to do anyway. Have heard the 1 o'clock news each day, but can remember very little of it. The oily, detached, disinterested voices begin to create that same feeling in me, so that the reality behind the tones slides off my consciousness as quickly as the sound fades from my ears.

Saw a paragraph in the <u>Star</u> which pleased me. "They" are doubtful about more eyewitness battle accounts, lest a chance remark in the "heat" of the moment gives any information to the enemy. Whatever the reason I hope they stop. It is an unthinkable degradation for listeners, this poppet-show attitude to an activity in which life is being wantonly destroyed. However much the Authorities may wish it to appear <u>necessary</u> to kill all Germans, they must avoid showing the "pleasure" involved if they want to keep women sane.

Comforting comparison between road casualty figures for last June and air raid casualties for this June. Nice to think we do ourselves even more damage than the Germans can.

My personal morale doesn't seem to have altered at all. Externally I go on doing things for the future in the garden and the home. Internally I still feel that the communal violence of the age I happen to live in has got little <u>real</u> significance; that individual souls are still the most important aspects of evolution and will disregard a dozen Hitlers in the long run. I'm not very much aware of any doubt that the British Empire <u>will</u> dissolve eventually, though it doesn't seem any weaker yet. But I am well aware of my ignorance of the real facts of the present situation. I don't know who <u>really</u> wields the power in the world. But does anyone know? I still <u>feel</u> that WE are bound to win the war, but I don't know why.

There is a big divergence in our family in the views of the men and the views of the women. I am thinking about it a lot lately and wondering why it is not reflected more in public life. Looking round, it is remarkable that women have faded out of public life a lot. On the surface this must be gratifying to men; but if they have any second thoughts about it, perhaps disturbing.

Why, oh why, don't women get together and stop all this killing! They know so well that force is <u>not</u> the final arbiter, even in household disputes. Surely we women are waiting [for] some important new movement of the sound common sense in us. Surely we can't let men get away with this everlasting childishness of fighting. It's ridiculous, in the pedantic sense of the word.

Monday, July 22

Lovely sunny morning at the office. Had another instalment of diary from VAD [Voluntary Aid Detachment: a nursing organization] friend this morning, in which is an outburst very like mine last night about the damn-fool ways of men and war, and the work and worry it creates for women.

Mother and Dad went to the bungalow again yesterday. Gardened. Saw even more soldiers and evidences of war, and were even less perturbed. Was kept awake myself last night by constant planes and the very bright moon, but at the office today <u>nobody has mentioned the war</u>—except once incidentally saying that traffic on the hill is less now.

Tuesday, July 23

Peg came last night. We read bits of VAD diary and enlarged on the man vs. woman aspects of the war. Enjoyed the sunset meanwhile. Listened to Haw-Haw and disliked being called "the enemy." Found cynical amusement in the mirror-likeness to BBC news. Decided that threats on the other are bad form and bad psychology. Peg said she has seen several letters in the press against the "eye-witness battle" episode. Good; that gives me pride in the country again.

This morning's news referred to an empty house in Thames Estuary being bombed. Mother feels sure it was ours. Nothing we can do about it—and it probably wasn't, anyway. Eric has come back from Wye Valley fortnight with a bad cold caught while sheltering from raids!

The previous week had generated much talk about the BBC's live report-ing of an air-battle on July 14. One of these opinions appeared in the journal of another Mass-Observation diarist in London. On July 17 she wrote:

There is a lot of fuss in the papers about two Sunday broadcasts, one an 'indiscreet' one by Priestley and one a running commentary on an air battle, which some people praise as stirring, thrilling, inspiring, etc., while others condemn it as being unpleasant and savage. I didn't hear either of the broadcasts—I never do listen in to anything in the way of talks or commentaries—so I can't judge. But on the face of it the treatment of any aspect of war as a sporting contest like football, a means of providing a thrill for the armchair listener, seems quite unjustifiable. That listeners did in some cases enjoy it doesn't affect the issue. B. told me about it when she was here on Monday, and said it was exciting in a way but disgusting when you stopped to think that it was lives, not goals or wickets, that were at stake—this was before all the newspaper discussion of the subject had begun. (Diarist no. 5427)

One of these newspapers, the News Chronicle *of July 17 (p. 4), printed a letter to the editor that conveyed this critical perspective. "There must be those among us who still retain some small measure of sanity," wrote Barbara Willard of Courtfield Gardens, London SW5, "and for them the BBC's extraordinary performance on Sunday night will have come as something of a shock. Have we really sunk so low that this sort of thing can be treated as a sporting event? With cries of glee, we were told to listen for the machine-gunning, we were asked to visualise a pilot, hampered by his parachute, struggling in the water. If this sort of thing is allowed to go unchecked we shall soon have microphones installed in any available front line, with squared diagrams printed in the 'Radio Times' to help us follow the action." Such on-the-spot, centre-of-the-action journalism was not yet fully accepted as normal.*

Women were, as a rule, less inclined than men to celebrate the triumphs of war. Rather, for them war tended to mean destructive stupidity and senseless slaughter. Women were more likely than men to find the particulars of combat repulsive and were more likely to wonder about the point of it all—even as (and this was common, even for the pacifistically inclined) they grudgingly accepted the need for self-defence. Perhaps, they conceded, war had to be endured; perhaps there was now no way out (short of complete capitulation). Still, the reality of war was frightful and heart-breaking. As one woman had remarked a few months earlier, "My idea of war is bound up with the thought of death, disfigurement and every other kind of horror" (DR no. 2413, February 1940). These were also Olivia's sentiments. In early September 1940 another London woman, in her early thirties, said that she had "Come to the conclusion that war is filthy, and just a release for the repressed emotions of most men. Things they would not be able to do in peacetime are extolled in time of war. I suppose all sides are the same" (Diarist no. 5250, 4 September 1940).

Olivia resumed her diary after a week's break.

Monday, July 29

Have not written for several days. Had a curious bland feeling. Saw an old dried-up little woman on the train last week, wondered to myself "Is it worth while going on, for what waits between me and that?" And for days a kind of numb distaste for life has kept me from any but necessary efforts. I've eaten little, slept much, lazed shamelessly and felt altogether bitterly thin.

But this weekend three girlfriends stayed with me. I had to bestir myself to feed and entertain them and do their beds etc. And we talked a lot and life seemed good again, though they agreed with me on the awful prospects some moods provide. I've almost rejoiced in the idiocy of war, in this mood.

Have been thrilled to hear the J.B. Priestley broadcasts [on Sunday evenings]. Each time I think "Will they let him talk again?" And, mild as he is, and milky sweet, it <u>does</u> seem a good sign that he's allowed to say such things in wartime. Is it dope? If so, <u>he's</u> being taken in too, for I dare swear he's sincere. Everyone at the office likes and admires his speeches and style, or says they do. But will it make any difference?

On the previous evening's broadcast Priestley had described the stresses and sacrifices of a young RAF pilot and his wife, and then pointed out what had been done to reward such young people who had served in the previous war. "We did nothing—except let them take their chance in a world in which every gangster and trickster and stupid insensitive fool or rogue was let loose to do his damnedest. After the cheering and the flag-waving were over, and all the medals were given out, somehow the young heroes disappeared, but after a year or two there were a lot of shabby, young-oldish men about who didn't seem to have been lucky in the scramble for easy jobs and quick profits, and so tried to sell us second-hand cars or office supplies we didn't want, or even trailed round the suburbs asking to be allowed to demonstrate the latest vacuum cleaner." Priestley endorsed co-operative over competitive values and the building of a more humane postwar society. (Postscripts [1940], pp. 42–43). Olivia almost certainly agreed with most of his political opinions.

On the day that Priestley spoke, July 28, Olivia had written a few lines in her "Baby Book 1934–1940" (a diary addressed to her future children) that pointed to how she was then feeling about the prospect of motherhood in wartime.

Feel very feminine but <u>un</u>motherly just now. Have written more M-O diary and made remarks about the everlasting childishness of men fighting, so I don't want you boys at the moment; I feel annoyed at your potential scraps and blows and trials of strength. And I don't want you girls unless you can get together and run the men in such a way that their pugnacity serves us instead of hindering us in our search for a more abundant life.

Her M-O diary continued for July 29.

Am still beatifically in love, still with insurmountable odds against marrying.

Have had plenty of work to do lately; so not a lot of office discussion to report. The Budget echoes on. Real heated disgust when the males worked it out that the under £400's pay 331½ more <u>in proportion</u> than the over £400's. General agreement, even among over £400's, that the poor man has the worst of it, but that he always <u>has</u> and always <u>will</u>, so what?

Amused to see the hasty efforts on the part of the Government to repair the "Silent Column" breach. Public opinion does still mean something. Rumours float here buoyantly, all believed, but none startling. Have heard several bombs about eight miles away; no panic at all, but a rather exaggerated calm. And silence as we listened to the planes.

1 o'clock news still going strong. But the holy church atmosphere has given way to snappy comments on bloodthirsty lines. A little more concentrated hate against the Germans—but not much, not hateful yet. I may have a little to do with the expression of that—I

fly off the handle uncontrollably at "warmonger" speeches. Also I've been reading Dostoevsky and J.C. Powys and feel my inhibitions all loosened up lately!

Garden is doing well. Have eaten beans and turnips and cucumber (very good 10/10) and lettuce and marrow and beetroot and onions from it. Family all progressing on same lines. No casualties so far among acquaintances.

Wednesday, July 31
Some excitement last night. I was in bed reading, about 10. Heard a heavy low plane, sounded unnatural. Listened. It got terribly close and then—brrmmm—machine gun! Slippers and coat and rushed down to baby-nephew. Stood with Mother near him and heard three or four more bursts, receding. Dad came up and said it was only the exhaust. We pretended to believe him—and went to bed.

Much overt excitement in the office about it today. Had been heard at most places across South London around 10 pm. Didn't feel at all afraid—just excited and not wanting the baby to wake.

The news is definitely losing popularity. Fewer people come to listen at 1 o'clock and they go before the end—just come to hear the first headlines. And several times it has been switched off after a few minutes. I've been disturbed about the Japanese news [thirteen British subjects in Japan had been arrested and accused of spying]. B says the British Empire stinks in the nose of the world over it. No discussion at all at office.

Had several people swapped round to different jobs in the last few days, caused discontentment. And everyone's grumbling. But the weather is so good, it's difficult to be cross.

In early August Olivia received a news update from Mass-Observation. Her next diary entry was largely a reaction to this communication.

Tuesday, August 6
Thanks for the bulletin of information. It was a pleasant surprise and spot of sanity among the "papers" and BBC and Haw-Haw. But it lacked that larger view one had come to expect of M-O. Perhaps I am carping. Perhaps the "larger view" at the moment is to be found

in attention to details of morale, to assist victory. But I—obviously, from the scanty records herewith—have found it distasteful to keep on recording the infinite variations of the same old fact that no one likes this war but that all my acquaintance take it for granted that we've got to win it. Your bulletin remarks about the easy-morale of the French people right up to the last minute may apply here. But if so it will be for something of the same reason: the Government keeps saying it's all OK so we must believe it is. And if it isn't, what on earth can we do? It's all very well for Hannen Swaffer [a prominent journalist who wrote for the <u>Daily Herald</u>, a pro-Labour paper] to say "If the Government doesn't reflect the people's opinion, we must have a General Election." That's bunk. How can we begin a General Election? It's treason to carp at Government. And most people are against changing horses in midstream—unless one breaks down completely.

So we all welcome the political truce, grumble at every restriction and comply with it, and hope for the hazy peace. But until a lot more of us are killed, it won't be "at any price."

Thursday, August 8

Every day, office, garden, books, lover, bad dreams at night. Constant "Will this be the last day I'll see" feeling. Surface cheery, better tempered than last year, healthy, optimistic, cynical.

Have just listened for the first time to the "man who uses such bad language on the wireless," as he was described to me when I was told the wavelength. A Cockney–East Anglian voice, street corner technique, clumsy delivery for microphone, not sincere; with the message of ten-year-back communism laced with references to Hitler's might, sprinkled with public house adjectives, addressed to the "workers." MUST fall rather flat on any one who knows it's broadcast from Germany, where the workers are supposed to be worse off than here. But probably would excite and appeal to any one tuning in by accident.[11]

Wednesday, August 14

Last weekend at the office. Home Guard began their night patrol; a squad of six with NCO each night. No uniforms yet, LDV

1 Olivia Cockett as a child.

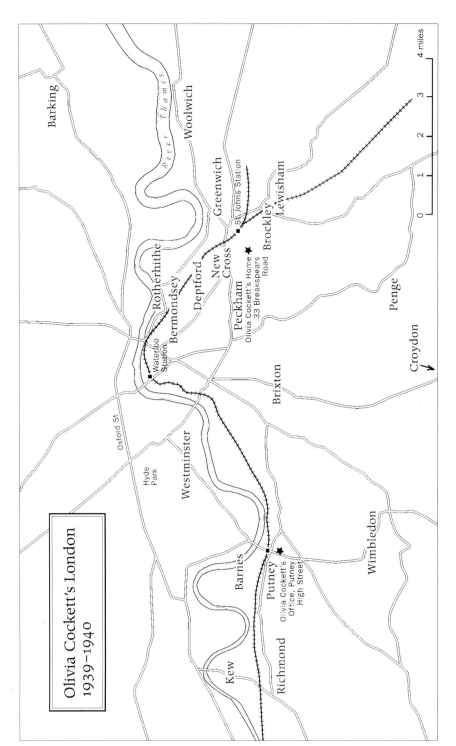

2 Olivia Cockett's London, 1939–1940.

3 Waterloo Station in 1941.

4 Bill Hole in 1938.

5 Olivia Cockett as a young woman.

6 "The Cut" market in 1938.

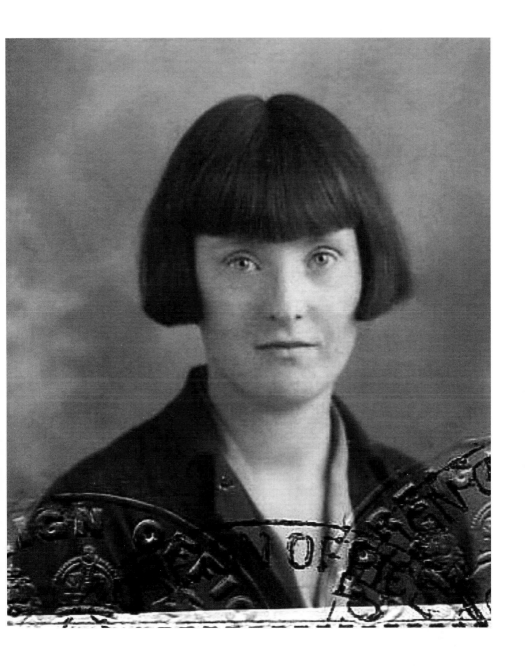

7 Olivia Cockett's passport photo, 1931.

8 Damaged houses on Breakspears Road, 1940–1941.

Southeast London sustained heavy damage in 1940–41, and many residents left for safer parts of the country. One man who returned to inspect the abandoned family home on or near Breakspears Road in February 1941 described the neighbourhood in a letter to his daughter: "Everywhere around here seems deserted and Brockley and Lewisham look every day like Sunday – nobody about as most of the houses which are not down are deserted by their tenants."

9 Rene Willmot at 33 Breakspears Road, November 1942.

10 Olivia Cockett in her mid-thirties.

[Local Defence Volunteers] armband, rifles and fixed bayonets. Heard some funny stories as each squad had its first turn. The first lot said "Oh, it was all right," the second lot said it was damn cold, the third lot began some real grumbles about food and sleep and discipline.

Two blokes patrol for 2½ hours in turn with fixed bayonets; the NCO visits them. Our bright 19 year-old, instead of challenging the elderly gentle senior officer who is his NCO, padded around behind him and let him walk for 1½ hours, looking for him, before challenging him on the wrong side of some wire netting. Ordered him to step forward and of course he didn't see the wire. Says he saw six hedgehogs; didn't kill them because he'd have to clean the blood off his bayonet; so kicked them instead. The NCO cooked their breakfast for them. The second lot were on Sunday. Didn't leave the guardroom except to patrol, although there is a lovely lawn out-side the dungeon. The third didn't try to sleep—gambled halfpenny nap all night; and didn't have any yellow warning, although the sirens were sounded five miles away.

Personal doings—little variant on the routine. Have read five books in last three days: Bax's <u>That Immortal Sea</u>, Ford M. Ford's <u>Rash Act</u>, C. Dane's <u>White Ben</u>, Sean O'Casey's <u>The Star Turns Red</u>, Casteret's <u>Caves</u> book. On Sunday went out at 4 to see a friend. Finding she was not at home I was at a loose end. So, although clad in old walking mac, felt hat, heavy shoes and laddered stockings, decided to walk in the West End. Found great crowds in Oxford Street, difficult to see in the shop windows for the rows of gazers. Wandered on to Hyde Park. Two men tried to "pick me up." Didn't persist after my blank stare. Listened with amusement to the Spouters. Found no embarrassing stares at my garb among <u>that</u> galère, all rather mad, with a glint in the eye. Bought a Wall's ice cream, too sweet, found it was a local fake Wall & Son and gave it to a small boy. Meandered on over the grass to the Serpentine; many people sitting on the grass and beginning to sit in the band enclosure half-an-hour before opening time. Lots of boats on the water. A few more religious meetings going on by the bridge, no political ones down there. Heard no really unusual remarks for record. All the old gags, little specifically war talk. But the various military encampments in the park were a great stare attraction. The queues outside the ladies lavatories were the next thickest density of population. By the time I got to Admiralty Arch, via Green Park and the Mall, the crowds had thinned. But clusters formed again to watch the sentry salutes as officers came and went at the Admiralty. A little, rather suppressed, giggling. I felt tragic-comic about it all. Home in time to watch the sunset and then contemplate till supper at 10. Felt personally cheerful, but communally dismal.

Thursday, August 15

Had a "night out" last night. Met Man at 6, Leicester Square. Spent a giggling hour at an all-funny news cinema—an aged Charlie Chaplin, very good—and went on to Snow's for best-steak-of-the-war, mushrooms, peas, chips, beer. Home soon after 9, after looking at the milling crowds of Piccadilly for a while. Pleasant twilight hour of lovemaking. Then to the station with him. This war in the air adds appreciable zest to such entertainment. We said "Last September we expected to be dead by August—not laughing at Charlie and eating steak!" And, contrasted with the blankness of death, zest comes.

One new habit since the war—<u>enjoying</u> cigarettes. Used to smoke occasionally, but now three or four a day regularly, and with plea-sure! Inhaling makes the difference, and the nicotine-treat which just detaches one's mind from one's body for a second or two after each breath. Shall endeavour to keep to this small number; don't want a habit, or the expense.

Friday, August 16

Met Mother [yesterday] and went to Lewis' and bought me a winter coat, £5 15s 6d. Mother pays £3 for birthday and Christmas present! Got caught in Trafalgar Square by siren and air raid—see separate account [this report did not survive]. Slept badly and this morning have spent the first hour and a half talking and writing about the air raid.

Met Man at Waterloo, talked air raid. Gave him my M-O typed account to read. Came down on the train with two girls, talking air raid all the way. Lovely blue-and-gold morning but it didn't get a mention. Have got plenty of work in, but don't feel a bit like doing it. Shall work hard this afternoon while Mrs S is at First Aid and we are quiet. [The rest of this handwritten page is blank. The same date's entry continues on a new page.]

Well, well, well!! I can't afford to post off accounts directly after air raids if they're going to be so frequent! But as I've just remembered, I posted the one two hours ago without my name and address. I might as well give it now and the next account.

12 noon. Mrs Smith and I walk down the hill to the High Street. Go into several shops, are in the street and hear the first note of the sirens. Look instinctively up at the sky, suddenly realise everyone is running! Mrs S says "There's a shelter over there." I say "I'm not going in there, I'm going back to the office." She agrees and we walk back. I stop to post my M-O. She looks back, wonders what happened to me. See a bus, begin to run for it, lights change and we miss it. So walk on up the hill. Traffic goes on. Most people have disappeared. A woman with a pram is running. We get to the gate and on the lawn a senior officer, white-faced and angry, yells to us "Get on inside, you two!!" We say mildly "We were out shopping." He says "I don't care, get on in, I tell you." We go to our room, collect coats and gas masks and lunch packets and watch. Go down to the cellars, where all the others are. They don't question us. We sit on a form [i.e., a bench] and giggle and eat our sandwiches. Various bells ring and people jump nervously. A man takes down a shutter and he is barked at to put it back. It is cold and gets stuffy.

We swap stories of last night's raid, murmur anxiously about our people at home. Someone brings the portable radio down and a groan goes up as choral singing comes through. It is turned down, loud again for 1 o'clock news, which seems remarkably out-of-date because it doesn't mention this raid. Quite soon the OK goes and we go up. Have discovered that the first-aid mattress and blankets are damp, so take them up to sun and air. Spend next hour chatting in our room. Then ten minutes hilarity when an old box of ping pong balls is found. They hurtle through the air in every direction. Then we settle, at long last, to work.

No, it's teatime!!! Now, it's 4 o'clock and still I've done no work—I'll have to stay late tonight to get through. Have had rumour that bombs were dropped on Woolwich and Staines.

In bed, 11 striking. I was on my way to the greenhouse at the office, to water. Heard the sirens, cursed. Found greenhouse door locked, so ambled back to the office and collected bag etc. Didn't go down to the stuffy shelter until ordered to by senior officer. Several people who had started for home came back to the office. Everyone cross about it coming at leaving time, nagging about broken engagements and meals waiting. Mrs S and I took cushions this time—hard wooden benches—and sat and knitted.

Were very relieved to hear the OK just after 6. Raced off down to the station. Had to wait 15 minutes for train, watched three fast ones pass. Then one stopped at the further platform—no time to get over the bridge to it. Another soon came, and proceeded with many halts to Waterloo by 7. A crowd of perhaps 900 people were waiting to get on to the 16 to 22 platforms, we had difficulty in pushing through them to get off. Heard rumours that the line was hit at Staines. Certainly the loudspeaker was advising people to go by Underground to Kingston and beyond; no certain news. But after the lunch rumours, Staines seemed 100% probable.

Found Man waiting for me—the dear. He had assumed I'd come, however late; and I did. We swapped news for ten minutes. He passed over a small parcel he'd bought for me at lunchtime and we decided to make our ways home as soon as possible in view of the crowds. But I was lucky and was home by 7:30! Quicker than usual.

Had heard a rumour of bombs on New Cross and worried, but luckily it was not true, and the house and garden were cool and calm. Dad had stayed at work for evening raid, been home to lunch at midday one. Mother was out in the afternoon, but came home at 8. Was at Ethel's (friend) at 5 and went in her shelter. Saw German planes, she says—at Penge [south London]. Heard bombs drop, in

Croydon area again. Listened to beginning of 9 o'clock news for once, in case they mentioned "our" raid. They did, but very briefly, so didn't listen any more. With this gorgeous moon we all expect more tonight. Am irritated by it, and have a headache slightly.

Saturday, August 17

10 am at the office. Everyone talking about raids again. Many rumours about. Direct evidence of some stations on Southern Railway hit. Three people had all their windows broken. One girl's aunt with six children, house quite demolished. Not hurt, because not there, but destitute now. Salvation Army helping them. One man on LDV [Local Defence Volunteers: that is, the Home Guard] sent home, as he lives by South Wimbledon station. Two men and a girl on bykes on the way home, bombs dropped near them on Common, stood behind trees, ran on to a trench as soon as a bit quieter. One of the boys coming up on a byke this morning nearly blown off it by a delayed action bomb.

Atmosphere cheerful. People pull faces and say "Pretty bad" and repeat rumours and facts and wonder when the next one's coming. At Dad's works they had a sweepstake, by quarter of an hour, as to when the next raid would come.

Man from another department has just been in, says over 100 killed at Croydon, 30–40 in a public shelter. Rumour 60 killed and 160 injured in Wimbledon area yesterday evening. One or two suggestions that Berlin ought to get it in the neck. A mild girl (normally) hoped their defences are worse than ours.

Strong feeling about everything, that it may be the last of its kind, so have and enjoy it. Was grateful for the moon, grateful for the sunny morning, grateful for a seat in the train, grateful for a comfortable body, grateful for being able to shut my eyes, and occasionally shut my mind, to present difficulties.[12] Came over my mind that that's escapism. I bolster up my self-esteem by reminding myself that I've worried and nagged and bored all my friends, since 1933 until Munich, with talking about Nazism and war and the menace to freedom. Went to meetings, read books, converted Conservatives.

So when the war came, I leaned back and let my mind wander. Now I'm beginning to nag and worry and bore people with talking about reconstruction after the peace.

Sunday, August 18

Stayed at the office for an hour on Saturday afternoon working on the allotment. Posted my warning and raid accounts on the way home, and wondered if I'd get home without another one. Met Man at Waterloo for ten minutes talk and got home by 3:30, after going through my station once on a non-stop train. Didn't get very cross because it was such a lovely hot afternoon.

Had a meal, decided to go up the garden in my deck chair. But Mother wanted it so I went up to my sitting room and read on the settee. Fell asleep awhile and woke with a start, feeling sticky. Had a wash and washed my hair, dried it in the sun. Listened to Mother chatting to two young girls (19) about clothes and make-up till I couldn't stand it any longer. About 7 went in and began cutting up an old silk frock; made one blouse and cut out another. Went down and had supper. Listened to <u>Music Hall</u> the while, was cynically amused at Suzettfe Tarry's patriotic tail to a sexy turn.

Then Gay came, having the weekend off from the hospital, VAD [Voluntary Aid Detachment]. Sat at my sitting room window watching the moonlight and hearing awful stories of the wounds and the bad grub and thirty cases of dysentry among the nurses—sacked all the kitchen staff for it. Even now Gay is making a collection of the blue bottles found in the fishcakes. When there are a lot she says she'll show them to the CMO [Chief Medical Officer]. She is very wild that neither nurses nor men get their fair rations; is sure the kitchen staff steal them. Told a lovely story. One VAD, moved from men's to officers' ward, snaffled a couple of open jam tarts and smuggled them over to her old ward. Gay cut them up for tea and sent her partner out to serve them while she made the tea. They came back soon, untouched. The other VAD said "The men say they don't want the officers' leavings." Gay cursed her for telling them, and took them out again. Told the men they were stolen for them, that the girl who got them would get the sack if it came out, that the officers knew nothing about it. The men ate them up to the last crumb—and Gay had hoped for a bit. They get very sore about the difference in the quality of the officers' food and the men's.

Another story. Warden I know was asked by a man, very sleepy, 2 am, if the All Clear had gone yet, as he'd been in this shelter half an hour and nobody else had arrived. Warden pointed to the roof and said "I don't expect they will either—this one ain't finished yet!" No roof on it at all.

At midnight we went to bed. Gave Gay her breakfast in bed. She went at 11, on [her job] at 2. Mother and Dad went off to the bungalow soon after. I had wanted to go down to Shoreham and walk a bit and sketch. Dithered about, looked up trains, packed a satchel. Am hoping period will arrive today; feel a bit headachy and a bit worried, having made so much "love" this month. Decided to stay home. Spent an hour trying to draw garden from my bedroom window. Believe I am a bit scared of going into the country alone (raids). So am now in the garden in deck chair, lovely warm sun and breeze and trees. Vaguely dislike the sound of planes in the distance, approaching like a headache in the sky. WELL I'M DAMNED—THE SIRENS.

I take my typewriter in and type on the kitchen table. Can hear whistles blowing, planes very close. Bert out on lawn watching, can't see anything. Wonder how far parents have got in the car—silly devils, they've gone down the Thames estuary. Three minutes pause in typing to listen to the swooping planes and hear the machine guns. Run up to my top window and hang out like a fool to stare at the heavenly blue of the sky. Run down again to type. Can hear the planes through my noisy typewriter. More machine guns. A BOMB. Mabel runs down to say "They're dropping bombs Paddy." [Olivia was known as "Paddy" to family and friends.] I say yes and type in the remark. Pause to observe that my typing is rather worse than usual. Heart beating a bit faster. Stop and listen. Planes further off. Neighbours' voices in gardens, "Spitfire," "Bombs," "Coming again." Zooom. Probably about five miles off—in Croydon direction.

1:20. Stand at kitchen door and listen. Still machine guns. Type again and wonder if neighbours think the noise is guns—too slow really! Wonder what Man is doing. Dad ought to go on duty. Hope they're in shelter. Lot of noise coming from that river way now. Distinct bomb [noise] closer.

Eight minutes later. The three of us went to the cellar after that close one. Plane seemed right overhead. More bangs. Ran up again for coat—cold down below. Got one of Dad's jackets from hall. Talked about Bert's eyebrows, cows' eyebrows, dogs and cows. Hoped parents and Bert's daughter are at bungalow by now. Swear at Germans. Guess that we were over Berlin last night. Decide the whole war's daft. Mabel says "The public are demanding so—that they should hit Berlin—but it's not worth losing lovely men for." I say "Seems quiet again now" and come up to the kitchen and type that bit and go to lav. Still no sign of period, but perhaps this will bring it on.

Listen in garden again. Very still. Leaves rustle in breeze, birds twitter. Distant fire to the north. Hope no delayed actions. Had that funny hot pain in top of head again, wearing off now. Trains still running. No voices. 1:40 pm. Planes again, distant. Car goes by. Church clock strikes three-quarters. I put kitchen clock right. As I wind it up I worry about Dad, who usually winds it. Shudder of fear for them. 1:50 pm. Voices about now. Faint clatter of pots and pans. Wonder how many dinners spoiled? Decide to get some food. Glad I didn't go to Kent.

Whistle as I get food from pantry "HAP hap happy day" and stop self-consciously to record the fact. The typewriter and dinner are both on the table. Decide to have a glass of plum wine. Feel I deserve it even if I don't need it. While preparing salad, sing all the words of "Miss Otis regrets she's unable to lunch today." Amuses me, and, I hope, the neighbours. 2 o'clock. No OK yet. Very distant planes now. 2:04. The All Clear is just sounding. Women's laughter in the gardens. Our local siren picks up. Funny the dogs don't bark at it any more. 2:10. Planes again. Hope it's ours coming back.

3:10. Finished lunch, washed up. Mabel brought me a cup of tea, so took it and fags and sewing and books up the garden. Very hot. Smoked a cig. And drank tea. Sewed one seam, lost scissors. Went down for kitchen pair and brought typewriter back with me. There were the scissors in the deck chair! Deep zoom of planes in the high sky still, almost all the time. Am watching the freckles come out on my legs. Ever since I can remember, I have hoped one day to catch one in the act. There seem to be more [barrage] balloons up now than there were during the raid. Perhaps they pull some down for reserves at the last minute.

5:42. Began clearing a border at 4. Just got nicely stuck into a very old rose root when the sirens go again. Fetch typewriter from top of garden (leave sewing) and come in to kitchen. Good deal of laughter came up from all gardens when the sirens began. Can't hear any planes. I go up the garden, collect bulbs into a bag. Put away deckchair, bring in rugs and cushions. Very distant noise of planes. Mabel brings me an apple. I am eating it as I type. I find a maggot in it. When my noise of crunching and spitting stop I hear planes a bit louder. Put on my gloves and did some more gardening. Heard next door 6 o'clock news. "Early this afternoon enemy machines tried to penetrate London's defences but were driven off." However, they're back. Can hear distant engines, faint gunfire. Feel annoyed, as Bert was helping with big root and has now gone indoors. Do some more raking. Wonder if this lunch-and-tea raid business is expected to put us off our grub. Find it certainly doesn't. The OK went as I'd got well down the rose root, so Bert came out and finished it off. Then spread two barrowloads of manure on the bed and dug it in a bit. Cleared all the tools away, swept the path, had a wash, and now at 6:55 I am typing this while waiting for the tea to draw—and do I need it!

Had a pleasant cup of tea (two mugfuls) and piece of homemade cake. Watered some garden. Cleared up. Came up to my own rooms, drew the view from my window, this time in black and looking out on a level instead of down onto the garden. Am now typing at a few minutes past 8. Shall listen to Haw-Haw at 8:15, to hear where they were trying to get. Biggin Hill, Sutton, Croydon. Gladder I didn't walk. [Haw-Haw was] Very cocky tonight. Mother and Dad came home so I didn't listen to the end. They saw a lot of fighting, 50 Germans coming at once. Saw three of ours go up, and Mother said "It was as though the Germans came up against a wall in the sky and had to swerve to avoid it; and once they were broken up they were shot down in flames. One seemed to fall on another and bring both down." A lone one dropped eight bombs fairly near so they went indoors, but were soon out again, Dad and Rene leaning over the fence to watch. Mother went out and put a mattress on their shoulders! The sirens went off several minutes after the planes went over.

Now the bath is running, for a quick one before supper.

Monday, August 19

Had the best night's sleep for a long while. Heard no planes at all. At Waterloo met Man. He had family visiting yesterday, raid at mealtimes, took meals with them to shelter. At office Mrs S (22) was at Club, swimming, near Crystal Palace. Crowded the diving boards to get better view; plane dived very near them, and they all dived, into the water! JM (19) was playing tennis at Club. Went on playing; so did the cricket team. (Have just broken off for a discussion on the Workers' Challenge station. I'm the only one who's heard it. I didn't tell the wavelength, and discouraged them from listening, saying it's a boring lot of lies and mildly bad language—which it is.) Miss F (25) was walking with girl friend in park near home, walked on home, though shouted at by Warden. Says the public shelters are her idea of Hell. One unpleasant feature is that one thinks every noise now will be siren or plane—keep catching oneself and other people with that "listening look."

Tuesday, August 20

Had best night's sleep for a long time last night; even better than Sunday's. Seems the coming of raids is easier to the nerves than the waiting for raids.

Was amused by Southern Railway notice at Waterloo—Owing to a mishap on the line trains will not run between Croydon and

Tadworth. Yah! The blackout on carriage windows is providing a new scribbling pad for them as likes 'em. "Blast Hitler" and "Down with Hitler and his (scratched out by later traveller) pals." The "Blinds must be kept down after dark" notice is varied to "Blonds must be kept down after dark"—and to "Knickers must be kept down after dark." Many pencil scribbles of no meaning at all, lines and dots and circles.

Peg came last night. The "What did you do in the raids?" is thin talk with intelligent pals, though it thickens into juicy gossip with acquaintances. Have not heard any really tall stories; but I know I've got a very sceptical eye, which may protect me from the best of them. We discussed the difference in propaganda, after listening to Zeesen [German short-wave station]. Decided the Germans MUST have beliefs, and are only happy when they all think alike, and strongly. And that many English are the same; but that there is a strong vein of agnosticism about EVERYTHING in a certain type of Briton, which is content to take the facts as they come, however odd they may be, and, whatever the previous "authority view," act empirically. We felt this New Statesman out of Tribune [pro-Labour periodicals] attitude a very useful standby, but a thorn in the flesh for Ministry of Information purposes. One of the best anti-Hitler inoculations though.

Have heard from two friends in Ministry of Labour that the figures for unemployed are up this month; and last night Haw-Haw put it at 600,000 more; disquieting. Probably due to need for skilled workers in the new jobs, while the old jobs which are closing down are throwing out unskilled people who can't be absorbed. But they must be having a lousy time on the dole with prices so far up. Mother says there is another penny on cheese every week now. And the purchase tax will be a big jump too.

So far I personally have been lucky. I have not felt any real pinch or lack although I'm well under £4 a week. But Mother is a very good food manager; and the garden has helped a lot. Have not bought lettuces or beans or cucumbers or radishes or apples all the year, and have a lot of tomatoes and greens to come. Spent some time last night making a frame for winter greens, on the Sunday-dug-up border.

Have just dug out the August questionnaire from M-O; feel that my diary covers the points mentioned. "General Feeling" [about the war] is difficult; can only hope it appears between the lines. Should say the raids these last few days have <u>increased</u> the enthusiasm for the war, odd as that should sound. But I happen to be lucky, I think, in living and working among people of good CHARACTER, who, having decided we've got to fight and win this war, don't think about it any more as a thing to "feel" about, but just to endure and slog at till it's over.

Government campaigns are not taken very seriously in Government offices. One wonders what bee is in whose bonnet at every fresh order, and hopes that in spite of the idiotic and confusing mess apparently made by every responsible official one has ever heard of or met, there are still some angels on our side to iron out the creases in the nick of time. The Somaliland fiasco was very much resented by two of my friends. It was not even mentioned in the office today. Personally I don't know enough about it to feel strongly one way or the other, but it seems to make some of our public ridicule of Italy look rather silly.[13]

By the way, my period arrived quite unmistakeably yesterday. Any woman reading this will realise the relief that means from worry and the consequent rise in spirits. May account for the good sleep more than any other factor. Having already experienced two "forced draughts" [i.e., abortions] I dread a third. Have done all the sensible things with the sympathy of a good doctor, but the fear is always half-alive, because the longing is so great. I keep a notebook going of remarks and records and thoughts for my future children. Wonder if they will find that unbearable sentimentality in a mother?

Olivia's "Baby Book" (1934–1940), which exists among her personal papers, contains some fifteen handwritten pages of remarks addressed to her future children, telling them of her hopes for them, of the sort of mother she'll try to be, of her suggestions for good reading—"When you grow up—16 say—I want you to read most of Galworthy's books" (October 6, 1934)— and, as the years go on, of her frustration and impatience concerning their delayed arrival. "My darlings, I ought not tell you but one of you got sent away this spring," she wrote in July 1936, and three years later, "More than one of you has been sent away by now and I tremble for the waste." Her urge to be a mother was and continued to be painfully intense—"I do so want you and need you and love you," she declared to her imagined children in July 1936.

In the absence of children, Olivia had sought out other outlets for her creative energies. "In the last few years," she wrote in July 1939, "I have spent you in political (left wing) theory and at Unity Theatre. In Mass-Observation. In Readers Union. In visiting America. In Mathematics for the Million. *In the* Psychology and the Religious Quest *[by Raymond Cattell, 1938]. In water colour dabbling. In new furniture and books. And most in gardening. All these shall go into you some time," she concluded, optimistically. Some months later, on March 30, 1940, she sounded much less hopeful. "Babies! I jeer at myself. Other people have babies, not me. I just happened to fall in love with a married man.... There's a war on now, anyway. But I'd jolly well have you, my dears, if I could—oh gosh I would! Garden, and room, and appreciating; some sewing; much dreaming: that's where your substance goes, my lovely kids. And I begin to feel bitter towards your first-choice-for-a-father. Dead End.... I am not so much sorry for myself as puzzled. WHY do I submit and submit and submit?"*

Her feelings on these matters ebbed and flowed, and earlier this summer, on July 22, 1940, her inclinations as reported in her private journal were running in a spiritualist direction. "Don't feel urgent regret, however real my longing for babies is. And it gets stronger in spite of the war. Been very lucky in friends and you, Bill. And in books—dear books. Mental effort, mental attitude, mental passivity, can change more, mean more, be more, last more than any other circumstance. I feel life flowing strongly and cool, clear and pure and bubbly, deep and dark and stony through this body, these habits, called Me. And I like it, give thanks for the experience of it; fret and kick as I may against fools of clever men with guns and bank balances."

Wednesday, August 21

9:30 am. Must take two minutes to record a succession of moments of thrilling happiness. No special reason, but on the journey to work this morning, they have been with me and given me breathless delight. The lines:

> Though inland far we be,
> Our souls have sight of that immortal sea
> Which brought us hither[14]

have been running in my head, reverberating with brimming meaning, flowing over my "core" with cool blessing. And now, in the office, the Home Guard talk is submerging me. Workaday cynicism, daily toughness, hardens and surrounds that throbbing emotion—heart, soul, spirit—call it by any name, it was real and lovely while it lasted.

Thursday, August 22

Thank you for the acknowledgement. Very sorry to hear about Joy Langley's husband. [Joy Langley was a staff member in M-O's London office.] If all our wishes count, he should recover. Probably his wife's presence has done him a lot of good. Please let us know, if you can, in the next news, how he is.

Spent an hour last night planting out lettuces in the new bed. Meal and talk to Mother. That sight of the fight on Sunday has played on her mind, she talks of it a lot. And we are all going down there again on Sunday next. Mother met a friend yesterday: heard that the scent factory at Croydon, where 46 people (?) were killed, has some wonderful deep air-raid shelters and that <u>if</u> the warning had gone they would probably all have been safe in them.

Rumour in the office this morning that Stoneleigh station was bombed last night. Can't get any confirmation, though people living fairly near heard nothing. This single raider method has got people on the jump. Obviously can't sound warnings for one at a time. 2:15 pm. AM (35), who says today what we all think tomorrow, has just exclaimed à propos of nothing at all "I wonder if this whole war's just a bloody farce. The blokes at the top on both sides just keeping us blokes under and getting us to do whatever they say." Chorus from the room "Coo blimey!"

Friday, August 23

10 am. Spent a pleasant evening, steak and kid and beer at Snow's. Then Devil's Disciple [by George Bernard Shaw] at Piccadilly. Home in bright moonlight by 11 and asleep by 12. Woke soon after 2, much plane noise. Lay and wondered and gradually got quite sure they were Germans. At 2:45 loud bomb noises and then gunfire. Mother came up and asked me to come down to the cellar. Feeling shivery and afraid, as our windows were rattling, I did. We woke the others, and all sat in the cellar, two of us smoking. Plenty of light hearted chatter and then the air raid warning came. But all else being silent, we went up to bed. Five minutes later the OK came. But it was difficult to sleep again, and this morning we all yawn.

Lee had the five bombs half-a-mile from him—Wealdstone. Feel sure there were some near Woolwich. Shall hear later. The shelling of Dover has been much talked of. People don't like it; hope not many people left there; and say there must have been many killed. "That's the limit." "The French again, you see, let us down again." "Sound nice, I should think, 16 inch shells whizzing over 21 miles of sea."

3:45 pm. Walked down the corridor just now with a tray of tea and suddenly all the walls melted away as I realised I may be killed tonight. 4:15. Just been discussing the fact that here we are in London, at HQ of an important fact-collecting organisation [the Metropolitan Police], and we still don't know all the places bombs dropped in Metropolis last night.

Saturday, August 24

On Friday met Man at 5:30 at Waterloo and walked along the New Cut. Saw a crowd of people listening to a pilot's description of battle. They all moved away when the BBC accent came on again with foreign statesmen's names and movements—or at least that's what it sounded like as we went by. Discussed the wickedness of government which tolerated the conditions most of the Cut people live with, and which then muddled its own distant affairs so damnably as to make these poor neglected trash their "heroes" when they could handle a gun.[14]

Home to a bit of gardening and a visit from my Auxiliary fireman brother. He said the whole squad turned out for the raid warning last night; luckily had to do nothing, so made tea. Asked after his wife and baby. They went to the Anderson shelter in their half of the garden. The other people in the house refused one when they had the chance, but are now glad to cram into it. In the Sunday raids they invited the next door people in, who had visitors, one man drunk. Nine of them got in a four [person] shelter and Bebe [sister-in-law] got very angry but could do nothing; not good for Mick aged 2½. She went to the Town Hall and they said the neighbours could still apply for a shelter for themselves; but she is trying to move away because of it! Still, she finds everyone difficult to get on with.

Soon after 9 we heard bombs and planes, but no warning. Mother wanted us to go to the cellar, but I was comfortably in bed with a Rawlings story [Marjorie Kinnan Rawlings, an American author] and didn't want to. Promised to come down if it got worse. Slept from 11:30 to 2:45, awakened by planes. Spent the next three hours quaking in bed, getting out every half-hour to pass water and look out at the moonlit sky. Felt really frightened, shivers, dry throat, swollen tongue, cold feet. Tried hard to will myself out of it; but only fell asleep after getting desperately tied up and thinking angrily "Oh blast them, if they come, they come; it's my nerve and philosophy against theirs, and I'm damned if I'll give way." During the day the thought of that fear came back two or three times and I shuddered. Hope to goodness my nerve doesn't break.

Didn't feel at all afraid, only annoyed, when the 8:15 am raid came on. Was in a full railway carriage, silently halted outside London Bridge. Heard the first faint siren against the rustle of newspapers, and uttered an explosive "DAMN." Was stared at in disgust by several gents, who, perceiving my "listening look," listened and then grinned and agreed with my Damn. Train went on to Waterloo and I hurried over and got my Putney train, thinking Man would not get there or wait. Found afterwards that he did, though he was glad I didn't. Got to office earlier than usual. Stayed in the garden instead of going in cellar. Wasn't caught by senior officer, luckily. Such glorious sunshine, couldn't leave it till I heard guns—and they didn't go off—so stayed till OK.

Then tried to phone Man. No reply from switchboard, so went to the phone cellar. No one there; looked with interest at the complicated board; all still and no one near. Longed to speak to Man. Touched various switches and knobs, heard a voice say "Number please" and GOT him. Open Sesame. Such a fascinating set of things, once I'd got the horn on my chest and a voice, I HAD to go on playing with it. Made several experiments when the little grey circles and numbers dropped. Nearly dropped myself when a voice came, a VERY SENIOR officer. I asked for "Number please" as I couldn't think what else to do. He recognised the difference and spoke, then recognised my voice; asked what I was doing there. I said "Well no one seems to have come" and expected a terrible ticking off. Instead of that got thanks and compliments on my helpfulness!!! By God's grace the operator came and got the number he wanted, or I couldn't have got away with it. Begged a lesson off the operator then and there, in case I should get caught out. Shall go down next week and have another go, as it is a big board, with several private lines as well as seven exchange lines and 60 interior extensions.

The things I've done for Love!

Man came home with me this afternoon. After two hours of the most heavenly love making we've had in all our eleven years (10½), Micky arrived and we played with him in the garden, tired, but happy.

Then the blasted guns and bombs and sirens at 4. Played picnics with Mick in the cellar, and forgot to be frightened in the joy of having Man and Mick and Mother—my three most important people—all in the cellar with me, playing childish games. I quite forgot why we were there. Went up to the garden after 20 minutes and no more noise, but dived back with Mick in my arms when a plane hummed towards us. The All Clear divided us up again. Mick had to go home, Man to station, me with him and then to library.

Home to meal (delayed lunch) at 6:30. Cleaned bedroom; washed hair; dried it in garden, listening to Rene going over her pros and cons for war marriage. Biggest con seems to be that the Government would buy the home. If they get married on Jack's week's leave, she gets 20 shillings a week and will save it, keeping at home and keeping at work, till after the war. Normally they would have to save for three years yet, as she's only 19. Hasn't made up her mind yet.

Sunday, August 25

1:30 am. I'm scared stiff. Sirens at 11:20 after I'd been to bed and got up once for bombs. Cellar; bombs very close; quiet later so [to] top window—big fire blazing high over the Rotherhithe Docks. Shivered for the poor souls near or in it. Trembled uncontrollably when the big bangs came. Had a fag. Seven of us, no one broke down, but we did not like it. Heavenly moonlight and peace out in the garden.

Up again 2:45. More bombs, no siren. Spent rest of night in clothes, on settee, afraid. Crawled upstairs and into bed again about 6. Slept till 10:30. Breakfast and dressed and Dad got car. Picked up Joan at Barking by 1. Went to Benfleet "the devastated" [bungalow in Essex], didn't see one cracked window. Picked several pounds of apples, beans and potatoes. Left at 6. At Rainham saw four bomb craters in a field. Three houses shattered [on] the other side; roofs gone, but windows not broken! The German plane was brought down nearby. Felt dreadfully sorry for the people—had a drink at the local and heard no one was killed.

Home and in bed by 9. Heard half of Priestley on next door's radio; sounded good. Slept till warning at 10:30, drowsed on settee for an hour. Back to bed, lay rigid listening till 12:30 next morning. Down again. Mother and Dad didn't get up (this is the first they ignored). Bed again at 1. Rigid with faint noises till 2:15. Three bombs and an approaching plane. Shot downstairs again without coat or anything. Up to bed again by 2:30. Too much tension—my top room catches every tiny sound. So down again on settee. Slept from 3:30 till 6:30.

In J.B. Priestley's August 25th Postscript on the BBC, part of which Olivia heard, he had talked about:

the best way of mentally coping with this war. But before I do that, I'll tell you the worst way—how to drive yourself half barmy. You do this—God help you!—by chaining your mind to the procession of events, by reading in ten different newspapers and hearing in five news broadcasts about the same eleven Heinkels and seven Messerschmitts, by never stopping wondering in a dreary kind of fashion—you know—"I wonder what they'll try next," by opening your mind to nothing but idiotic rumours or lying enemy propaganda. Now the best way is the opposite of this. Don't be dragged along in that slow procession. Sometimes, take your mind clean away from the whole business, just break loose from it. But then, come back to the War and instead of rumouring and wondering, really *think* about it, cut through the surface, and try to discover what's behind, pulling the strings, in this vast lunatic puppet-show of armed men and machines. In this way, instead of the War—as people say—getting *you down*, you get *it* down, to take a good look at it; and you begin to exercise, to be part of, that free, enquiring, searching mind that not all the bombs in the world can destroy because it's unconquerable and indestructible. (*Postscripts* [1940], 54–55)

Monday, August 26

In to office quite normally, after meeting Man at Waterloo and hearing his tale of bombs <u>after</u> the OK, killing two people at Barnes. First hour at the office, all raid gossip. Junior staff getting fed-up with senior repetitions.

2:35 pm. Feel sleepy; heavy eyed; hot head; back aches; nervous shooting pains. Can hear sirens in my ears all the time again, as in first week of war. Everyone's sleepy but not cross—all kind to one another's tiredness. Keep hearing news of the weekend raids. A lot of damage and death; spoken of coolly.

4:15 pm. Just come up from half hour in the air raid cellar. Heard first note of warning—knew it wasn't the one in my head. All ran round putting up shutters. Put on coat, took bag and book and gas mask and went to FAP [First Aid Post]. Filled bottle with clean water. Sat on blankets and read. No sound from anywhere till All Clear.

Tuesday, August 27

10 am. Met Man at Waterloo last night, half an hour's sleepy chat. Home by 7. Gardened, lettuces and radishes and cress for winter salads. Listened to 9 o'clock news. Ran a bath with lots of foam. Came the sirens. Couldn't bear to waste the lovely hot water, so bathed; but it was a quick one! Then downstairs, darning stockings. Into the cellar as planes came closer, took darning with me. Willmotts had three visitors, so there were ten of us down there, four smoking. Played solo till 2. Wandered round the garden, lovely moon. Tried to sleep on settee; couldn't get off. By 3 everyone had wandered back to bed. Heard six bombs and went into cellar. No more, so settee again, after OK. Slept till 7.

Whistled my way down the road, felt extraordinarily cheerful. Bit set back when Man didn't arrive; rang him, no reply but phone buzzed so house is still there. Rang as soon as I got here, found he had only overslept, thank goodness. Remarkable cheerfulness at office, due to absence of fires or bombs near us last night.

2:30 pm. Many yawns. Worn mine off a bit by spending an hour flat out on the grass. Drowsed restfully. Heard from man in another department that Ashstead was badly bombed last night. Rang Man and told him, as he has friends there with a baby. LALH's sister was at the pictures—came home to find the back blown off her house.

Wednesday, August 28

9:40 am. Everybody looking weary today. Trains not so cheerfully tired—more bored. Instead of sympathy for others' yawns, a faint disgust.

When I got home [yesterday], found sister-in-law and nephew had come to stay the night, regarding air raids. Both slept with me on the dining room floor. Or rather, didn't sleep till 3:30 am. Then so stiff and dull, went up to my bed and <u>slept</u> (!) till 6:45. Talking to Man at Waterloo this morning, found our air raid times differed. We had a second warning (9:35, 12:35) with no All Clear between. Home Guard here saw German bomber being chased across by Spitfire at 5 am. No warning. Heard several people commenting on the <u>idiocy</u> of us bombing them, while they're bombing us. Begin to feel furiously indignant in spasms myself.

More talk last night of dreading the winter coming if night raids go on like this. I suppressed a horrid fantasy of fears on the lines of—sewers and water mains gone; gas gone; daren't drink water (typhoid); then gas from cruising planes; and nowhere to go. Endless possibilities of horrors, difficult to dismiss during those listening hours in the night. 4:45 pm. Very weary now. Head and eyes ache; throat sore, back aches; last few days much dandruff and leucorrhea [vaginal discharge of mucus]. A bite from an insect six days ago has not healed yet.

Had a visit from DBP (24) today, late clerk, now PT instructor in RAF. Having "grand time" but would rather be in civvies. Thinks everyone is now determined to "see it through." Said "Morale is very good all over England." (Has been moving about a lot with batches of recruits.) Wonders how London will stand up to many more night raids. Enjoys making "straight backs and short hair" out of "hands in the pockets and hair over the collar." A thoroughly charming good natured lad, probably popular with his men.

Thursday, August 29

9:40 am. Met Man at Waterloo last night; talked sleepily for half an hour. Home by 7:15 to read Micky to sleep. Supper, garden for half-an-hour. Then bath and made up bed on settee; in it by 9. Then, of course, the warning. Got Micky down on to cellar camp bed without waking. Sat around sleepily till midnight, after the supper etc. was cleared off normally. Then crumps began and I slid into the cellar, Mick woke and we played games. Eric was trying to sleep on a camp bed in the coal cellar, beyond the cleaned-up part, and he sighed noisily when Mick chuckled loudly. There was a constant coming and going among the nine people present; deciding to lie down, hearing things and coming back again. I gave up the attempt until the All Clear went at 4:05 am. Then had sound sleep till 6:45. Up and lovely wash and freshen. Because of my fear, sweat is extra stinking, needs much more cleaning up.

Was surprised how empty my usual train was. Usually ten sit, five to ten stand; but only four in it today. And London Bridge and Waterloo both remarkably empty of people. Seems to have been a joint decision to be late—didn't see any difference yesterday. (Only two people out of 20 late in office.) I was whistling; a porter nearby was whistling; I stepped up and said "The tune for today is <u>Serenade in the Night</u>, please." We both laughed, and I amused myself jingling rhymes topical in my head for the rest of journey. Got a carriage to myself on second half of journey. Stretched out on seat flat for a while, as I have done all this week when possible.

Olivia's exchange with the railway porter brings to mind the remarks of an American woman in her twenties who volunteered for and served in the Women's Auxiliary Air Force (WAAF). In her wartime memoir, Mary Lee Settle recalled that in World War Two "the British talked." During the War, she thought, "they were, for once, the most direct people I had ever seen. Perhaps, being such a phlegmatic people, they needed the edging, the slow nightmare reality, to draw them out. The English were discovering each other with the freedom of strangers, lurched by war out of their silences, often friendly, sometimes with the direct belligerence of the stripped down."[14]

The sleep-time chart in with this packet is accurate according to people's own estimates—obtained without their knowing I noted it, of course. It's an easy question, "How many hours did <u>you</u> get last night?" [This chart does not seem to have survived.]

11:15 am. Miss C in next Department had six bombs near her house last night; all the windows blown out; feeling very shaky. Bomb on Chelsea F.C. ground. Bombs on Old Kent Road near Bricklayers Goods Yards (that must have been our worst window-shake). The news filters round with the work; is accepted with Dear oh Dears. Facetious comments in this room, but gloom in the next.

2:05 pm. Went down the High Street at noon. Bought pair of shoes which I can't afford, but if I live they'll be a bargain and if I die

I die broke. Came back to sleep on the grass for half an hour, very good—wanted more. L came in to chat. Bombs near him did less damage than he thought from the noise. He expects "big" ones soon. For the first time this summer the "gang" didn't play stump-cricket in the lunch hour. But four stalwarts slammed a tennis ball over the net.

Very fair attitude to "random" bombing. Every spot we have personal acquaintance with is acknowledged to be "not far" from some military objective. But that must apply to all England now. The "Blast it, let 'em come" attitude is still to the fore. But signs of a break are there in tone, if not in word. Read somewhere "Few Governments make much difference to the amount the ordinary man eats or sleeps." An out-of-date classical remark now. What next?

One of the most trying things is the way we all react to possible danger signs. My heart misses a beat whenever a car changes gear-up, or when someone runs, or walks very quickly, or suddenly stands still, or cocks their head on one side, or stares up at the sky, or says "Sshh!" or whistles blow, or a door bangs in the wind or a mosquito buzzes in the room. So taken all round my heart seems to miss more beats than it ticks!! Skin feels all puckered round bomb-crater eye sockets.

Have had two immediate calculation jobs in today, involving £60,000. Found my additions needed careful checking. It doesn't matter so much if I nod over a few accounts, but I feel very sorry for those who want to nod over a steering wheel or a cutting machine. Or even over cooking and washing and keeping the baby quiet.

Friday, August 30

10:50 am. All had good normal night last night, after spending an hour making the cellar extra comfortable. I slept on dining room settee again, still not brave enough to listen at top of house. But slept well with only two breaks when planes went over.

Saw RJW (55) last night and heard his account of the incendiary bombs on Bermondsey. He is ARP [Air Raid Precautions] casualty car owner-driver. Was up and waiting at door with car in street.

Dived in as they came down all round his house. Then out again to deal with the damage. Far more cars than casualties! So after the raid the CO rearranged things and now they don't move from spot until messenger fetches them, if the need is not in their own street. They picked up or reported 180 bombs, all 2½ lbs, in their area. Five which did not go off were marked "Made in England." He saw this himself—said he wouldn't have believed it if he'd been told. Wondered if it's propaganda or Dunkirk.

The demolition squad in the Council yard were not to be seen. The CO shouted for them; they are all on the roof watching! He tells 'em a thing or two, but is interrupted by the batch of incendiaries. Two flicks and they are all in the dugout! Except one little one, the butt of the squad and last down—sees one flaring in middle of yard. Scoops up handfuls of sand and piles it three feet high, topping off with a dustbin lid. Of course it was on concrete and would have done no harm, but today he is a hero, thumbs in braces, cock-a-hoop, and he deserves his pat on the back!

Several householders put their own bombs out, before the officials got there. Nice work. (Dad fixed 60 feet of hose pipe on to the bathroom tap after hearing RJW's stories.) No one was killed. The excitement has had a really good effect. The damage was so very much less than anticipated, and the precautions and help were adequate, so that morale has improved tremendously. I felt much better too, after hearing about it, though I reserve my opinion of high explosives or <u>big</u> incendiary bombs. Or of possible bombardment.

Noticed a good many amulets and crosses and charms being worn lately. Wristlet identity discs seem to come in the same category, from owners' remarks!

I have a bus map in the office. Am putting blue crosses where there is fairly reliable news of bombs dropping. As I have a certain amount of official information this is a bit unfair, but it will be interesting to keep as a souvenir. (That shows how I unconsciously assume we win!!) No, I shan't send it in for M-O; probably have better knowledge (and map) already.

Found myself biting my tongue this morning, to keep from "imparting information." A little girl (8) sat next me in the train; seemed unacquainted with London. The female in charge didn't tell her much, and I was longing to say "Look, that's the Tower and that's St. Paul's" etc. Acknowledged to myself that I enjoy "imparting information." Must say I rarely do it! Probably one of M-O's attractions for me; and a safety valve. Because M-O is rationalised gossip, after all! But just think what a lot we'd know if only this grand everflowing river of human activity had been canalised a hundred years ago by some such organisation! I envy the blokes who'll find or use the records in a hundred years time.

1:20 pm. As it was such a sunny day I decided to air the office first aid equipment. Put all blankets on railings in sun. Opened four shuttered up windows. Just got up the stairs in time to hear the raid warning going. Swore and tore around putting them all back. Took water round to people in shelters. Four out of 30 had a drink. Some were quite annoyed at being asked. Stayed down for half-an-hour. Remembered a packet of valuables on my desk. Crept up on my crepe rubber (sorry!) shoes and fetched it. Read four pages of a novel and then the All Clear. Nine people took their work down with them. They're doing overtime—very busy. Lot of grumbles about spoiled lunches.

Feel annoyed with the people who <u>will</u> go out in the evenings for amusement <u>this</u> week. Cinemas, theatres and Prom concerts are all very well. But what about the bus-drivers etc. who're expected to get you back home. And the apprehensions of the people at home as to how you're doing, out. Heard some amusing stories of the goings-on in public shelters and cinemas etc. during raids. But I won't pass them on in detail, as you probably have first-hand reports; "fraternising" of artists and audience mostly. Have just rung up the branch of this Department near my home, on a footling query; really just to finish up by asking if they "heard" anything. They didn't.

3:55 pm. Very short warning, didn't even have time to settle down, after fetching blankets from the garden again. A rumour that bombs dropped five minutes before the warning at Barnes. As my worst enemy lives there, I try halfheartedly to suppress a wicked hope. [She was probably referring to Bill's wife.]

Home 8 pm. Had another raid 4:50 to 5:50 at office. Heard gunfire. Walked around and joked and made a stranger (caller) welcome after being told she had been neglected. Met Man at Waterloo 6:30; talked twenty minutes. Very crowded train home. Micky is here to sleep again tonight. Feel terribly apprehensive about tonight, somehow. So much so that I'm scrawling this on kitchen table and will post it before eating. Catch myself saying "Oh God, Oh God" over and over again, on the stairs and places. Terrible tummy shooting pains too. Am joking and witty to people still, on the surface. But <u>horrible</u> underneath. A man apologised for shoving on train tonight. I said "That's all right—it's as bad as a good dance." Cheeroh M-O—good luck.

3

Bombs, Busyness, & Hoping for Babies

September 1940–October 1942

September the 7th, 1940, was a Saturday. On that Saturday, a warm and sunny day, there occurred an event which had been dreaded for years, expected for over twelve months, and which now had been awaited with mounting certainty throughout that hot summer of battle, and defeat, and death. On September the 7th, 1940, the German Air Force set out to destroy London.

These were the opening words of chapter one of The Blitz *by Constantine Fitzgibbon, first published in 1957. For those who lived through them, these early days of Germany's assault on London were unforgettable.*

On that September weekend in 1940, Phyllis Warner, a woman in her early thirties, was living on Tavistock Place, London WC1. On Sunday the 8th, she wrote in her diary, "Last night was a night of horror, a hell on earth. About one o'clock I heard the sound of an approaching bomb for the first time, an appalling shriek like a train whistle growing nearer and nearer, and then a sickening crash reverberating through the earth."[1] Vera Brittain's diary for that day conveyed a similar tone of horror. She, too, was in central London (specifically, Kensington).

Terrible night—10 solid hours of bombing from 8:00 p.m. to 6:00 a.m. German bombers circling overhead—now far—now nearer, with bomb crashes as they came. One very loud one broke glass in shelter window, already shattered by previous night. Between 2.0 & 3.0 bombs seemed to drop every 5 minutes. Lay in shelter most of night face downwards with pillow over my head. Worst night yet.

In afternoon (& also early morning) went round & saw damage done last night. Warwick Gardens was a devastated area—no glass anywhere. House at corner of Pembroke Gardens & Earl's Court demolished—windows all round broken; clock & windows smashed on St Philip & St James's Church.[2]

"The squalor of destruction," she remarked elsewhere, "has made a temporary slum of these once prosperous middle-class homes."[3] *"All the sky was lit up by a red glare of burning buildings in the distance," wrote one woman in London to her friend in Scotland, early in the morning on September 9, after walking home from work late at night, "and nearer buildings were silhouetted against it. You felt you really were walking with death—death in front of you and death hovering in the skies."*[4]

This was the start of the Blitz on London. Massive German bombing of civilians persisted, relentlessly, and nightly, and sometimes in daytime as well, for almost all of the next two months. Landmark buildings were engulfed in flames; walls collapsed, roofs fell in, roads were blocked, rail lines were blown up, glass was shattered and sent flying in all directions. To be on the receiving end of a direct hit usually meant death. Hundreds of thousands of people took shelter as best they could, in cellars, tube stations, bunkers, and specially built shelters. The normal quiet of nighttime became a thing of the past. While all this was by no means unanticipated, to actually live through the chaos and feel intense fear, to experience the violence of battle on the home front and be constantly on the alert for the safety of oneself and one's loved ones, was, if not without precedent, certainly novel in its suddenness, scale, and concentrated deadliness. Heretofore such destruction from the air had existed mainly in people's minds and in works of the literary imagination. As Phyllis Warner remarked on September 9, two days after the Blitz began, "The bombing of great cities is now an old story, but—God help us—it's new when you see it with your own eyes what it means in terms of human suffering." "How fantastic life has become," wrote the novelist Rose Macaulay on September 11 from her flat on Luxborough Street, London W1. "I wonder if London will soon lie in ruins, like Warsaw and Rotterdam."[5]

   This was a moment in London's history that concentrated diarists' minds. "What an awful night!" wrote a middle-aged married woman in West Hampstead on September 9. "From the window, we saw, again to the east, large fires, and as we gazed, holding our breath, swift stabs of flame shot down from the sky in quick succession. Every stab sent up a vivid flash of flame, while, already, a high wall of pure, lightning-coloured fire glowed for miles along the Eastern horizon. The rest of London was aflame with search-lights, bursting shells, floating flares and the quaking radiance of Molotov breadbaskets—and the noise! Booms, bangs, pops, crashes, screams, Wardens' whistles—while below, in the inky street, the traffic crawled, dim-lit, ghost-like—I gasped, shut the window and suddenly felt we should no longer remain in the flat." She and her husband retired to their basement shelter.[6] *("Molotov breadbaskets" were cluster bombs. They split open in the air, scattering dozens of incendiaries.)*

   The first intense bombing of western regions of London followed a few days after the initial raids on the East End. Vivienne Hall, a diarist in her early thirties who lived with her mother in Putney, wrote the following words on September 18. "What can I say? Last night, from before 8 until 6 this morning, heaven and earth went mad with noise. The barrage spat into the air booming and bursting shells and all manner of other horrors. All night long the swish and whistle of things falling from the skies kept us on the alert; at times the whistles seemed so near that we were certain that the bomb was to hit our house—but it passed over. The flashes through the curtains looked like endless lightning and the beastly planes purring overhead made a fantastic accompaniment to the crashing night chorus. We lay in bed, lucky to have beds to do this in, and listened and watched—and so the night went by."[7] *These raids went on some nights for eight hours, ten hours, or even more. Sometimes bombers were heard overhead—or seemed to be overhead (a few diarists kept count)—every five or six minutes. "It did not seem as though bombs were falling," wrote one London woman, "but as though they were being slammed down, like the lash of a whip."*[8] *Another diarist, a woman born in 1901 who lived in Notting Hill, vividly remembered the first days of the Blitz a year after she had first been exposed to it. On September 10, 1941, she wrote: "Exactly a year today that I returned to London to face the blitz…. I shall never forget the next fortnight as long as I live … sleepless, terrified nights, and days when you could fall off your chair for weariness, and yet somehow held on … the tense look on the faces of all the inhabitants of Notting Hill Gate—for, of course, I ventured nowhere else!"[9]*

Olivia Cockett kept no M-O diary for these weeks of the Blitz. However, she did respond to two questionnaires in September that asked for details on how the bombing was affecting her life and other people's lives. She offered the following reflections on Wednesday, September 11, just four days after the Blitz began.

Wednesday, September 11

There's no word I can start off with to give the mood of these ghastly days and nights of bombs on London. In a way it's not yet as bad as I feared. Yet that it has come at all tears away good from life. And makes good all the more important. I've not lost my nerve— yet. Had a good cry one day last week and sent off a bulletin ending hysterically. Now, my nerves are steady after seeing one strong man I know crumple up and cry like a baby after living through those two nights and Saturday afternoon [September 7] in Rotherhithe near the Docks. (There are terrible explosions going off somewhere still, 30 minutes after the OK of the second afternoon raid. Books have just slid off the desk here, and the house shudders.)

Material record. Sunday night I put out an incendiary beside the coal cellar. Monday night a high explosive at the end of the garden brought all the walls down and made a crater ten feet deep and thirty in diameter. Of course broke a lot of windows. No casualties. Have mended windows with cardboard and also those of lone lady opposite. Reported damage. Have had no official notice taken at all. The Ministry of Information local boards have a notice: local damage, two houses hit, no casualties. Bloody farce. There are literally hundreds of houses down in this borough of Deptford. (During these last few minutes planes have gone over. Now I can hear bombs going off, but there is no warning.)

Luckily I am on leave this week. Should have been walking in Buckinghamshire—am very glad to be at home. Have tried to get in touch with the office, but since Monday morning the trains have not run and the phone is off. They can get me if they want me. I'm not going if I can help it.

Every night we have been in the cellar. I cannot sleep, especially since I was the only one awake to hear the incendiary bomb and was able to put it out within two minutes of landing. I daren't sleep now. I roam around the house and garden and keep going back to the cellar when the lights are overhead, and report progress to the other ten. Yes, ten in that little cellar now. A cousin of 40 with his Mother over 70 have come to us from the riverside, only just in time. Came late one evening through a raid and that night their flat was wrecked. And sister-in-law with 2½ year-old Michael come each night. Brother a hero in the AFS, doing rescue work and laughing and joking and looking 20 years older in three days, during which he had seven hours off duty.

Since last Saturday I've not been more than a half mile from home. Have seen two churches, six houses, wrecked; windows out of about two hundred; traces of 15 incendiary bombs. The terrible fires I see from my high window along the river valley will haunt me for ever.

She went on to portray the behaviour of each of the eight other adults who at that time resided at 33 Breakspears Road, followed by some observation on her own state of mind.

Old Aunt sits still and says little. Trembles. Doesn't move all day. Prefers to be let stay in the cellar. Bert (50) takes it quietly. Can't rest. Swears. Keeps sarcastically cheerful, except in private to me when he says "God, it's bad, girl; we've all been barking up the wrong tree for years." Mabel (47) fidgets and fidgets and won't wear soft shoes. Keeps everyone on edge tapping up and down the stairs. Thinks the Germans are very clever and says so till we all yell at her. Mother (46) says she doesn't care what happens to her now. Hopes she'll soon be hit and out of her misery. Eyes generally with tears. Only keeps up because of baby Mick to be cosseted. Dozes. Dad (49) works hard all day among the wreckage. Will be on voluntary night duty every third night. Says "Things are very sticky, m' dear. I'm glad you are home to keep your Mother going." Sleeps a bit now and then. Sam (40) working twelve hours a day repairing gas mains. In a mask a lot. Looks very tired. Is quiet and cheerful. A dear. And so glad to have got his Mother up here to us. Eric (24) a damned shirker. Wouldn't even try to go to work till we bullied him today. Had to be coaxed to help me mend Mrs W's windows. Sleeps all day and all night. Probably scared stiff inside and ashamed so I try not to get cross. Rene (19) tough dear girl. Keeps us laughing at her wisecracks and we have a good hug now and then and understand one another. She walked to her city warehouse but was sent home because of unexploded bombs there. Tried again next day; wasn't back again. Shivers as bombs hiss by (and by golly they do, on their way to the mile-off docks) and takes aspirin. Sleeps a lot.

I can't sleep. But I don't feel terribly tired. Living on nerves I suppose. Am terribly worried about Man. We were to have met at Paddington on Monday at 11. I couldn't get there or let him know and I've had no word from him. Bang goes our week's holiday again.

Keep philosophising to myself. Dreaming of a better world to come (where from?) and still not hating the Germans. Still getting up on my hind legs when the others curse them. Still can't keep quiet when I hear shallow pessimism, or optimism. Still glad to be alive, and still expecting to be dead. And trying not to think of gas, or mutilation. Won't admit to myself that I'm worried to hell that Dad is not in. Those blasted big ones two hours ago were near him. And I fear.

Shall post this out of sheer bravado, after telling myself a few times in the last three terrible days that I couldn't possibly do M-O. For God's sake pass on anything to the officials which will bring peace. Nerves won't stand much more. And the housewives will go crazy soon. And fever will come from the docks. They have no gas, water, light or sewage at Bob's, in Bermondsey. And the people are cracking there.

*A few days later, on September 19, a woman who lived a short distance
southeast of Olivia, on Ladywell Road, took a walk in Lewisham with
her Mother and was shaken by the destruction she saw. She wrote in her
diary, "We went up the High Street shopping. There is not a shop that isn't
damaged. It is terrible, most of them uninhabitable and down to the ground.
It's heartbreaking to see. It looks as if a battle has been fought there. All
was done by two land mines dropped by parashoot."[10] These bombs had
been dropped around 11:30 pm on September 17. In contrast to individuals'
perceptions, the voice of the censored press was less alarmed (newspapers were
expected to help sustain morale, and not provide facts for the enemy). On
Tuesday, September 10, just after the massive bombing raids on London had
begun, the* Lewisham Borough News *presented a calmer report. "During
Sunday night's raid it appeared that very serious and widespread damage
in SE London must be inevitable. A tour of a large area yesterday morning
[September 9] revealed that the noise had no relation to the actual amount
of damage done. Some properties, mostly private dwellings, were damaged
and partially wrecked, but one remarkable factor is that the casualties are
light."*

*Some weeks later, probably just before October 9, Olivia responded to
M-O's September questionnaire, which had asked informants about their
experiences of the Blitz. She began by describing how her life had been
changed by the air raids.*

September, M-O September questionnaire

My lover is afraid. So I see him once a week instead of twice
a day. And I am so annoyed about that, that I am on the verge of
saying goodbye to him. He expects me not to mind, and to make
love physically with complete abandon after having only phone
calls to comfort me all the week. I wouldn't mind if he was away,
or kept from me by outside agencies. But it's just "carefulness" for
his own skin. After I ran around for ten days keeping ten minute
appointments with him at a risk I didn't give a second thought to, he
stopped even that, for his own convenience and caution. I knew he
was socially a conservative coward, but this new safety has "got my
goat" and I cannot disguise the fact from either of us.

In her private journal, which was not sent to Mass-Observation, Olivia said more about her strained romantic relations at this time. She was writing on October 6, 1940.

Monday, October 6

Arranged another week with Bill. Again it fell through, though this time [in contrast to May] he went and I didn't. Since he's been back (September 14) we've met about five times, the last time yesterday afternoon. He came home with me, and I didn't want to make love, and he went very hurt. Said he could sense my complete indifference to him. Perhaps he could. I have been once more de-illusioned about him, since he's chosen comfort and safety rather than being together for these last weeks—even being together for a few minutes in public places has gone since he was offered car-lift instead of bad railway service. <u>Of course</u>, he's sensible. But he can't expect me to go on being romantic for ever, when each time there's a choice he chooses "sensible."

And, there was, in all honesty, an incident with a young man on the train, since followed by a letter from him, which left me—wondering. He is six years younger than I am. Very brainy. Not ordinary. Not at all "fresh." But happening, it seems, to have read all the books and thought many of the thoughts which I have. And it's extraordinarily refreshing to be taken at one's mind value rather than one's body-sex value for a change.

She concluded these reflections of early October with the following musing.

My room is clean and warm and quiet. Outside there is pouring rain and howling gale in the blackness. No sirens yet. The door rattles, the draughts moan. I am content and contained, <u>in spite of</u> Bill and the war. I bow to Powys and he bows back. Aldous [Huxley] leers and whispers "New man?" and I put out my tongue and reply "So what?"

I'd still marry Bill tomorrow.

Her report to M-O from early October went on to describe other aspects of her daily life during the first month of the Blitz.

September, M-O September questionnaire continued

I have not slept in my own bed all night for over a month. At first it was the settee in the dining room, then a bed taken down there. For a week it was my sister-in-law's cellar on a camp bed, rushing round there as soon as I got home as she was afraid to be alone. [Olivia's brother, Freddie, his wife and their young son lived nearby. Because of his work in the Auxiliary Fire Service, Freddie was at home at this time only about one night in three.] Now she has people in upstairs and so for the last two nights I have slept in our own cellar, on a bunk Dad has put up, four feet up, with him and Mother on a spring mattress on the floor underneath. And four Wilmotts on mattresses and camp bed also in the cellar. So that my distaste for many people about me prevents me sleeping. I have slept in a room alone as long as I can remember, and the sound of others near puts me to much irritation. (Just imagine if the selfish little devil had to sleep in a public shelter!) At about 4 am, if I am sure Mother won't hear me, I slide out and go up to my room under the roof. I am aware of the idiocy of this but get so nervously chafed that I'd brave fire to be alone awhile.

The office goes down to the cellar at the sound of a whistle blown by a spotter on duty after the sirens. My life has changed by the constant running up and down. I'd much rather be allowed to decide for myself and stay put. We went below more than six times a day <u>every day</u> last week (sometimes without sirens), and so far not one pane of glass has been broken in our building, nor can any damage be seen for a quarter mile around. So you can guess how "careful" our spotters are, and how annoyed we all get.

Air raid damage mucked up my travelling arrangements—ten miles across South London night and morning—so that one day it took four hours to do an hour's journey. But this last week the trains are almost normal again—and everyone has had the travel problem. So I won't particularise.

The second question that M-O put to its observers in September was: "Has the intensified air war affected your general attitude at all? Do you

dream differently? Read more or less? Care more or less for the radio?"
Olivia's response was as follows.

Yes, it has. On the first night of the Blitz I put out an incendiary bomb, alone for some minutes, though help came after I had dealt with it. This incident has come back to my mind on unexpected occasions. I was being "put on" by my boss, and had resented it for some time. After the bomb, I stood up to him, thinking, "If a blasted incendiary didn't frighten me and I dealt with it, why should I be afraid of <u>him</u>?" This has resulted in a general boldness of thought and action, a kind of sparkle on my usual cheek, which I have been quite surprised (and pleased) about. I don't know whether it will last, but it has worked so far.

Also, I have been less careful of other people's feelings, John Blunting, where previously I might have agreed for politeness. And I am not so apprehensive about the air war as I was before it started, because, bad as it has been, it has not been as bad as my Spanish-War-begun imagination painted for me [she was thinking of the destruction of civilians in the Spanish Civil War in 1937–38]. I don't think I am mentally afraid at all now (except gas). My flesh still shrinks from the thought of pain, but not my <u>mind</u> shying away as it used (again, except gas).

"The Blitz on London has been on since late August," Olivia noted in *her private journal for October 6, "and we are all still alive—the 'all' I know,* *at any rate—though 10,000 Londoners are dead." Her direct experiences of* *falling bombs alerted the senses, and she spoke of "night after night of expect-* *ing another [bomb] through the thunder of guns. As well as many daylight* *raiders. Have seen literally hundreds of houses down, probably thousands* *uninhabitable. Feel sick, but not sick to death. It is not so terrible in the* *present, as it was in the future."*

Overcoming fear—or, perhaps more accurately, putting fear in perspective *or at least putting on a good face—was often remarked on. On September 18,* *Phyllis Warner, who experienced the bombing of London in Bloomsbury, a* *few miles west of where Olivia lived, wrote of how her feelings had changed* *over the previous ten days. "I'm glad to say that I'm not as frightened as I was. Last week I couldn't sleep at all, and found the greatest difficulty in getting through my day's work, but this week I feel much stronger. I think everybody is the same, it's just a case of getting over the first shock. During the first three days of intensive bombing, I heard quite a bit of 'stop the War' talk in buses and trains (all from women and all very bitter), but I haven't heard any for at least a week now."*[11] Women had various ways of defending themselves, psychologically, against the terrible events around them. Diana Brinton Lee, who was a volunteer driver in London in 1940, recalled sitting in a group of other women drivers in late September. *"We spoke of the Blitz in a casual, matter of fact way, as if it were the weather, till I longed to break down the reticence and decency of my companions, and ask them whether they were not as frightened as I was, and what they felt about death, whether they had ever thought about it before this happened, and if so, whether its actual imminence had changed their ideas. But I was not such a cad as to do anything of the kind, and we retained our English assumption that every-thing was all right."*[12]

Other women spoke of how their nerves became steadier and they learned to manage their fears. A twenty-eight-year-old woman, a mother of two chil-dren, who lived in Maida Vale, London W9, felt better about herself as a result of September's air raids. *"I feel much more certainty and self-confidence, and much less shyness and 'inferiority complex,' as a result of the discovery that I am not the coward I thought, and have more good in me in the way of 'taking it' cheerfully and uncomplainingly than I would have believed."* She also found more value to others in her own existence. *"I have a greatly increased feeling of personal responsibility all round—as head of the house, as a mother, as a citizen, and simply as an individual human being."* She was discovering within herself a *"comparative fearlessness (touch wood)."* (DR no. 2500, September 1940.) The novelist Rose Macaulay (aged fifty-nine), noticed changes in her own feelings during the Blitz. *"I am getting a burying-phobia,"* she reported on September 23, *"result of having seen so many houses and blocks of flats reduced to piles of ruins from which people can't be extracted in time to live, and feel I would rather sleep in the street, but know I mustn't do this."* Three days later, on September 26, she was feel-ing less anxious: *"as to burial phobia, I don't think I shall have it under the stairs; in fact, it is already wearing off, and may have been a passing disease, induced by seeing too many ruins.*"[13]

Olivia spoke of some of the other changes she had experienced during the early weeks of the Blitz.

I'm not sure about the dream point. [The question in September was:"Do you dream differently?"] As you may remember from my record I was a regular and interested dreamer, but now I hardly ever remember dreams, if I have them. And I sleep so very lightly since the above incendiary (which would have done a lot of damage if I hadn't happened to have heard it) that perhaps I don't get to my dream level.

Reading is about the same again now, after not reading at all for a couple of weeks. That was a big change, because I read a book a day on the average. Care very much less for the radio, since it drivels so; not much good music either. And I have let Mother and Dad have my super-set downstairs as theirs went wrong and it didn't seem worth mending during all this destruction. So that I have to listen to the Forces [radio service, which offered mainly light entertainment] for their sakes, if I listen at all, as they don't like talks or plays or classical music.

This month's questionnaire also asked respondents to describe the "alterations you have made in the disposition of your household furniture, in your eating times, sleeping times, working times" and what if anything had been "done in the way of making your shelter comfortable, your basement safe, etc. What differences have you made in the times you amuse yourself, see friends, etc?"

Rolled up the rugs upstairs. Have a good midday meal instead of having main meal in the evening, since my homecoming time is so uncertain. Sleep—well, that gets in when it can, still between 11 and 6. Working times not changed, except when I get in late. No official change. Cellar has been strengthened with 4 x 4 balks. Fresh whitewash, then paper tacked over it where we touch. Mattressed bunks for three, floor mattresses for four, after a month of chairs and cushions.

Have had no amusements beyond the Blitz since it started, apart from playing with baby nephew (2½) because he won't go to sleep. Have only twice in a month seen friends, where normally I should have exchanged about 15 visits. And that twice was a flying visit at a railway station in early evening, and the other, all night sleeping visit from friend with hole in the roof.

Other readjustments. Done very little cleaning and polishing. Wear very old coat and no hat. Keep a rucksack in the dining room with change of clothes in. Leave my windows open all day while I'm away, whatever the weather, for blast help.

On November 8, 1940, before answering a M-O question on how she "felt" about such matters as the Vichy Government and the Free French Forces, and such peoples as the Jews and the Americans, Olivia remarked on the difficulty in talking about "feelings" during the Blitz. "I am writing at the moment in the cellar. Last night two houses in sight of mine were blown down. Already more than a dozen bombs have come within ducking distance tonight. One's 'feelings' are apt to become numbed, I find." She also offered a brief update on her current circumstances and failure to keep a diary.

Friday, November 8

Sorry I've done no diary lately. Have begun a new job in the office which takes all my mental energy. [She was no longer working in Putney but rather in central London.] So that cellar-bomb nights don't conduce to diary.

Next week I begin a six day shift—3½ days and nights at Whitehall, 2½ days at home. Will try to record a few impressions. Have been travelling by official tender this past month—thank God—the public travel appears to have been rotten, from the crowds seen along the road. Am not sorry to be missing it by staying at the office.

So far, none of my friends or relations have been killed, though several homes damaged and two destroyed.

Others experienced personal loss more acutely. Phyllis Warner's diary for Monday, September 30, 1940, reported that "A letter waiting for me here," after a weekend in the country, "told me that G_____ was killed by a bomb in a London hostel last Tuesday. She was a pretty laughing vital girl of twenty, and her parents, thoroughly decent good-hearted people, were wrapped up in her. Owing to difficulties of identification they didn't even know till Saturday. It seems impossible to believe that one's friends can just be written off like that, especially so innocent and lovely a victim—this brings war home as never before."[14] *Whether one lived (as most did) or died (some 60,000 civilians in Britain were killed during the war) was mainly a matter of luck. Feelings of fatalism were, understandably, commonplace.*

Olivia never again found the time or the energy to keep a sustained, detailed diary of the kind she had produced in the summer of 1940. In part she was distracted by work. She had been given enlarged responsibilities and had less time on her hands to write about either her introspections or the events in her life. Her intensity was no longer channelled so single-mindedly into a daily journal. Henceforth she reported only on the occasional day, or a few consecutive days, in comprehensive detail. More commonly she reviewed the character of her previous three to four weeks, in a summary form. A sense of regularity and routine came to loom more prominently, and this, for her, was not the right impetus for dedicated diary-keeping. However, she continued to be candid in her self-revelations, and her private life was a mixed story of pleasure and pain, of various upheavals, and of a seeking for a secure personal identity. As for the war, she almost came to take it for granted; and in the rest of her intermittent writing for Mass-Observation she turned her attention mainly to private matters and to her struggle for a future that would give her the fulfillment she craved.

On November 12, 1940, Olivia resumed her "Diary (of a sort)," as she titled it. She was writing from the office at 7:45 that evening.

Tuesday, November 12

Promised I would try to describe the office sleeping-in system. We come in on Day 1, at 10, work till 6. Sleep in shelter, after hot supper at 1s 3d. Work Day 2, 8 am to 6 pm. Sleep. Day 3, 8 am to 6 pm. Sleep. Day 4, work till 4 pm—home. Days 5 and 6 off and sleep at home. Day 7 = Day 1.

Am now on the second floor in Rest Room—blessedly alone because there is a lot of noise, guns and planes and bombs, and the others prefer to be below ground. Last night I went to bed at 9, read till 11. Slept between 5 and 5:20. Up at 6. Very stuffy and a narrow uncomfortable bed. Grumbled a lot at having 19 in same room. Have had a smaller room provided tonight for the five in our Branch. Should be much better. The women who had been sleeping in before we began did not welcome us. Were quite unpleasantly rude and surly. Another reason we are glad to be moved. Expected to be cold—brought hot water bottle and borrowed Dad's thick pyjamas. Was much too hot, so bought some silk pyjamas at lunchtime!

This is a bad account—I can hear bombs whistling and exploding close and a plane coming ever closer. Am not afraid, only can't concentrate.

My biggest "nuisance" is unsociability. I <u>must</u> be alone sometimes. And the others in my gang (I'm senior but not oldest) are of herd-tendencies. I prefer washing alone—and reading and writing and sleeping. Can't have the last, though I've begged to sleep upstairs. Can be here alone now, as the others are afraid. The men (about 500 to 20 women) are cheery to us. Any among them who feel as I do must have a thin time, as their shelter dormitory is full and crowded.

Am beginning to worry about people at home. They are sure to [worry] about me. What an extraordinary <u>waste</u> worry is! Yet I suppose it eggs us on to take survival precautions. Shall take a "composure tablet" as given by doctor and smoke a fag and look at a mag and then go for wash and bed.

Friday, November 15

8:25 pm. At home again after the first sleeping shift at the office. Looking back on it, it was the stuffiness, lack of baths, and lack of privacy, and the (for me) continual effort at sociableness, which were most nuisance. I don't look forward to several months of it but I'm not so upset that I'll refuse.

When I got home last night I found more refugees! So I left my bed in the cellar for them and slept under the roof again—first time since Blitz. Only woke four times all night! And it was quite a noisy one I'm told. Heard several bits of shrapnel hit the tiles, and my window is broken, but it was good to have 3 feet 6 inches to kick in instead of 20 inches of bunk.

Sunday, December 1

At the office again—on night shift. 9 pm. Have just been out with one of the men and had two half-pints of beer. Am feeling unwontedly cheerful in consequence. Have walked up Whitehall and down again, in the pitch blackout, feeling rather a devil and listening to his account of his wife's nerves. Stood on Westminster Bridge for a few minutes and giggled away his vague advances, thinking sententious thoughts about Thames being the same in spite of war, except for the strands of coloured lights of peace/business/war advertisements. Wandered back into the lonely dugout bedroom, determined to make an effort to be nice to the horrible B's. But they weren't there, so I played myself a game of shuv 'apenny (board donated by male staff) and am now scribbling in the typists' room.

Have been reading M-O's book <u>War Begins at Home</u>.[15] Found myself longing to read the documentation of the Blitz and blamed myself for not doing <u>my</u> share lately. Have answered each directive—briefly—but not kept up my diary or dreams. Had girl friend visiting me last week—found she <u>also</u> had had plane and bomb dreams on Night 58 as her first dreams of the Blitz. [The Blitz in London lasted for 57 consecutive nights in September–November. German bombing then became intermittent, though sometimes intense, up to May 1941.] Suppose that's psychology—dream danger on the first clear night. Should like to hear more versions.

Was shopping in Rye Lane, Peckham last Friday at noon when two bombs fell, no warning on. Heard the scream coming and ran. Man shouted "Lie down!!" I thought "Not in my new coat." Ran into C & A's glass arcade, realised the glass, laughed at two or three others who'd run there, ran out again. Bomb appeared to have dropped 150 yards away down a side turning. Walked on down the Lane feeling sorry for the people who were still looking for official shelters—after the danger. Then the warning came on. Much chatter at the bus stop—mostly aggrieved that bombs could fall before the warning. Two women began a discussion on Christmas. One was the "Well we must look on the bright side" type. The other said "What the hell's the good of getting ready for Christmas when all your family is split up—I shan't bother." I had my arms full of Christmas shopping, after deciding not to do any, and began to wonder what is the good of it. I've taken money out of Post Office for presents, mostly useful ones, but I suppose it's not the Government's idea of good citizenness. Expect to be working over Christmas. Am really giving presents because I don't want to be thought mean. [The next sentence is unintelligible because the bottom of the page is torn.]

Shall now read <u>Ulysses</u> in bed, after a wash, I think, and giggle until I sleep. Have done a lot of work today and feel tired.

Wednesday, December 4

At home again in bed. Have just spent two hours on December Directive. Interrupted by much noise outside. Got a special edition for SE London tonight it seems. Have heard more than 20 bombs for certain.

My two leave days have been pleasant—this shift system is helpful for shopping. After only Saturday afternoons for years, a Wednesday morning is like heaven in the shops.

Yesterday did housework till 4, then sewing till 7; then bed and slept till 10:30. Then read and wrote letters till 1 and slept till 7. Today, sewing and shopping till 1:30, lunch, and afternoon visiting bereaved cousin at Chislehurst. Walked among silver birches and joyed at mosses and brown bracken. Home to tea at 6. Chatted till 7. Then bed and Blitz and M-O till past 9. Now shall read. Good luck, M-O, hope you're having as little trouble as I am. Oh—Happy New Year.

In her responses to M-O's December Directive, mentioned above, Olivia reflected on her feelings about the coming year as war unfolded over her head.

December, M-O December Directive

How do I feel about 1941? I stopped typing for two minutes to listen to an extra noisy enemy plane. It dropped a bomb which puffed my curtains in and made the house shiver (I am in bed under the roof) and now the guns are galoomphing at its back. There are craters at the bottom of my garden, and a small unexploded bomb. Four windows are broken. Can see the ruins of 18 houses within five minutes walk. Have two lots of friends staying with us whose homes have been wrecked.

About 1941, I feel that I shall be damned glad if I'm lucky enough to see it at all—and that I'd rather like to see it. Still kid myself that I prefer quality to quantity. And that the quality will depend more on how I take it than on what is dished out. That's how I feel, cheerful at rock bottom. But I THINK differently, think we'll be hungrier (haven't been hungry yet), think many of our young men will die abroad. Have a cousin in the Navy, another in Ireland, a friend in the HAA [Anti-Aircraft], two more in the RAF. Think it unlikely they'll all be alive next Christmas. THINK this war is bloody silly. FEEL we must down Hitler etc. (Another bomb puffs the curtains—bad night tonight it seems.) THINK I ought to go down to the cellar. FEEL I am warm and happy in bed. But I don't see enough sense in long-term policies or prospects to make it worth while giving up the certain present warmth for the uncertain chills of uncertain safety.

Gift plans [for Christmas] go ahead as usual, on cheap and useful lines. Mother deals with food; she says it's to be economical. But as Dad and Son and I are all nearly certain to be at work on Christmas day, we are not planning anything of a celebration. Shall try to visit the London bits of the family in the next two weeks, not having seen any of them since the Blitz began, and take them small gifts. Expect to spend £4 on presents. Slippers, tobacco, diaries, blouse, hankies, hold-alls, books, calendars.

She also responded to the question "What do you consider the main thing which leads you to form your opinion on current events at present?"

My political and philosophical and anthropological reading in the past. Also M-O bulletins. My scrappy knowledge (not opinion) of current events comes from BBC news, and Ministry of Information, as does yours. The small specialised secret knowledge I get officially confirms my previous "left" opinions.

The final question in December, "What are the main things which determine your day to day feelings?" was to be answered on a separate form, to which Olivia joked:

God knows what the Government will do if everyone says "Love Life 100%"!

It is clear from her diary that Olivia had little use for deference. She spoke some months later of her "Deep rooted suspicion of leadership, on the lines of 'power corrupts'" (DR, September 1942). She found power distasteful, and concentrated on seeking strength within herself.

Olivia's diary began again after a gap of almost two months, though now in a different form. Mainly she summarized her activities of the previous month and highlighted, with some intensity, her current frustrations and unhappiness.

February 2, 1941

Can't remember last entries. Will review January as it looks now.

Began with a slightly intoxicated party at the office for New Year, as I was on sleeping shift that night. Two bottles of port, one of gin and vermouth, three dozen beers, between nine men and six women. Four girls provided sandwiches etc. One backed out and one had to pay her share. Came to 7s 6d. But I still think the evening was worth it. Cheerful foolish party games in a dingy office setting, camouflaged with paper chain. A little dancing and flirting to the BBC's miserable programme.

Became friendly with a man that night, middle-aged and married, who has been nice to me since, and cheered up the dull shift evenings with a mild flirtation, my first for ages. Have let him kiss me but didn't enjoy it much so shall not repeat. Anyway, I've had enough heartaches from married men! THE man was much shocked by the little I told him about CB, so have told him no more. But as HE has been my heartache for ten years, I am amused.

The desire for children has been growing in urgency in me for the last few years, until now it is an angry longing I cannot evade. Have told Man—who cannot oblige but adores me etc.—that I feel so strongly about it that I can no longer consider myself bound to wait for the mythical happy future we have so long looked to. The above-mentioned flirtation was the last little push in this direction. Have no person in view, and feel rather foolish and helpless, after reaching and announcing this great Moment. Resent the advantages any man in a similar position would undoubtedly have over this female. If M-O has aspirations toward match-making, now's its chance!

Mentioned this terrifying ache for children to my VAD friend. She wrote back: "I quite understand the frustration you write about—maternity—and should think there's a general human reason for it these days, apart from your personal reasons. You differ in being conscious of it, from some other women I know, here and elsewhere. What can I say, except that the war will be over some day, and in that possibly saner, and certainly more tranquil future, perhaps you will realise yourself." Personally I have little time to spare—first, babes at over thirty are not so attractive as in the twenties. But her words made me wonder if M-O could ask some questions about this. It may be a common problem. The birth rate figures wouldn't show at all the same proportions as the number of women who wanted babies in wartime, however impractical that wish might be.

This very day, the Man and I went walking in Kent, and discussed the birth rate. He has a Victorian attitude to sex, in word but not in deed, and spoke furiously about the modern vice aspect. Not worth quoting remarks in detail, as they are so exactly like The Times letters on the subject, conventional Major (Retd.) variety. I replied that what annoyed me most was the pity of it; that the more intelligent folk—just intelligent enough to contraceive efficiently anyway—didn't seem to realise that they were helping wipe out intelligence, and leave this astonishing adventure of life to the morons. But I sense a growing awareness of this point among professional people I know. Fifteen years ago they were boasting of no family. Now they are "afraid" they can only "afford" one child. I want three at least, four if possible on the income. If anything in life is worth while, poetry, music, food, sunshine, then Life is worth transmitting. And if you've ever felt that the human mind and spirit is creating some new value, some aspiring soul, then you MUST see that the raw material arrives, and consciously and willingly too. All this may be only a rationalisation of my own Mother-urge, but it is rapidly becoming the most acute problem in my mind, invasion included!

Went down to Petworth [Sussex] to see evacuated nephew and sister-in-law (the other Cockett, she wrote about your mix-up) and had twenty-four pleasant hours. Stirred up all my above longings of course. Was surprised couldn't get <u>any</u> sweets in Guildford when changing buses, and only allowed two ounces in village store, from a newly arrived jar. Appreciated quiet green fields as rarely before. Loathed striped uniforms and army motors all over the place and wicked boy scouts at play. Of course not so wicked as the UNSCRU-PULOUS Germans but damned silly all the same.

Have been to <u>no</u> public entertainment the whole month. Three meals at Strand Corner House, too dear for me really, but was momentarily desperate about canteen grub. Dirty, badly cooked, ill-chosen meals for four days on end can irritate one far more than rationing. Food is wasted daily, hourly, in our Government canteens, quite stupidly.

Had a tremendous shopping bout, in the Sales. Two dress-lengths, two undie lengths, two pairs of shoes (no, three), one pair of silver sandals in case I get asked to a Victory Ball! A blouse, a woolly coat, a tailored costume being made. Total, under £10. So that I shall probably spend no more on clothes for at least six months. And the things I've bought have been good of their kind, leaving a "wise" feeling.

Have spent just under £1 on other people and charity in the same period. Horrified shades of St. Francis! And 8s 6d on books. But good value again, ten Penguins, and Pelicans, T.S. Eliot's <u>East Coker</u>, [J.B.] Priestley's <u>Rain on Godshill</u>.

Have spent a day walking in Kent. Have had friends to stay home twice. Have spent one evening playing solo; lost one shilling. Have made a frock and jacket. Have done a lot of mending for self and brother. Have spent about twelve hours on housework. And about the same writing letters. Have worked hard, but not very conscientiously, at the office. Let some stuff go through which could have been rechecked and old papers found perhaps, but felt the new cases had better have new attention instead of old precedent, so didn't bother. Civil Service sin.

Have had no quarrels with anyone. A marked cool silence with two girls on the shift, but as it would only be replaced by false geniality I didn't bother to "check" that either. Don't like 'em. Six love makings with Man, only one complete for me. Twenty-four lunch hours, with him, walking and talking rather sadly and worriedly. Drank beer on six days, twice a whole pint!

Had seven incendiary bombs on house and garden (second lot). Small damage. Dug an anti-aircraft shell out of top lawn (or rather the bomb removers did) as tall as the kitchen table, as big across as a dinner plate, and over twelve feet down. Ruined the tennis lawn. But we never had a net. Helped clear up at midnight the wet mess resulting in our office from three fire bombs on the roof above. Jabbed hole in the ceiling for the streams of unnecessary water the amateur firemen drowned them in. Watched the anti-aircraft pompon on top of Admiralty Arch firing at enemies in my lunch time! Mug. More than a hundred other mugs did the same. And fire bombs were dropping at the time, by the Temple in the Strand, though we didn't know it as we stood in Trafalgar Square. Have learnt to play the mouth organ. Simple tunes only.

Don't look forward to this Spring Offensive much. Still fear gas intensely. But feel I have had a good month in January. Much better than might have been expected, so don't upset myself about February. East Coker made me feel genuinely philosophic for a while. And the feeling is renewable. Have prayed no prayers, except to Trees and Sun. Have felt amused at all this eager Wish Upon A Star singing, and gone on reading [Sir James Frazer's] Golden Bough. Have begun to grow my hair. To make me look more motherly? Or is that the wrong bait?

February 28

Another skeleton instalment. The sleeping rota at the office finished halfway through the month, to my relief. The evening boredom had got me into mischief, and I was emotionally humiliated in getting out of it. So upset in fact that I tried to wangle a few days sick leave, but was shamed into going back as my opposite number really went sick. Had a couple of teeth seen to, and a few sleeping tablets from my Doc, and gritted my teeth and forgot my cheap emotions.

The war? Growing conviction that the boring part is over, that the coming action will be conclusive, and probably victorious, as the spirit of our people is so completely undaunted. The resentment piling up against Germany in the occupied territories must be worrying the lads. And the Balkan moves are out of the Plan, which will worry Hitler. [The Germans were expanding their presence in the Balkans in preparation for their planned spring invasion of the Soviet Union. In February, Britain was searching for ways to bolster the pro-British government of Greece.]

Food—better now I'm at home. Enjoy it more as I know it's clean, which it was not at the office. Still losing weight, but only five pounds this month. Travelling—much better than last autumn, improving daily as the light grows. Clothes—have made a frock and petticoat; with stuff bought in January. Amusements—one news film, half a dozen detective stories, BBC. Have put radio beside my bed again, and go to bed about 9 and listen to late programmes. Friends—had two girls here to sleep, two nights. Peg another. Spent one night at Peg's, one at Joan's. Chatty evenings, no sheltering, no notice taken of warnings or guns! Camberwell and Barking.

Went walking with Man three times, north Kent. First time just happy. Next discussing parting. Third, on St. Valentine's Day (!), intended to be our last together. Said sad goodbyes, after eleven years of hoping things would come out all right. After four days he told me on the phone that he had been so miserable he had at last persuaded his wife to consider divorce seriously. So now we meet again at lunch time for conferences on ways and means. But we are both in the same

Civil Service office, have sent a test note on official reaction, as nothing will be possible if he gets the sack. Have had no reply yet.

Have begun feeling interested in the garden. Bought some seeds. Stirred the earth a bit. Planned places. Still too wet to do much. Went down to Petworth to see Michael for his birthday. Adored him for two hours, playing with his new toys. Was glad to hear from Bebe [her sister-in-law] that M-O had sent her a book token—it has pleased her tremendously. Felt sorry my February Bulletin and Directive came so late—wrong address, but have explained that on Directive reply. [The M-O Directive Replies for 1941 have not survived.] Still reading Frazer's <u>Golden Bough</u> and being comforted thereby. Obviously, human beings have come a long way, so can hope to go a lot farther yet. Prayers? To the west wind, to one or two sunsets, one or two blue skies, to children.

March 25 [approximately]

Have been to no public entertainments, no churches, no pubs even, since last diary. Have read three detective stories, two long "interior" novels (Myers), two books of modern poetry (MacNeice, Sassoon), and more of <u>Golden Bough</u>. Listened to some music, Haydn, Bach, Mozart. Half-listened to a lot of news and nonsense. No plays, no talks. Done no creative sewing, just a bit of necessary mending. Bought a cotton dress length, 4s 6d; six linen tea towels, 18 shillings.

Had Joan and Nancy to stay two weekends. Nancy stayed on for ten days, as she was ill, and Mother looked after her. Nuisance, but we made the best of it. Don't like her much. Went to Peg's for one night. Had supper together at 8 in the canteen. Walked out into the light of the full moon. Were so thrilled with its beauty we walked to Brixton, through gunfire and all, admiring the effects of shadow and light and liking the empty quiet of the streets. As Peg said, the war and the guns did seem trivial, essentially frivolous, against that solemn splendour. Played her recorder and sang old songs till late; then cocoa and biscuits (treat) and bed in a room with the ceiling down. Talked philosophy till sleep overtook us.

Sex? Divorce is the topic of the moment. Will she, won't she, the angle on the topic; money the balance on which we swing. She insists on half his wages <u>and pension</u> (!) and he wonders, can we manage children on the rest? Still waiting for the office reply as to either or both of us getting the sack. Had two afternoons of pleasant passion, one or two thrilling moments at work, at risk. Coffee and cigarettes and civilised talk each lunch hour. Evening walks across St. James's Park, wishing it was the real country, but appreciating it all the same. Swapping library books and opinions and waiting.

War? Two shoals of fire bombs last Wednesday and three high explosives near, within 50 yards, one 50 feet. Both cars (working ones!) buried, feared wrecked, but later salvaged. A DA [delayed-action explosive] through the railway bridge went off the next evening at 8, with a terrific bang. Got eight windows mended the next Saturday, but the roof has some holes in still. At 11 the backs of two houses across the road down, beds hanging over the edge, but no one hurt. Not so lucky half a mile away. Block of flats hit several times. Seventy dead out, still digging. Comment useless.[16] When the BOMB CENSOR (so he said) called later here for particulars, he told us that over seventy high explosives, two land mines, and countless incendiaries fell on Deptford ground that night. Dad's lorry was driven into a crater, and he fell into it at 4 in the morning. Found it was full of water under the lorry. Quite cheerful after he'd sworn for a few minutes.

It was a horrible night really, yet no one was anything like as frightened as last September. We walked in and out the house the whole time, laughing and joking and sweating and swearing. Calling out to neighbours and policemen and wardens, excited but completely unafraid. Ducking when whistles bombs heralded, saying "That's gone over—that's gone off." Cursing the explosive fire bombs, cursing the light they made, cursing the people who didn't get them out by the time ours were out. Losing count of how many we'd dealt with. Glad it wasn't a wet night. Making cups of tea and cocoa. Deciding to sleep a bit—not to—waking up on the dining room floor in Dad's big driving coat. Stumbling up to the top floor to bed, finding the windows gone again. Very tired next day at office, and huge amounts of work to do. Called at brother's Fire Station on the way. Thank God he was all right, but dog tired and filthy dirty. Home that night to no gas or water. And then told would have to leave, regarding DA. I hung around and luckily it went off before bed time. Made a lot more mess though.

Have had trouble with acne on my skin. Since Christmas it has got worse and hurts. So I took advice and went to hospital for treatment. All the usual silly waste of time at every stage. Eventually saw the doctor, after three hours. But the results are very cheering. Have had only six treatments so far, in a fortnight. GLB and Tungsten local, and all the pain has gone and most of the scars. Glad of HSF too, saved a lot of fees.

Am worried that Michael has measles. Hope Bebe looks after him properly. She talks well and writes good letters, but she's damn careless about cleanliness and impatient of Mick's babyness. As she is pregnant again she'll probably get all wrapped up and withdraw and neglect poor Mick. Gosh I do miss that infant! Waves of hot and cold go over me when I think—suppose he died. And then I want my own children with such a longing that I can't sit here typing any longer.

Olivia's reports now ceased entirely for three months. Not until June 21 did she write again to Mass-Observation, and then with news of great personal importance.

June 21

Sketchy I'm afraid. Been living too much to spare time to write about it. Believe the last instalment covered April [in fact, the last one was in late March].

Most important points: mid-May, the Man left home and came to live a few doors away from us. Consequently spends every evening with me, which we have waited twelve years for with longing, and now like even more than we expected to. Spent the second week in June walking round Gloucestershire hills together, in the seventh heaven of delight all the time, in spite of food and lodging and weather difficulties. The divorce has been discussed with lawyer, but seems very unlikely. I am to get a transfer from this Department to another, to avoid possible scandal.

We have been twice to a film, choosing a "comic" each time. Not at all restrained in our laughter. Once to theatre, <u>No Time for Comedy</u> [by Samuel N. Behrman]. Not very good. No concerts, except on the air, but a great deal of piano playing and singing. I am being taught to play—just my favourite Bach prelude. Refuse to learn by scales or "easy bits." Just want to play that for my own ear, so shall learn it.

Have attended the Registry wedding of a mutual friend. Drank too much sherry and got heat rash.

Have made love much too often but with beatitude.

Family affairs have changed but little. Blitzless nights have provided much needed extra sleep. Mother, Dad and I share two nights a week fire-watching. Son [i.e., her brother Freddie] still comes home to us every sixth night from AFS, spending the between time (three day shift) with wife and child in Sussex, facilitated by £6 home-produced motorbyke and sidecar.

The homeless WINTER family has left us, taking over our Essex bungalow for the summer months. Makes the house seem bigger.

The office has been bombed, causing much extra work, as a million index cards disappeared. But no vital damage really. No personal injury.

Relations with office colleagues very cordial, perhaps because I'm so much happier, having Man to care for. Do his mending and ironing and feed him sometimes.

Gardening takes up a lot of our time. Have planted two dozen tomatoes, four rows each of beet, carrot, spinach, parsnips. Sixty bean plants up. Twenty marrows. Several dozen lettuces. Two rows radishes, American cross. Brussels, water cabbages, raspberries, blackberries. Not bad for London [a very large back garden was attached to 33 Breakspears]. Oh, and five laying hens, with one broody for a dozen chicks, all healthy. Spent three hours last night watering and hoeing.

This last fortnight has been the happiest and healthiest of my whole life. And I look good, too. Perm has settled down and skin is clear and lovely, but freckled. Ration slimness suits me too.

So—or but?—damn the war.

Clearly, Olivia's zeal for dedicated diary-keeping was diminishing. It would not have been easy to sustain the sort of energy and commitment that had characterized her daily writing in the previous summer. Perhaps the new routines of her life were unconducive to the kind of relentless self-exploration that had fuelled so much of her earlier writing. By the summer of 1941 these new routines included much more time spent in the company of Bill Hole, who continued to live in a boarding house not far from Olivia's home. He, as she often testified, made her happy. His presence also probably diminished her desire, or her need, or her opportunities to devote herself so resolutely to the rigours of keeping up a personal diary. She resumed her contact with Mass-Observation in late July, at which time she provided a brief summary of her recent and current activities and offered more information on her altered personal circumstances.

July

WORK. A month in my new Department. [Olivia had transferred to the recently-established Ministry of Works, where she worked for the Chief Licensing Officer of Civil Building. Bill Hole continued to work for the Metropolitan Police.] Feel quite at home. Am working harder, but quite cheerfully.

HOME. Mother has been away this last fortnight on holiday, so I have been busy doing laundry on Sundays, cleaning, cooking; and on top of more travelling to new job, am feeling rather fagged. Have catered for brother and Man for a good many meals, very difficult on just my rations. But lettuces and eggs from the gardens have helped out. Have done a lot of work in the garden too, and kept the chickens cleaned and fed. Mending, but no making this month.

FRIENDS. Have had letter and one Sunday visit from Joan, from Gay; two letters, two evening and night visits from Peg, who is "moving" as well as Gay. General restlessness among my friends, makes my new position of having the Man here all the time seem extra solid.

He is healthier and I think happier but hates being broke—he didn't remember income tax when he fixed her [his wife's] allowance.

We have been too busy in house and garden—also playing piano (I've learnt the <u>Prelude</u> at last)—to do much lovemaking; and are occasionally a little surprised and regretful that we seem to have "settled down" to our bodies at last, after twelve years of being electrically excited by them.

BOOKS. Three novels, still <u>Study of History</u> [by Arnold Toynbee], now Vol. IV; De la Mare's <u>Behold the Dreamer</u> anthology; Clare Leighton's <u>Sometime Never</u>. Nothing like so much reading as usual—in fact probably less than any other month in my adult life—due to garden and Man.

No "entertainment" apart from BBC two evenings, and Eric's gramophone one evening, and some piano every day. Went to Thesiger's exhibition of pictures in Bond Street [Ernest Thesiger, 1879–1961, was a painter in oil and watercolour]—good to see line and colour, though sad to see the bombed church subjects.

WAR. Very little in my mind. Deliberate concentration produces vague haze of "better than this time last year—only a couple of years to go now." Still fear gas, hope winter doesn't bring more blitz.

The character of the war for Londoners had altered dramatically. Germany was now deeply absorbed on the Eastern Front—the part of the world where Hitler planned to make his most visible mark on world history. The ferocious Nazi assault on the Soviet Union meant relief for England, in more ways than one. Bombing largely ceased, and the skies over England were free of enemy planes. A new sort of normality came to supplant the peculiar normality that had come to be known as the Blitz. On July 6, 1941, Phyllis Warner remarked in her diary that "There has been nothing to write in this diary for a couple of weeks because life has been so blissfully uneventful and almost pre-war. We've had the lovely feeling of being able to sit back in the knowledge that there will be no heavy raids for a bit. Of course, I'm terribly sorry for the Russian people, but after all we've 'taken,' it wouldn't be human nature not to rejoice in this respite. Then the sun shone consistently, and what an effect sunshine has on morale—I'm sure that their morale must be super in California." A couple of weeks later, on July 24, the new exuberance of the English was actually making her a little concerned. "People are awfully cheerful, almost complacent, now that Russia has put up five weeks of ferocious resistance, raids here have been almost non-existent, the RAF have been battering Germany, and we are being constantly told that American aid is tipping the scale. I do think that we slip into a false sense of security too quickly. A few weeks ago there seemed to be every expectation of Russia being crushed, and an invasion here in September. Now we're all more certain every day that it is the German H.Q. which is in a jam."[17] She and many others felt that London and other British cities were probably off the hook—at least for a while.

In mid-August Olivia Cockett sent in another monthly digest, which conveyed a marked sense of the post-Blitz mood of serene normality.

August

AMUSEMENTS. Home made only, and BBC. Piano, singing, almost every evening.

FRIENDS. See the Man every day and all every evening and weekend. Have been served with divorce notice. Arranged to meet solicitor's clerk at the flat of Peg, who lives near his office, to keep expenses down. Was not so unpleasant a ten minutes as we had feared. Have seen notice in local paper of Charles Madge's divorce [he was one of the founders of M-O]. Felt a fellow feeling wondrous kind, and envied him, being through with it. Stayed the night at Peg's, and committed the offence for which we are indicted, very happily. The next evening we spent with Mr and Mrs C, pleasant friends who are newly married after Mr C's divorce was obtained. Our only two "outings."

Had Peg to visit us, twice. Chatted and gardened and sang. Joan came for a Sunday; we all ate a lot—no meat, but lots of vegetables from the garden. Laughed a lot, about wartime difficulties—rations and clothes and travel.

READING. Still <u>Study of History</u>, Toynbee; and De la Mare, <u>Behold the Sleeper</u>. Half a dozen detective stories. One H.E. Bates novel. Sacheverell Sitwell's <u>Sacred and Profane Love</u>. Llewellyn

Powys, <u>Bakers Dozen</u>. Freya Stark's latest travel book.

FAMILY. No change. Health and spirits all good. Father had his 50th Birthday—took Mother to Town to see blitz for a birthday treat!

CLOTHES. Made a housecoat for the winter evenings—to save office clothes. Curtain material, no coupons, £1 2s. Bought TWO HATS!!! A velour for winter, 5s 11d, and a summer straw for 1s 6d! Couldn't resist such bargains.

GARDEN. Eating lots of beans and marrows, carrots, beetroot, spinach. No tomatoes ripe yet. Praying for sunshine.

WORK. No remarks. All normal. Not very busy.

WAR. Fear gas and winter but generally forget it.

The people of London and other bombed cities had largely adjusted to being in a state of pressing war. Their mood altered as they learned to face what they had previously thought impossible to endure. Phyllis Warner had already detected this changing state of mind a fortnight after the start of the London Blitz. On September 22, 1940, she wrote in her diary, "Finding we can take it is a great relief to most of us. I think that each one of us was secretly afraid that he wouldn't be able to, that he would rush shrieking to shelter, that his nerve would give, that he would in some way collapse, so that this has been a pleasant surprise. I make no excuse for writing so much about this side of our experience, for the situation is so full of horror in this continent of lunatics that only in the contemplation of what men can endure and can rise to is there any consolation."[18] Another woman, also in her early thirties, who lived in Birmingham, made a similar point the following summer. Writing on July 20, 1941, she reported that "Almost all my friends agree that the war, even after the bad winter we had, has not upset and really disturbed their lives half as much as they expected when it was only a dreadful possibility. We really can take it, and the best thing is so many good things remain untouched and untouchable—unless one is killed of course, but the relative smallness of that risk, spread out over the years and months one manages to remain alive, makes it seem entirely unimportant" (M-O Diarist no 5307). Women had learned to live with risk, to manage and get by, and thus felt confident that they could confront new dangers without falling apart. While the prospect of sudden death was always there, as a backdrop for daily life, war took on a business-as-usual quality.

For the six weeks from late August, Olivia discovered renewed energy for diary-keeping and she provided a fairly detailed account of her feelings and activities.

End of August. Went to see <u>Target for Tonight</u> [about a bombing raid on Germany]. Had not wanted to, but Man was keen, so went—first pictures for some weeks. Was interested and not too much moved. Had expected to hate the violence, but found it was skillfully overlaid by the "human interest" of the crews, as <u>has</u> to happen to keep us sane. Laughed at <u>[The] Devil and Miss Jones</u> on with it, and came out at 8:40 into moonlight and cool peace. Dislike the tiring stuffy noise of cinemas.

Spent pleasant weekends in the garden. Killed a lot of slugs and snails and ants, squeamish about it, but thorough. Finished knitting pullover for Man's birthday. Also bought him Rolls Razor, borrowing £2 from office petty cash over a weekend, as the shop wouldn't accept either order or deposit.

The landlady at his boarding house made a birthday party for him. We celebrated at lunch time with a large sherry each at a pub in Oxford Street. Were invited for two more sherries at 5:30 by friends. Got home with ten minutes to spare to change for the "party." Used 20 minutes and then had 40 minutes waiting for the gang, doing a X-word and playing with the Rolls Razor.

Descended to find the dining room transmogrified into a buffet. Jellies and trifles and sausages and waffles and cakes and cake—most in wartime and unexpected abundance. Tea to drink. Hovered for 90 minutes pecking at slippery sweet foods, face aching with grateful smiles. Had collected about twenty people, mostly strangers to me, for the "party." Proceeded to drawing room. Sat about looking pleasant in hard light. Whispered suggestion to host to swap for soft lamp by the fire. Great improvement. All listened to two of the men, one in the Army telling the other what he'll have to have in the way of clothes when <u>he</u> joins the Army next week.

Pianist was persuaded to tinkle. Thin chorus joined in a mixture of songs—<u>Daisy</u>, <u>Beneath thy Window</u>, <u>Bycycle Two</u>, <u>Butterfly</u>, <u>5th Symphony</u>—dibbled out to chatter again. Daughter-at-the-house, 15, shepherded talkers into some round games—spin the plate etc.—which led to laughter and childish fun and loosened us up a bit. "Grunt Piggy Grunt" was followed by tricks in the hallway in which we got wet and vulgar. At 11 several people went, for trains. The rest of us played an unsuccessful Murder game. I drew M, but had to throttle three people before one would scream. They said afterwards that they knew it was me and thought I was "only playing!"

Half of us then lounged in the drawing room and the others chatted to the Doctor about their feet in the hall. At 2 I wanted to go home but Man said "Just wait a bit—we're the guests of honour, can't go first." But after another half an hour I was almost asleep. So we collected the flock and stamped out Auld Lang Syne and had a lot of rousing cheers for everybody. Went out into the moonlit cool dark road with jellies, a cake balanced between us. Both remarked on the relief it was to our cheek muscles to relax from our party smile.

Kissed goodnight and washed a lazy face and hands. Read Toynbee on Persian history for twenty minutes and then slept well.

I had my hair "set" on Thursday morning for the party. First time ever. And it looked very nice and I didn't really grudge the 6s 6d until Sunday, when it all fell straight and I realised the girl had cut out all the "perm." Got more and more miserable about it till in the early evening I wept! Never considered myself vain before, but it really was pure miserable injured vanity. Man cleverly realised it and suggested going on the Monday morning for a new perm. Otherwise I'd be so sick for the three days precious leave beginning that day. He was even angelic enough to come to Town with me! Had a successful perm and went to Flemings for lunch. No meat left at 2, so he had fish and I had treacle pudding only. Walked across Hyde Park to the Serpentine enjoying the sun, and caught a bus from Victoria just before the business rush.

Spent a pleasant hour playing with nephew Mike 3½, who is staying with us while my sister-in-law has her second baby.

Tuesday, September 9

Caught 10:20 for Knockholt. Walked through grey September mists and nutty woods over the hill to Shoreham. Drank a pint of beer and ate some sandwiches. Walked on over the hills to a lovely lost valley. Ate more food and then slept in the sun while Man picked blackberries. Woke to machine guns stutter (practise range) and helped pick. Filled basket, 4 lbs. Meandered over and through Otford. Had half pint instead of tea at the Polhill Arms and caught 7:14 back from Knockholt. Ate hot meal and made love and went to bed early.

Wednesday, September 10

Arose at 8, hour later than usual. Played in the garden with Michael. Picked elderberries when Man arrived at 11. Wandered down to Lewisham with Mick and Man, trying to buy some sausages for lunch. No luck. After vegetarian lunch played again with Mick. Put up his tent in the grass and fooled around. Played the piano. Sang. Mended a lot of socks and stockings. Marvelled at how quickly our three days holiday had vanished.

Man's landlady having hurt her back, she refused to feed anyone over the weekend. Brother and Mick at home for weekend and food shortish, so rang Joan and asked to be invited for weekend. Was. Took Man and beans and marrow and eggs and butter and had a happy weekend and two lovely nights. Went to Hainault Forest and were pleasantly surprised with its rurality. Misty rain added to its solitude and we came home to tea feeling happy.

Came up to office via Ilford and Liverpool Street and saw some of the East End and City damage from a different angle. Have lost the "shocked" feeling and just view the ruins speculatively now, comparing this and that corner of London.

Was duly gratified to get a copy of <u>Change</u>. Feel I have not really deserved it, hence the effort to send a rather fuller envelope this time. Have already discussed points from it and found the general interest in clothes coupons has died down. [<u>Change</u> was the <u>Bulletin of the Advertising Service Guild</u>. This issue, published in August 1941, dealt with clothes rationing.]

Intend to ring the London M-O phone number and discuss income tax. I come in contact with a number of so-called money experts, whose tax I deduct at source, and they are abysmally ignorant of the impact of the new tax. So I am troubled about the reaction in November, when so many workers will <u>have</u> to pay income tax for the first time. There will be very bitter resentment, and it will be a fearful shock. A <u>lot</u> of poster propaganda, showing how income tax helps, is vitally necessary—and <u>soon</u> so that people do not have this dreadful sudden cutting down of their pay packets without <u>any</u> word of thanks and explanation from Authority. This is a job which, if there is time, M-O might get a rough reaction for in October Directive—to compare with the pre and post compulsory deduction attitude. LATER. Phoned; hope I made a strong enough impression in 40 seconds. Anyway, here's a reminder—<u>may</u> save a revolution.

The budget of April 1941 raised the rates of income tax and significantly reduced the number of earners exempt from tax. As a result of these changes, which were designed to yield another £255 million per year in revenue, many working-class people became, for the first time, payers of income tax. A total of some four million new taxpayers were created. Some of these far-from-affluent taxpayers were undoubtedly shocked by their new liability.[19]

Sunday, September 20

Diary will peter out now for a bit. Have a lot of work at work and Michael at home. Have an hour free now but must spend it doing Directive and darning. Have had many "happy" moments since last weekend. Find myself singing as I walk along on my way to work. Am grateful, wherever they come from. Man and I seem to fall in love all over again every couple of months—very enjoyable.

War? Keep forgetting it. Can't do any more to help than work and save and economise and keep cheerful.

Friday, October 3

This and the last three mornings I have walked from Big Ben to Berkeley Square across the parks. Pleasantly brisk with mist sun-shot, dewy grass, smell of damp leaves. First morning saw a black and white patched blackbird. At one place by the London Museum there is a manhole, with always a murmur of rushing water from it. For a moment I am among all the thwaites and fells of Cumberland, with splashing waterfalls and grass and trees. I walk on basking in conscious happiness, glad to be alive, along my bones and in my nerves.

10:45. Break for cup of tea. Have spent last hour fuming at people over income tax. It is APPALLING the dismay caused as they gradually admit one's figures are correct—figures they should have budgeted for since last April. I spoke on the phone to M-O about this and mentioned it in last month's Diary but it cannot be overstressed. One little man on £3 10s, to pay five shillings income tax, says bitterly "The Guvmint ort to pass a bill abaht it—me a married man!" He thought at first that five shillings was all he'd have to pay—said he couldn't live on it when he found it was five shillings every week till next March. Have now discussed it with colleague. Both agree Inland Revenue should have more imagination and use PUBLICITY.

2:20 pm. Introduced two mutual friends over a coffee at lunch time and was glad they liked one another. Funny how often women of about 30 say together "As one grows up one realises…" this that and the other.

Saturday, October 4

Last night walked to Victoria across Green Park with Miss D discussing her family. Queued five minutes for a bus and blessed the queue system once more. Watched with disgust the scramble of the strongest at stops en route.

Found Mother up the garden feeding chickens. Baby nephew went back to the country that morning and already she was missing him. Had some toast, jam, custard, and coffee for evening meal. Sat afterwards reminiscing and hearing news from Dad of old friends who have been blitzed. Later, 8:45, Man and I walked in the moonlight to a fried fish shop, to find it shut, so that Mother and Dad were disappointed, having suddenly fancied a fish supper.

Listened to the end of the 9 o'clock news and then Man and I went upstairs. Sang London Pride—like it—then he went on playing piano. I stared dreamily at the bookcase and decided to browse in the Bible. Soon the lovely prose demanded to be read aloud, and I did, rather to Man's surprise. He seemed faintly shocked when I laughed at a verse about the "stork knoweth her times" and I enunciated later "Women don't feel that awe of the Bible that men do, because women are so remotely unreal in the Bible. We don't feel it applies at all to <u>modern</u> women. The threats or promises do not apply. Men may have much the same attitude, but not so strongly as women." Few women who work and earn can "feel" the Oriental attitude to women.

At 10:30 Man went, and we stared at the moonlit cloudy sky for a few minutes. Soon to bed and read C.E. Montague's essays for a while.

Not such a nice morning [Saturday, October 4], so went by bus. Plenty of work; left at 1:20 though; home on crawling buses by 2:30. Found Man in garden with Mother. Went to Public Library, got music. Bought buns and back to Man's room for tea. Joined by Social Service spinster from the opposite room. Chatted about imbeciles for 40 minutes. Home, changed, packed and again to Man's by 5, ready to go to Joan's for weekend, at Barkingside. Miserable journey through blitzed East End in deepening twilight, with weary women packing the buses and shrill children who ought to have been in the country.

Found Joan doing two days washing up. Helped and had some supper off the pork pie and tomatoes we had brought. Talked and sewed and felt sleepy and ready for bed with Man. To bed at 10:30 to sleep at midnight. It's incredible that we're both still thrilled so much—after so long.

Sunday, October 5
Had cup of tea in bed at 9:30. Misty damp morning so Joan suggested breakfast in bed. Didn't get up till 11. Wandered round the flat in pyjamas helping Joan prepare lunch, while Man occupied the bathroom very leisurely. Lunched at 1:30 and hurried off to concert for the Navy at local cinema. Joan's office boy was singing. Quite enjoyed the

two hours of popular songs—one very excellent piano soloist. Walked part of the way back through dreary Ilford streets, to enjoy tea and chatter and then help Joan learn her part in a new play. She is very active in arranging amusements for her young people's club.

At 9 Edna, who lives with Joan, came home. Had fallen down some steps in the dark and cut her knee badly. Was very annoyed at tearing her last pair of real silk stockings.

Had supper and talked. The three women agreed in detesting the "real life" descriptions of war horrors on the BBC. Man thought them "interesting" but we squirmed. Got more and more sleepy till bed at 11:15. Still, we didn't sleep for an hour, even so. How inadequate words are for one's gratitude for complete love!

Monday, October 6

Slept fitfully, in strange jerks. Up soon after 7 and rushed around. Got dirty late train through dirty misty wet London, into the more bearable parts about Bond Street.

Was surprised by the lovely sun and warmth at lunchtime. Met Man in Piccadilly and perambulated dozily in the sun, hearing news of old friend he had met for a drink. His landlady has suddenly announced "No more dinners" and so I'll have a problem to cope with. Don't like to ask Mother to provide, but what are we to do?

Busy afternoon, try to find last quarter's errors [in the accounts]. Left 5:15 and walked across Park to Victoria. Almost fell asleep on the bus. Chatted to Dad about chickens and garden and Man's meal problem; peeled potatoes and had a game with Betty, Mabel's eight year old niece visiting, while they cooked. Man came at 7, ate happily. Read an old Times Dad found—1805—accounts of Nelson's death. Early to bed and overslept well. Heavenly moony ramble round garden at 10.

Tuesday, October 7

Bus to work. Cold grey mist. Plenty to do, but small interval for tea chat with new girl. Has same tastes as I have. Lunch time, ten pence in canteen, soup, bread and semolina pudding. Then met Man and bought some sausages and apples for evening meal. Walked down

Bond Street and stared avidly at opals, my one delight among jewels—no, my one personal covet among jewels.

Walked across the Park again and home to cook sausages—they all burst—thick skin and thin meat. Had potatoes and tomatoes with them—good. Cup of tea and Dad, Man and I listened for a bit to a daft BBC revue. Bored, so upstairs to play piano (Man) and darn socks (Me). Eric called and stayed an hour talking music and home-making and books. Bed 10:30 and slept well.

Wednesday, October 8

Up at 7, Dad having put the alarm clock outside my door when he went at 5. But still was a bit late leaving, as I lingered around washing up etc., thinking I had plenty of time. Walked across the park again and saw my white blackbird. Lunch time met Man, after long traffic block in Piccadilly, and went to Foyle's. Bought modern-photo complete Shakespeare for five shillings. Bargain. Have two copies but like having clear print one, and several are good for play readings, which we enjoy. Birthday present too. Back via Soho Square. Once more called to see if my radio is repaired. No. Sorry, no labour. Soon. Had it eight weeks. Left 5:30, walked across Park to Victoria. Sleepy in bus again. Home 6:45. Prepared garden salad and cold sausage supper. Man came 7:10. Finished and cleared by 8. Then an hour's ironing while Man played piano. After I'd done he pressed pair of trousers. Listened to end of news and then lazily to harvest programme, which we enjoyed mildly. Was worrying about money, though at the back of my mind. Man thinks Russian prospect gloomy and worries about that. But I know nothing of their strategy and try not to "worry" except clear-headedly making ends meet. For war-effort I'm trying specially hard to save light and fuel and water.

Thursday, October 9

Up 6:55. Alarm clock again. Apple and bread and butter and coffee, wash up, wash down and 8:30 met Man for work. Giggly good spirits on the way to work, but the rain decided me to tell him not to come out at lunch time, but _if_ it was fine 1:10 [at] Swan and Edgars.

It was wet, but of course he was there, saying so readily "D'you think a drop of rain would stop me seeing you?" I feel scared, sometimes, of the jealous gods.

Bought eight cards of darning wool. Wandered up Regent Street and down Bond Street looking in all the opal shop windows. My heavenly earrings are still there, like immobilized sunsets. Raining at 5:30 so no walk across park. Home by 6:40 and by 7:40 we had <u>eaten</u> steak and potatoes and beans and tomatoes I'd cooked, but Dad had prepared the vegetables for me. Mother arrives at 8, full of laughter and having enjoyed her few days in the country. Ethel had done her hair a new way for her and it looked very funny. Told us that there was a lot more food and sweets in Southend than London—got ¼lb butter in a shop by chance.

We went upstairs at 9 and heard the news. Were <u>intensely annoyed</u> by Monty Norman's talk—expect that what he spends on cigars or drinks or ties would keep us for a quarter—every sixpence indeed! [Montagu Norman, 1871–1950, was Governor of the Bank of England.] We're by no means as badly off as some people. But I can't save at all on present prices and income and income tax. Find it quite difficult to keep up insurance payments. Soak the rich has still a long way to go before they're as near the border as we are.

Bed by 10:15 and read Toynbee on the Internal Proletariat of Hellas till 11. Slept well, dreaming of Man's kisses.

Monday, October 13

Have just read over these pages. Seems silly to keep it up, it's so pompously dull. Don't think you'll have much value from it. Shan't continue, as this sample really covers the "lull" feeling—until a change comes in the atmosphere.

With this abrupt self-dismissal, Olivia's regular efforts at diary-keeping ceased. She offered one further observation for the month, which is added at the bottom of the page, in much smaller handwriting, and dated October 31.

October 31

Change came. The twelve-years awaited divorce was a failure—suspected collusion. The world seems in bits and I can't bother with

M-O report this month. Sorry. If I possibly can I must earn some money to pay the £80 debt, perhaps by writing.

October 1941 was the month (in Olivia's own words) of "the divorce that didn't," for the judge had refused the petition for divorce. Apparently Bill and Olivia's solicitor had revealed (unwisely) the agreement already made concerning maintenance payments to Bill's wife, and thus the verdict of "collusion." Thereafter Olivia had "Several days of unhappiness, with friends' kindness unexpectedly helpful." She had a "sudden change for the better when I tried to earn some money by writing. Didn't even get as far as sending it to any editor—short stories and poems—but found the effort intensely diverting and when I came back to life again was very amused." Writing, for her, was clearly a means of self-therapy. She described November as "Mostly quiet and reading history and philosophy." In December she "registered for National Service"—unmarried younger women were from that month liable to be conscripted into some form of wartime work—and "Began to make love again and enjoy it. The man and I spend more time than ever together, though we don't see any way out of this divorce mess and have a big debt hanging over us." They were together most evenings. On February 20, 1942 she described a typical weekday evening. "Home by 7. Wash and eat high tea. Into housecoat or gown by 8, when Man arrives to find me (apparently) calmly knitting on settee. Kisses, crossways chatter on day's events, finish Telegraph *X-word. If BBC good, listen, and I knit. Otherwise Man plays piano till 9 o'clock news. Then listen, turn out light, snuggle. Three or four times a week make love passionately. About 10:30, he goes, after, occasionally, cocoa or tea and biscuits. Me, teeth and eyes and hair; bed by 11 to read till 12 or past."*

"The war," Olivia reported on February 20, 1942, "is just a nuisance, like cold weather or toothache." She sometimes even forgot to acknowledge momentous occurrences. In her "Brief Diary" for January 1942 she wrote, "Was amazed when I re-read my December brief diary that I had not mentioned USA coming into the war." The war did, though, have a deeper impact on her state of mind. A few weeks previously she had compared her current with her prewar attitudes. The war, she thought, "has steadied me tremendously. The tension of continual prewar crises was very unbalancing. I thought

and talked wild extremes in my anxiety. Now that it's here and still here and everywhere I accept it and dismiss it as a phase of social illness we may live through." Reading had helped her to become philosophical. *"Toynbee's* Study of History *has pulled all these puzzled anxieties into a pattern for me and calmed me considerably. I am not really as horrified of the suffering as I expected to be."* She was able to push the suffering of war *"out of my mind"* and *"balance it against hunger and illness and cruelty in peace and it doesn't seem so very different. The foolishness is aggravating—but all foolishness is. Slums and strikes and slavery are only peacetime forms of war"* (DR, January 1942). As for thoughts about death and dying, she felt that *"the war hasn't made much difference to my feelings. I am surprised that, being in Central London throughout the blitz, I have not seen one dead body. Not even a wounded one!"* (DR, May 1942).

Her life continued to have its ups and downs—and Mass-Observation was well suited to capture some of this turbulence and these uncertainties in private lives. From mid-March 1942 Olivia experienced *"Periods of depression over the war, and lately [she is writing in mid May] a growing certainty that it will be over by next Christmas. Based on a little 'official view' and a lot of hope."* As for her personal life, she reported in late January 1942 (*"Brief Diary"*) on *"Love: Man and I have thoroughly enjoyed our three nights together. Abandon and experiment have brought us into closer and closer tenderness. We spend every evening together, every lunch hour, travel to town together—and we don't seem to get bored yet."* Later in May 1942 (further *"Brief Diary"*), she was finding the *"Situation re. Man very depressing: no money and no hope of divorce being re-heard. He hates boarding house. We have ecstatic moments and then fearful deeps. I keep wanting to join the [Women's] Land Army, and shall if he goes back. And if the Civil Service will release me."* None of this happened. *"Feel very domesticated with Man this month,"* she said in September 1942 (*"Very Brief Diary"*). *"Only one really passionate night. But a constant affection."*

Routine, lack of drama, repetitive labour, plugging along and getting by, digging in for the long haul (perhaps while hoping for a quick peace), waiting and enduring, enjoying whatever (usually small) pleasures came one's way: these were the characteristics of many people's lives, including Olivia's, during *the middle years of the war. The ordinariness of existence is the dominant theme. Olivia records in detail what she did on Wednesday, February 25, 1942—and this is the last full description of a single day's experience that she gave to Mass-Observation.*

Wednesday, February 25 1942

Switched off my light soon after midnight, having read three critical essays on modern poets. Thanked God for comfort once again as I snuggled down into my pillow. [She had been suffering from a throat infection for much of February.]

Awake at about 4 with a discomfort. Throat still very sore. Sipped some water. Couldn't regain sleep. Made water, back into bed, still no sleep. Reached for a lozenge, switched on the light, sat up and read two more essays. Then sleepy again and off till 6:30. Lay hating the thoughts of getting up, and the clamour and effacement of the office. At 7:20 dragged myself up. Dressing gowned to wash in the warm kitchen and Mother already making coffee. Talked sleepily but fond of one another. Ate toast and two prunes, porridge and coffee. Listened to the 8 o'clock news, from in the lavatory. Was once more amused by the "Dear Russia" instead of damned Reds. Didn't think the news startling. Up to bedroom to dress and tidy, out of the house as the clock struck the half-hour.

Waited two minutes for Man, in his boarding house porch. Stared at the plaster broken down by the frost. Hated the bitter East wind. Felt sorry for myself avec throat so sore. Kissed Man good morning. He didn't sleep well either. His clock stopped in the night "Because it was so cold." Waited just round corner out of the wind for a tram, glad to catch a through one and avoid five minutes waiting in the wind. Felt cold and weary and watched the iron grey streets of SE London lurching by, still blitzed curtains struggling in the wind. Arranged to meet at lunchtime. Stared at the other people, tired girls and women, muffled up oddly against the cold. To Big Ben by 9:05. Ran dangerously across the wide road, hating the wind, to catch a bus. Found a seat empty near the front, warmer. Watched two Military Police questioning a soldier in Trafalgar Square. Bus didn't stop at right place, and I had to walk right back from Oxford Circus in the teeth of the wind.

Went to Boots as I was early. Asked for some mild throat pastilles. Offered only Thymol, which are strong and upset my digestion, so had the walk for nothing. Gritted my teeth and down Conduit Street longing for sun and warmth. Vaguely remembered a Chemist in Bond Street. Decided to go there if I could see it from corner. Could. Did. Was helpfully served with Glycerine Jujubes—1s 2d— but really mild and kept me moist. Wish this throat and sore tongue would heal. Doctor's treatment doesn't seem very effective.

Into the office on time. Muttered hoarse good mornings to colleagues. Pretended voice quite weaker than it is, to avoid daft conversations. Coat and hat off and hung on cupboard behind me. Blotter, calendar, basket, index, ledgers out onto desk. Immersed myself in the arrears of work my fortnight sick has left me. After an hour of it stopped gratefully for beaker of weak hot tea. Found my hands freezing and liked holding hot china. Girl next to me told me she'd had a poor night's sleep. Asked after her Mother's twisted ankle. Told one another how our joint job is going—satisfactory. Listened to three senior men innuendoing about a radio programme last night, Fanny Adams and so on. Didn't join in though they threw out obvious "Don't you think so?s." Went to cloakroom, soaked hands gratefully in hot water. Back to swim in figures, clicking my sore tongue to myself in calculating, until lunchtime. With next girl down to canteen. Beef sauté baked and cabbage—good gravy but couldn't eat meat—tainted gristle and fat. She talked food all the time, what she had yesterday, Sunday, last week; and told me a recipe for a sweet, cocoa and breadcrumbs. In fifteen minutes of the steamy, sweaty, stinking, noisy canteen felt a lot warmer and more human, but, oh, the knife edge of the wind on the stairs again!

Hat and coat and gloves and out to Bond Street. Kissed Man happily, and to Lyons for the rare extravagance of a cup of coffee. Cafeteria service sensible. He told me that an acquaintance, O

(45), had cut his throat yesterday, after a month's illness. Wasn't very shocked or upset. Wondered what had driven him to the step one so often contemplates thankfully as at least <u>one</u> way out.

Coffee finished we marched up Bond Street with the wind cold and piercing, west along Oxford Street out of its bite. A break in the clouds provided a blue background for Selfridges' flags, tearing to fly away: Union Jack, Stars and Stripes, French, Netherlands, and HAMMER and SICKLE! Laughed and laughed and exclaimed that this time last year Nobody Would Have Believed etc. I thought "And as soon as the war's over it'll be the same again." Since the BBC brouhaha for USSR my pride and private thrill about it have declined a little! I must prefer lost causes.

Stared into a flower shop window. Daffodils, narcissus, pussy palm, cinerarias, carnations, freesia. Daren't even wonder "How Much?" Walked on the <u>sunny</u>! side of the street. Noticed that Sylvia, balloon in Square, was well tied down. Were asked by Canadian Army lorry driver where Berkeley Square was. Told him. Walked down Mount Street. Stared at some lovely jade, Chinese pictures, and old china. Wondered how such shops can keep going. Stopped in surprise to feel a little warmth in the sun at a sheltered place—thoughts flow to gardens and green leaves and Dig for Victory. Huddled into coat at next corner, East Wind whipping. Kissed Man Goodbye and looked forward to seeing him tonight. Such a tender amusement in his eye—the bright shine of a loved eye is a heartening sight.

Into office, cloakroom on the way. Nose began to be wet as soon as the warmth indoors touched it. Sucked another pastille and settled to slogging again solidly. Headache and eye ache. Damned stink of oil stoves. Always artificial light; never any fresh air. Stopped soon after 3 for another mug of warm weak tea and a biscuit. Talked a bit, the weather, mutual acquaintances, scandal about the chief clerk and the new girl. Asked if any new scandal while I was away—not very interesting. Worked again, less accurately now, eyes and head aching, and throat damn sore. Decided to go early. Did, without asking permission. Really my Medical Certificate covers several more days sick leave, but I knew the work ought to be done this week. Still, I have a pleasant feeling of heroism and so of independence and come and go without asking.

Walked ten minutes to bus detesting the wicked wind all the way. Wondering how the poor devils in Russia could fight at all. Pitying the poor and the French prostitutes I passed on the corners—short fur coats and long silk stockings. Waited miserably for a bus. Got on the first that came though. Had to go on top, coughed in smoke. Sucked another lozenge and worried about my throat. Stared at the dirty buildings and longed for green trees and meadows and streams and summer. Overlooked headlines in paper. Parliament fussing again. Heard no comments on news.

Warmly welcomed by Mother and Dad. Hot rice and cabbage soon ready, then coffee and piece of bread pudding. Stayed for wiping-up. Then to my sitting room to write this. Three quarters of an hour of writing—Man came. Talked of day's doings, nothing much. Turned on wireless for news. Was feeling sorry for myself and throat and unprepared for lovemaking. But satisfied him. Then half an hour's laze in firelight and by 10:30 to bed, to read for an hour, Milton, and sleep.

In September 1942, in response to Mass-Observation's questionnaire that month, she offered a few comments on how people were then feeling about the war.

September, M-O September questionnaire

People seem to sway in the breeze of the last headline. Their reason sees no near end to the war, their feelings want a quick end. The slaughter of foreigners by foreigners doesn't seem to matter. The English casualties are not yet gloom making. The absolute assumption that we shall win in the end seems untouched—it is so much taken for granted that I seem to be the only person who ever mentions it. The young wives of soldiers (I work with seven or eight) are usually quite cheerful. If letters are delayed there may be some gloom, but, although the atmosphere here is emotional, I've never yet seen tears.

Olivia was a very inner-directed person. Sometimes she spoke of life in a decidedly psycho-spiritual manner. In 1942 she was still striving for a sense of spiritual well-being. Her goal was "to make my 'security' an inward feeling, on Powys lines: a sensation of being at one with the essence of whatever Is, except cruelty."[20] She searched for other words to describe this pursuit of meaningful security. Its objective, she wrote, was "A general and deepening 'awareness' of oneself: a feeling-oneself-into the smallest flower that blows— the usual mystical sensual guff in fact. But for me it works" (DR, September 1942). For her this was a way of finding some repose beyond the buffeting blows of political events. However, the war, she acknowledged, had altered some of her values. "My first analysis for M-O of my own philosophy laid stress, I remember, on 'self-detachment.' Since the war I have begun to think that these detached individuals will have to learn to cooperate to achieve what they dream in lonely hours. I have not got far along that road," she admitted, "because I fear that it would upset my private life, and I am not yet unselfish enough to let it. Also I cannot persuade my Man to share any of my desire to 'do something' and I dread a real clash between us. My ideas can't be very persuasive if they have no effect on someone who loves me" (DR, October 1942).

October 1942 marked the end of Olivia's wartime writing for Mass-Observation. While her personal life was still unsettled, she expected to be promoted at work and she had been given new responsibilities. "I was put on to a job where I really have to use my brains for once. I shall be happier for a few weeks until it has become just another routine." Her career was becoming more important to her, partly because she thought it might give her an opportunity both to bring about beneficial social change and to advance herself. Through her job she might, she hoped, find some a sense of achievement; by contrast "my personal life after the war is very foggy," she lamented. Her birthday in October 1942 seems to have signalled a change of outlook, and perhaps a step in a new direction. On the second last page of her diary she wrote the following words. "I had my 30th birthday this month, and friends came and we feasted on the old cockerel and laughed and were gay. I was given books and gloves and money, and felt warmly grateful to everybody for being so nice to me. For a long time I have thought something different should come into my life after 30. I seem to have decided to flaunt myself officially and try for a Civil Service career (!!) as it seems my real desire—to marry the Man and have children in the country—is quite unattainable."

In Olivia Cockett's diaries, personal matters outweighed matters political. This may have been partly or mainly because her personal life generated most of the fuel for her writing. She was driven to write—aided, no doubt, by encouraging letters from Tom Harrisson at Mass-Observation—by how she felt at a particular time, and how she felt was strongly influenced by the immediate circumstances of her personal life, especially those involving her relationship with Bill Hole. This, for her, was the crucial variable. She was most likely to write both when she and Bill were apart and when the daily tasks she had to carry out did not absorb all her time and energy.

However, Olivia was by no means uninterested in public affairs or indifferent to issues of public policy. There is, in fact, evidence of the sorts of inclinations that would suit a career in the civil service. During her twenties she sometimes commented on public issues, even though during those years she did not exercise much in the way of independent responsibility. Her sympathies were almost always in favour of social reform. In August 1934 she wrote of the improvements she would like to see come about: "the making of new laws respecting work, wages, housing, marriage, birth-control, education, leisure, old age and cemeteries. With a special extension for foreign policy and international cooperation." She wondered, though, about how she could contribute to the cause of beneficial change, since "better people than I have workable plans ready, needing only enthusiasm and energy and cooperation for them to become operative. Can I do anything towards providing this sort of help? Especially as I have a profound disbelief in organisations, while yet realising their necessity as things are." She was attracted more to imagining a better future state than to those nitty-gritty political processes that were apparently required to bring change about. "Nothing, I suppose," she rather glumly conceded in these reflections, written when she was twenty-one years of age, "can be done without leagues and petitions and bills and laws and officials." And obviously, she declared, "there are so many staring absurdities awaiting redress."

Four years later she wrote again about her interest in reform and thought that some of her attitudes and aspirations were changing: "my personal gropings after an Ideal Life are becoming more concrete than ever—Naomi Mitchison's Moral Basis of Politics *has given me a vigorous shove in a definite direction" (August 14, 1938). Her new responsibilities in 1938 with the Metropolitan Police introduced her to social problems that she had not previously dealt with, and these new challenges, she found, were invigorating. "Especially with a technical library at my disposal," she remarked about her new opportunities at work, "I ought to make myself an efficient and informed person on the outcast woman problem. It is, I hope, a problem which would automatically disappear on the establishment of a socialist state. The little I have heard on the matter in USSR seems to confirm that hope. But, meanwhile, it exists; and is still inadequately dealt with; and is alleviable."*

Bill Hole did not share her visions for the future. He was, in fact, opposed to them and was unsympathetic to her efforts to be (as she saw it) forward-looking. He criticized her interest in joining the Left Book Club—this at a time when she was keen to do as much reading as possible (August 1938). On August 14, 1938, in the evening, she was about to read a History of the French People in bed. "I really know *so little. Once I do begin action I shall never have 'enough' time for reading, and so I ought to do that now, especially as Bill has dropped objections to my choice of books lately. Though he still looks them over and sniffs." She was hoping for more enrichment for her "social mind," which, she felt, was "starving and disappearing at the expense of my emotional attachment to Bill, or of his demands on me. And each time his pitiful longing (and mine) draws us together again." She wanted greater independence in order to "lead a fuller and more interesting, I'd like to say more useful, life. Socially, politically.... Some change* must *come soon— though I acknowledge that soon may still mean years. And I want the change to be in Bill's attitude. My heart is still his, but less and less my head. If only he could suddenly see the value of the future State!"*

A telling indication of Olivia's taste for social policy and public admin-istration was revealed four years later. Mass-Observation's Directive for August 1942 asked its panel members several questions, one of which was, "Have you any ideas about how the medical services should be organized

after the war? If so, outline them." Olivia, it turned out, was full of ideas.
She recommended:

… more men and women trained in positive medicine—to keep
people fit. Many centres of the Peckham type.[21] Always a regular
inspection and an easily available doctor for all employees, at office,
shop and factory. Ditto dentist. To be paid by regular contributions
from employer and employee, with convalescent homes run by them.
But hospitals run by Civil Service method, state supported, with a
month at lectures for every qualified practitioner every year.

More information widely spread about new techniques. No patent medicines on sale except through the easily available plentiful
doctors' prescriptions.

This was not the end of her proposals. She also thought advisable:

A local home service for housewives with visiting doctors for
regular inspections. And a central pooling of family histories—from
home, hospital, factory, school, whenever a doctor asked for it,
through a National Registry—quite as easy as Military Service registration. But the whole scheme NOT COMPULSORY. A good
publicity campaign and the innate sense of the scheme would soon
make it practically universally desired.

*After a further paragraph of suggestions, she concluded with a PS:
"Didn't realise I felt so strongly about it, till I answered the question!"*

*Another question posed in August 1942 was "What changes do you
personally hope will be brought about by the war or after the war?" which
allowed Olivia to put on record some of her ideals. "I hope the Sankey Rights of
Man will be met.[22] I hope the widows and orphans will be well treated. I hope
old-age, unemployment, hospitals, schools, health services, will be adequately
dealt with. I hope ostentatious luxuries will be cut out. I hope international
federation will cut the silliest sort of politics away. I hope industry will serve
the needs of the people instead of using those needs for its own gains."*

*Olivia, then, continued to be committed to an agenda of social reform,
though she was not optimistic that major reforms would actually come about.
While her hopes for postwar reform might have been high, her expectations
were low. She predicted "Very few changes—the present 'arrangements' will*

lapse into the overriding needs of oligarchy, with sops they can't avoid" (DR, August 1942). In November 1942 her thoughts concerning the possibility of postwar change in England were decidedly gloomy.

November 1942

Since the last Conservative party meeting I have more "forebodings" than beliefs. The re-assurances that private enterprise will not be strangled are not indicative of a New Order. And the way a Government spokesman quickly negatives any bright suggestions as soon as possible—similar process to the "Raids, Yes we will, No we won't" game. My office job since July has been in close connection with commerce. I realise now that the Big Firms and Big Names are <u>more</u> firmly in the saddle since the war, not shaken or afraid at all. They have no intention of allowing changes let alone helping them. Even winning the war, right now, must not interfere with their sacred rights of profit.

One of the questions posted to Mass-Observers at this time was "How have you formed your own plans and desires about what you want after the war?" Olivia's reply pointed to the principal components of her own progressive attitudes.

I have formed my hopes of future improvement (a) On personal experience: from seeing the standard of living acquired by my own family and "class" and realising how many people are worse off, and wanting them not to be. (b) On history: largely on Toynbee's interpretation of cycles of civilisation and the realisation, pressed home by Wells and Russell and Powys and even Joan Grant [a novelist], that we CAN if we WILL improve the "housekeeping" of the world. (c) On the possibility of getting into a Ministry where I can do something about it, and also get responsibility and promotion for myself.

Almost her final words for M-O were, "I am getting more and more restive for action" (DR, October 1942).

Epilogue

Olivia's Life ~ 1942–1998[1]

Olivia's intelligence and questioning mind, and perhaps her strong feelings as well, allowed her to develop professionally, to be promoted, and to enjoy a fulfilling career in the public service. She spent her entire career in the Ministry of Works. During most of the latter half of World War Two she worked for "Buildings Materials Licensing": she dealt with (as she remembered when she was eighty) "Appeals from local refusals and travelled to all bombed areas for several years, reviewing needs. Got to know UK under difficulties." Her work involved the allocation of building materials to various regions of the country, taking bombing damage into account. In 1946 she was a staff officer (Licensing) in the Ministry's Labour, Licensing and General Division. Her responsibilities were carried out in a unit that dealt with "Policy, Parliamentary Questions, Instructions, and General Matters."[2] After the war, to advance her career, she wrote the Civil Service Reconstruction Exam, and by 1947 she had been promoted to the minister's office, where she served as his assistant private secretary—and earned at least triple the salary she had been paid in the early 1940s. "Enjoyed state visits and Parliament," she later recalled. For most of the postwar years she worked closely with the minister of the day, whether Labour or Conservative. One official invitation in 1951 was to a reception held by the prime minister, Clement Attlee. "Marvellous experience with Ministers and Houses of Parliament; ran Museum and Science vote till voluntary retirement." She helped to prepare the minister for Question Period in Parliament. She also had responsibility for the upkeep of much government property, including royal palaces and historic buildings. During the years before her retirement in 1964, she was one of the most senior women in the Ministry. (Her office, in Lambeth Bridge House, SE1, overlooked the Thames.) In the New Year's Honours List for 1965 she was awarded the Order of the British Empire (O.B.E.): "Miss Olivia Elsie Sarah Isabel Cockett, Lately Principal, Ministry of Public Buildings and Works."[3]

Olivia and Bill Hole remained partners after the War. He never did obtain a divorce. By the 1950s they were living together in Olivia's own house at 43 Breakspears Road, just a few doors away from her wartime residence (which had been rented). Both properties had huge back gardens, which were points in their favour to Olivia and Bill, who were avid gardeners. Olivia suffered some health problems in her late forties and early fifties, and in the early 1960s she was misdiagnosed as being terminally ill, which prompted her early retirement. She expected to live, at best, only a few more years—and probably not beyond her fifties; her own mother had died, unexpectedly, at the age of fifty-nine, from complications after surgery (Olivia suspected medical malpractice). Upon her retirement, Olivia and Bill moved to the coastal village of Charmouth, Dorset, where she had purchased a pleasant modern cottage, with a view of the sea. At Bill's request—perhaps at his insistence—Olivia had at that time changed her surname by deed poll to Hole and was generally recognized in and around West Dorset as Mrs. Hole.

Despite their differences, Olivia and Bill had interests in common and mutual pleasures, and family members remember their relationship as mainly happy and harmonious. They both enjoyed walking, rural life, music, watching cricket on television, amateur dramatics (Bill had been in "The Comets," the Dramatic Society of New Scotland Yard (Civil Staff) Sports and Social Club, and was treasurer of the Society in 1950), and gardening, and both were wardens on the National Trust's Golden Cap estate to the east of Charmouth. Olivia's niece, Hilary Munday, recalls that Bill, in his sixties and seventies, was deeply attached to Olivia and "was very devoted to her when she was ill" prior to their move to Charmouth. Bill was, as Hilary remembers him, "very conventional," and it was "out of character" for him "to live openly with Paddy [Olivia's family nickname], a woman he was not married to." Olivia described Bill as "the last of the Victorians." He was, however, no patriarch. She was the dominant partner and she did most of the talking. She also had a lot more money than he had, partly because she had earned more, partly because of his continuing payments to his separated wife (which took half of his pension). Olivia's strong preference for sleeping alone continued all her life, so while she and Bill acted toward each other much like any married couple, they always had separate bedrooms, whether in London or Charmouth. Bill died suddenly in August 1972, shortly before his seventy-seventh birthday; he suffered an apparent heart attack while walking in Charmouth and was dead a few hours later. "I felt cut in half after 42 years with him as the centre of my life," Olivia wrote in a January 1990 letter to the Mass-Observation Archive. (From 1989 she became a contributor to the new autobiographical Mass-Observation Project that is based in the Archive at the University of Sussex.)

Olivia, with age, did not lose any of her intellectual vitality. Indeed, she was seen as a force to be reckoned with. "She had the keenest of minds," her nephew Michael Cockett recalls, "a sharp interest in politics, and a fierce debating style until her first stroke in the 1990s." Her niece Hilary reports that "I (and many others) thought she had a very sharp intellect and an incisive mind, and was able to maintain a logical debate or argument." Michael remembers vividly his aunt's relentlessly questioning mind and the lively discussions that he had with her in the 1950s. "As a child and later a teen I talked to her because she treated me as an equal. She influenced, I absorbed. We loved the exchange and each other. I learned debate, the delight of words, and the flashes of understanding—the 'Eureka! Moments' from her." Her sparkling adult mind was, for him as a youth, a challenge to orthodoxy and a prod to enlarge his perspectives on life. "She could hold the dullest child entranced with the glitter of her imagination." She treated children as people and did not talk down to them.

Olivia continued to see herself as "a wordsmith," and her style of self-expression in communications to the Mass-Observation Archive when she was in her late seventies continued to be direct, blunt, and concise. She took words seriously. "Words words glorious words!" she wrote in April 1990, in a letter to the Mass-Observation Archive. "I play around with strings of them, throwing them like dice across the board of my mind. Some seem new-minted like old gold coins re-issued. Bless their creation." Michael Cockett remembers "her insistence on clear use of language. One of her favourite phrases was 'It depends on what you mean by _____.' She gave me a book called Language and the Pursuit of Truth *which I kept by me throughout school and University." (This book was written by philosopher John Wilson and published in 1956.) Books remained very important to Olivia, and the diverse intellectual interests that were apparent in her youth continued to be evident in her middle and old age. She read philosophy (she belonged to the Fellowship of Meditation and went to its annual retreat), mathematics, sociology, history, and natural science—especially geology. She also enjoyed poetry, particularly that of Thomas Hardy, Oscar Wilde, T.S. Eliot, and Sylvia Plath. She had a special fondness for women poets. Late in life, when her eyesight was failing, she gave her entire poetry collection, assembled over half a century, to her nephew.*

Olivia was a free spirit and free thinker (she belonged to the Euthanasia Society), readily entertaining unconventional views. She had no trouble speaking her mind—her father, according to the family, had declared that she "was born out-spoken." "My father used to tell me that what would embarrass me would turn a tram over," she wrote to M-O in 1990. Perhaps her remarks were sometimes cutting; some people may have been struck by what they saw as her eccentricities, even her "outlandish" behaviour, and may have seen her as "a character." Certainly, she had no fear of being seen as different. As a child, Hilary Munday saw her aunt as exciting, entertaining, sophisticated, and though she had little interest in clothes or fashion, "almost glamorous." To Hilary's eyes, Olivia "always had interesting things" and her flat and later house in London "seemed modern." Olivia was living quite comfortably by the 1950s, even affluently from the vantage point of others in the family. Her sense of adventure persisted until late in her life, and was manifested in various ways. In 1978 she embarked on a second passionate love affair, which lasted until the early 1990s, and she started again to keep a candid private diary (not unlike the one she had kept in the 1930s relating to Bill) that talked mostly about this intense relationship of her sixties and seventies. Not all about her, though, was unusual or exotic. As a child, her great-niece Danielle Blyfield (born in 1963) learned from Olivia "that you should find small satisfactions in everyday tasks, such as keeping the dishwater as clean as possible by emptying the dirty as you worked, and that such simple pleasures contributed to a happy life."

Olivia liked to work and had a successful career, enjoying most of her tasks in the public service, but while she followed her own muse and was certainly no intellectual conformist, she was always attached to "home." Home meant a lot to her, during the war and after. She savoured daily pleasures and enjoyed the sensuousness of everyday life at home. One of the questions asked in Mass-Observation's Directive for October 1942 was "What does Home mean to you?" Olivia had replied: "Mother. Books. Cushions. A good bed. Food, warmth, laughter. Appreciation. Flattery even. A garden. The nephew and niece. The reason for working at things I don't much like. Music and friends and the Man. Housework and cooking and wearing old clothes. Quiet. Sleep." In Charmouth she liked to sit outside, feeling the sun and the sea breezes, her eyes closed, letting nature get inside her. To touch and be touched—these were important sensations to her.

Olivia's life in Charmouth from the mid-1960s until the early 1990s was active, energetic, and productive. She sailed her small boat (Bill watched from the shore), she swam, and she walked a lot. She learned to fly a Cessna (though her health and perhaps age did not permit her to get a pilot's license) and belonged to the Exeter Flying Club. She joined the Women's Institute; for several years she was president of the Charmouth Society, founded in 1973, which was affiliated with the Council for the Protection of Rural England; she was instrumental in setting up the Heritage Coast Centre in Charmouth. Olivia was strongly committed to the protection of the natural environment, and her "green" disposition was evident in a variety of ways (recycling paper, membership in the National Trust). From the 1960s she also became a dedicated and capable photographer, and photography became her major hobby. Her niece Hilary recalls that "She took thousands of slides recording village life and the changing coast line. Paddy's slide shows were very popular, mainly because she put together collections of images suited to her audience and gave a witty and succinct commentary." (In a letter of December 1989 to the Mass-Observation Archive, Olivia herself said that "After my Bill died in 1972 I took to carrying a camera as an excuse for refusing all the kind invitations from other lone women here. 'Must just catch the sunset—the tide—the gulls—.'")

Olivia died on October 29, 1998, shortly after her eighty-sixth birthday. She had been in failing health for several years. Her remains were cremated, as Bill's had been, and they were buried alongside his in the Charmouth cemetery, which lies just outside the village. Near the entrance to the chapel, a simple flat gravestone testifies to their lives together—and also, in their last years, to the fact of their shared surname, Hole. Since Olivia had spent her last three decades in West Dorset as Mrs. Hole, she had at least appeared to be "married to the Man" and they "lived in the country" (two of her principal goals in life). She had no children. As Hilary Munday has observed, "A bungled attempt at divorce ruled out her greatest ambition of being a mother. She had a choice between Bill and having children and she chose Bill." She also chose to write, and in this writing she preserved a part of herself, putting on record her entanglements with history and her immersion in the challenges of living.

Appendix

Mass Observation

Mass-Observation was created in order to meet a need; and that need, in the eyes of its founders, was to overcome Britons' ignorance about themselves in their everyday lives. Given that many basic facts of social life were unknown or barely known, how could the citizens of Britain, whatever their class or status, adequately understand themselves? This ignorance was thought to be especially pronounced with regard to the beliefs and behaviour of the majority of Britons: that is, those who lacked social prominence, and who had little political or intellectual influence. It was essential, according to Mass-Observation, to study the "normal and everyday behaviour problems of our own lives, as actually lived in the houses and factories, pubs and chapels and shops of this sort of civilisation." The goal was to help establish a "science of ourselves."[1] Science had to be based on evidence, methodically and laboriously collected. As M-O's leading figures wrote early in the war, "our first job is to record and publish factual data to enable other students, in other countries and other times, to get from our work a fair objective picture of what was happening, and to use these data to fit in their own ideas and re-interpretations."[2]

In order to pursue this science, M-O recruited hundreds of volunteer "Observers." These Observers were asked to collect facts, to describe, record, sometimes count, listen, and perhaps ask questions.

These efforts at social recording were thought to be similar to those of an anthropologist in the field. Mass-Observation, with hundreds of data-collectors working in many different parts of the country, aspired to make a major contribution to social science. Initially M-O was especially interested in casting light on matters of social life that had previously been largely ignored, such as jokes, superstitions, pub-going, betting on football pools, "smoking as a social habit," and "Doing the Lambeth Walk" (a popular dance). While a persistent objective of M-O was to describe events in detail, there were other and larger goals. One of these aims, as the preface to M-O's first book declared, "is to see how, and how far, the individual is linked up with society and its institutions."[3]

Volunteers were vital to M-O. Without them, it would not have been possible to acquire most of the facts on which a "science of ourselves" was to be based. These volunteer Observers were likened to "cameras with which we are trying to photograph contemporary life. The trained Observer is ideally a camera with no distortion. They tell us not what society is like, but what it looks like to them."[4]

This acceptance of subjectivity as a legitimate dimension of social science must have been one reason why diary-keeping came to be promoted from 1939 as a promising tool of both social and self-observation. A diary was another form of recording—and it was a form that inevitably tapped into the temperaments, personalities, and inner lives of the individual diarists. The pursuit of science, then, facilitated the production of a particularly personal form of writing.

The following accounts of Mass-Observation and its work are particularly valuable: Tom Jeffery, *Mass-Observation: A Short History* (University of Sussex Library: M-O Archive Occasional Paper no. 10, 1999); Angus Calder, "Mass-Observation 1937–1949," in Martin Bulmer, ed., Essays on the History of British Sociological Research (Cambridge: Cambridge University Press, 1985), 121–36; and Dorothy Sheridan, Brian Street, and David Bloome, *Writing Ourselves: Mass-Observation and Literacy Practices* (Cresskill, NJ: Hampton Press, 2000), especially 21–38 and 79–95. The biography of one of M-O's founders, Tom Harrisson, includes much pertinent information: see Part 3 of Judith Heimann, *The Most Offending Soul Alive: Tom Harrisson and His Remarkable Life* (Honolulu: University of Hawaii Press, 1998). Easily the most knowledgeable person about Mass-Observation is the director of its Archive, Dorothy Sheridan, who has published both commentary on the Archive's holdings and helpful anthologies and editions of M-O sources. See, for example, *Speak for Yourself: A Mass-Observation Anthology 1939–1949* (Oxford: Oxford University Press, 1985), which she edited with Angus Calder, and her edited book, *Wartime Women: An Anthology of Women's Wartime Writing for Mass Observation* (London: Heinemann, 1990). Tom Harrisson himself later wrote Living through the Blitz (London: Collins, 1976), which was based on findings and testimony generated by M-O.

Notes

Preface & Introduction

1 M-O Archive, diarist no. 5182. His wife, diarist no. 5406, produced an excellent and detailed diary for the last four months of 1939; thereafter she wrote only occasionally.

2 Angus Calder and Dorothy Sheridan, *Speak for Yourself: A Mass-Observation Anthology 1939–1949* (Oxford: Oxford University Press, 1985), 151.

3 See, for instance, Charles Madge and Tom Harrisson, *Britain by Mass-Observation* (Harmondsworth: Penguin, 1939). This study predated the writing of diaries by M-O's volunteers.

4 M-O Archive, diarist no. 5396. She was writing from Tadworth, Surrey.

5 These details are found in school records in the archive of Haberdashers' Aske's Hatcham College, Jerningham Road, London SE14 7N7 (I am grateful for being allowed to examine these documents); M-O Archive, H.2160, DR for Winter 1992; and the Metropolitan Police Museum, London SW1H 0BG.

1 War in Name Only ~ October 1939–April 1940

1 The preparations for war in London, and the initial responses to the outbreak of war, are well described in Philip Ziegler, *London at War* (London: Sinclair-Stevenson, 1994), chapters 3 and 4.

2 She was probably reading *Mathematics for the Million: A Popular Self Educator,* by Lancelot Hogben, F.R.S. (London: Allen and Unwin, 1936).

3 Tom Harrisson was one of the two chief driving forces behind Mass-Observation. See Judith M. Heimann, *The Most Offending Soul Alive: Tom Harrisson and His Remarkable Life* (Honolulu: University of Hawaii Press, 1998), Part 3.

4 Lin Yutang was the author of *The Importance of Living* (1938) and other works. Olivia had mentioned in her diary for September 9th that she was reading Lin Yutang in bed before falling asleep.

5 She is referring to Arthur Askey's program *Band Waggon*, on the BBC.

6 Hitler had proposed a European conference to settle the current conflict. On October 12 Britain rejected the offer and the various implications of this German "peace offensive" (including the liquidation of Poland). See Ian Kershaw, Hitler 1936–1945: Nemesis (London: Allen Lane, 2000), 265–66.

7 Gracie Fields performed with the BBC Variety Orchestra and the Revue Chorus on Wednesday, October 11, 8:00–8:30 pm.

8 On October 14 a German submarine had sunk the old British battleship Royal Oak, which was anchored in the naval base at Scapa Flow in the Orkney Islands.

9 Dorothy Richardson (1873–1957) adopted a stream-of-consciousness approach in her multi-volume novel *Pilgrimage*, the first part of which appeared in 1915.

10 Olivia and her mother left for the United States on April 22, 1939. They stayed in and around New York City until their departure for home on June 5. Such a journey would have been most unusual at that time for members of the lower middle class. (Private papers, held by Hilary Munday.)

11 Dachshunds, which had been considered "enemy" dogs in 1914, were regarded more tolerantly in 1939. See E.S. Turner, *The Phoney War on the Home Front* (London: Michael Joseph, 1961), 114.

12 Myra Hess, the concert pianist, had launched a series of midday concerts at the National Gallery. They were designed to offer serious music to listeners who, because of the blackout, would have trouble attending evening concerts. They also afforded employment to musicians who might otherwise have been unemployed. Mollie Panter-Downes, who wrote from London for the New Yorker, described these concerts in an essay of November 24, 1939. "People pack into them daily, sitting on chairs if they are lucky and on the floor if they are not. Sandwiches can be bought for threepence each, but most of the office workers bring lunch with them and munch dreamily while listening to Bach and Schubert.... The applause at the end of the programs is tremendous and moving. People hurry out into Trafalgar Square, shouldering their gas masks and looking all the better for having been lifted for an hour to a plane where boredom and fear seem irrelevant" (Mollie Panter-Downes, *London War Notes 1939-1945*, ed. William Shawn [New York: Farrar, Strauss and Giroux, 1971], 26. See also Marian C. McKenna, *Myra Hess: A Portrait* [London: Hamish Hamilton, 1976], esp. chap. 9.)

13 Marie Stopes (1880–1958) was a sex educator, advocate of birth control, and author of various books, including *Married Love* (1918) and *Enduring Passion* (1928).

14 Diana Athill, *Instead of a Letter* (London: Chatto and Windus, 1963), 120.

15 On February 16, 1940, a British destroyer entered Norwegian waters and removed some 300 prisoners from the German transport ship *Altmark*. In early March Olivia remarked on her feelings about this naval initiative. "The Altmark incident amused and stimulated me, more as a cheeky adventure, a piece of inspired common sense, than as 'encouraging news.' I was glad that 300–400 men were rescued, glad that red tape did not,

for once, prevail; glad that so few people were killed in the game" (DR, February 1940).

16 *The Artist in the Witness Box*, with Eric Newton and Herbert Hodge, was aired between 7:40 and 8:00 pm.

17 To get to work at this time, she normally travelled from St. Johns station to Waterloo station, where she changed to another westbound train that would take her to Putney station, a short distance north of her relocated office.

18 *Housewife*, which began in February 1939, was oriented to the "modern" woman and designed to fit in a handbag. Its contents were diverse. The two issues for February and March 1940 included one short story each, along with articles on baby care and child-rearing, honey-making, jealousy between children, gardening, knitting, home decorating, the plight of British women married to enemy aliens, "Life in a Cottage," "Corns—and their cure," wise budgeting, making and keeping friends, kitchen gadgets, games for children, skin care, headaches, homemade bread, "A Housewife in the Holy Land," shoes in wartime, "Hens in Your Back-Yard," using vegetables, and "Catering for Your Family on a Rationed Budget."

19 A man in a "reserved" civilian occupation, or older than a specified age, was not liable for conscription. Given the increasing demand for military manpower in the early 1940s, call-ups of men in previously reserved positions became more and more common.

20 The English pianist, Solomon Cutner (b. 1902), did not use his surname professionally. The *Radio Times* indicates that he was to play Beethoven's *Concerto no. 2 in B flat*.

21 This issue of *US*, for March 2, 1940, included a five-page article on conscientious objectors, who comprised about 2 percent of those men who had registered thus far.

22 Olivia is referring to the "Winter War," the war between Finland and the Soviet Union. The latter had attacked the former on November 30, 1939. Declarations from Britain and France in support of Finland were merely rhetorical, as the Finns were now concluding. They signed an armistice with the Soviet Union on March 13, 1940.

23 *US*, no. 6, for March 9, 1940, had asked readers what they liked and disliked about the magazine, and what changes they would like to see (45). An analysis of the responses was printed in *US*, no. 9, for March 29, 1940 (82–84).

24 Olivia rarely mentioned religion or church. She recorded her most blunt observation in September 1939: "Find religious broadcasts physically sick making" (Wartime Directive no. 2).

25 See Keith Bell, *Stanley Spencer: A Complete Catalogue of the Paintings* (London: Phaidon Press, 1992), 456 (Bridle Path, Cookham was painted in 1938). This reproduction cost Olivia almost two weeks' wages.

26 On March 19th and 20th the RAF attacked the German North Sea air base at Hornum on the Island of Sylt near the German-Danish border. Olivia's opinion was that of a minority; most people approved of the raid (M-O Archive, FR 63).

27 The Arctic port of Petsamo, which the Soviets had captured during the Winter War, was returned to the Finns in accordance with the peace treaty in March.

2 Real War ~ June–August 1940

1 Imperial War Museum "The Second World War Diary of Miss Vivienne Hall," Ref. No. DS/MISC/88 and Con. Shelf.

2 Olivia's sister-in-law Beatrice Cockett, known as Bebe, who started writing for Mass-Observation in October 1940, spoke about this security issue in a letter to Tom Harrisson on November 12 of that year. "My husband is interested in Mass-Observation but is rather afraid of what he considers its dangerous possibilities in war-time. He thinks that it would be a fairly simple matter for an enemy agent to be on your staff and the knowledge which he could have of the people's views and wishes would be a very valuable weapon in the enemy's hands for use. We do know that the psychological factor has been used successfully by the enemy so far in this war. Please answer the query for me! It certainly seems a sensible point to raise and I only hope we can be reassured" (DR no. 2465, October 1940).

3 "The main objects" of this move to Putney, according to the short official history of the London police during the war, "were to give elbow room at the Yard for any additional activities the war might produce and to spread the risks." (H.M. Howgrave-Graham, *The Metropolitan Police at War* [London, 1947], 47.)

4 Flying Officer E.J. "Cobber" Kain was a twenty-two-year-old pilot from New Zealand who had already distinguished himself in combat and been honoured with a DFC in March. He was killed in a flying accident.

5 For Bertrand Russell's changing views on peace and war, see Ronald W. Clark, *The Life of Bertrand Russell* (New York: Knopf, 1976), 465–68.

6 *Addresses and Messages of Franklin D. Roosevelt*, U.S. Senate, 1942, 52–53.

7 J.C. Powys (much admired by Olivia) was the author of numerous books, including *In Defence of Sensuality* (1930), *A Philosophy of Solitude* (1933), and *The Art of Happiness* (1935). See also Part 3, note 20.

8 The Cockett family's bungalow was in Benfleet, just west of Southend. The entire coastal region had been declared a defence area, "and visitors, including holiday-makers, who cannot prove they are there for business or for other good reason will be told to leave" (*Southend Standard*, June 20, 1940, 6). The local civil defence authorities had the power to restrict movement into the region.

9 In his radio broadcast on Sunday, June 23rd, Priestley declared "that about Hitler and the Nazis I have always held the same opinion—the opinion that they were evil, and that the time must come when either we must destroy them or they would destroy us; they were no more to be compromised with than typhoid fever is to be compromised with." Nazism, he asserted, "is not really a political philosophy, but an attitude of mind—the expression in political life of a certain very unpleasant temperament—of the man who hates Democracy, reasonable argument, tolerance, patience and humorous

equality—the man who loves bluster and swagger, uniforms and bodyguards and fast cars, plotting in back rooms, shouting and bullying, taking it out on all the people who have made him feel inferior." Olivia almost certainly agreed with these sentiments. She may, though, have been unconvinced by his final declamation—"England will be victorious"—and perhaps, too, by a sentence that cast Britain in an especially favourable and heroic light: "If the kindness of England, of Britain, of the wide Empire forever reaching out towards new expressions of Freedom, is overwhelmed by that vast dark [Nazi] face, then we all might as well decide to leave this world, for it will not be a world worth living in." (J.B. Priestley, *Postscripts* [London: William Heinemann, 1940], 14–18.)

10 Later that year British Railways ensured that managing the lighting on trains would no longer depend on the judgement of passengers. An advertisement circulating in November, under the heading "Reduce the risk of attack on YOUR train," advised that "Trains showing lights are targets for bombs and machine-gun bullets. It is for YOUR protection that train lights are extinguished during Air Raids. There is sufficient light for reading during All-Clear periods. For your own safety please see that blinds are kept down during black-out hours. The enemy raiders have a maxim: 'Where there's light there's life'" (*Kentish Mercury*, November 29, 1940, 21).

11 Olivia had listened to *Workers' Challenge*, a German propaganda station that targeted British workers and their perceived discontents. It was noted for its use of foul language. See M.A. Doherty, *Nazi Wireless Propaganda: Lord Haw-Haw and British Public Opinion in the Second World War* (Edinburgh: Edinburgh University Press, 2000), esp. 23–24 and 74.

12 Another woman recorded in diary a similar sentiment. "In war-time there is only the present moment, and if it offers a brief Halt in Paradise, one enjoys it with intensity unknown in days of peace" (Imperial War Museum, "Journal of Phyllis Warner, September 1940–February 1942," Ref. no. 95/14/1, September 1, 1940).

13 Britain had been forced by the Italians from British Somaliland. As for the significance of this retreat (yet another in mid-1940), the *Manchester Guardian* thought that "The immediate question is whether the Italians, by acquiring a long stretch of coastline and the port of Berbera, looking towards the exit from the Red Sea into the Gulf of Aden, will be able by sea or air to impair our control of the passage from the Mediterranean to the East. That would be serious and it is that which has to be prevented" (August 20, 1940, 4).

14 These lines of poetry are from William Wordsworth, "Ode: Intimations of Immortality from Recollections of Early Childhood," lines 165–67.

15 The New Cut, renamed "The Cut" in 1936, was a shopping street with open-air market stall near Waterloo station. It was a poor neighbourhood and considered by many to be rough and grim. See Mary Benedetta, *The Street Markets of London* (London: John Miles, 1936), 61–63.

16 Mary Lee Settle, *All the Brave Promises: Memories of Aircraft Women 2nd Class 2146391* (Columbia, SC: University of South Carolina Press, 1995; 1st publ. 1966), 90.

3 Bombs, Busyness, & Hoping for Babies ~ Sept 1940–Oct 1942

1 Imperial War Museum, "Journal of Phyllis Warner, September 1940–February 1942," Ref. no. 93/14/1.
2 Vera Brittain, *Diary 1939–1945: Wartime Chronicle*, ed. Alan Bishop and Y. Aleksandra Bennett (London: Gollancz, 1989), 53.
3 Vera Brittain, *England's Hour* (London: Macmillan, 1941), 164.
4 Imperial War Museum, Ref. No. 95/8/7, "Letters of Mary Eleanor Allan to Mary Chalmers," September 9, 1940.
5 Rose Macaulay, *Letters to a Sister*, ed. Constance Babington-Smith (New York: Atheneum, 1964), 111.
6 Imperial War Museum, Gwladys Cox, "London War Diary 1939–1945," Ref. no. 86/46/1(P).
7 Imperial War Museum, "The Second World War Diary of Miss Vivienne Hall," Ref. no. DS/MISC/88 and Con. Shelf.
8 Imperial War Museum, Diana Brinton Lee, "It Happened Like This: A Housewife's Diary of the Blitz," Ref. no. P178,100, week of September 22–28.
9 *Few Eggs and No Oranges: The Diaries of Vere Hodgson 1940–45* (London: Persephone Books, 1999; first publ. 1971), 210.
10 Lewisham Local Studies Centre, "Diaries of Miss Violet Gladys Tyler," vol. 4 (Ref. A98/9).
11 Imperial War museum, Ref. no. 93/14/1.
12 Imperial War museum, Ref. no. P178, 108.
13 Rose Macaulay, *Letters to a Sister*, 112-13.
14 Imperial War Museum, Ref. no. 93/14/1.
15 *War Begins at Home*, edited by Tom Harrisson and Charles Madge and published in 1940, was based largely on the evidence collected and testimony given by M-O's observers and investigators (some full-time, others part-time) and diarists, during the last third of 1939.
16 This was the worst single incident thus far for casualties in southeast London. A later source put the death toll at thirty-seven. The raid of March 19 left at least 150 dead in southeast London, making this night the second most lethal during the entire Blitz for that part of London (after April 16). See Lewis Blake, *Red Alert: The Story of South East London at War 1939–1945* (privately printed, 1992), 82.
17 Imperial War Museum, Ref. no. 93/14/1.
18 Ibid.
19 On wartime income tax, see R.S. Sayers, *Financial Policy 1939–45* (London: HMSO, 1956), 77–79.
20 Olivia was much impressed by the now largely forgotten "primitivist" writer John Cowper Powys. She had almost certainly read his *In Defence of Sensuality* (London: Victor Gollancz, 1930), in which Powys championed a sort of "mystic-sensuousness" (153). "To philosphise," he asserted, "is to gather up all your happiest sensualities and to associate their united mystery of life and death" (186). "The world is pluralistic and full of magic; and it is a grievous mistake,

and one of the chief and most obstinate causes of man's present misery, that people have given up polytheism" (89). He thought that "when you try to analyse the contents of your deepest and most individual self,…you will find there a great deal of the primordial passivity of rocks and stones and trees, and also, at rarer moments, certain fleeting feelings that seem to connect you with the super-human" (8). (For a brief account of Powys's work see Lawrence Millman, "An Irresistible Long-winded Bore," *Atlantic Monthly*, August 2000, 88–91.)

Olivia's "Too Brief Diary" for October 1942—her last diary instalment—testified to just such a sensuous outlook. She had spent a short leave from work at a friend's farm in Sussex, "very, very happy. I am soaked to my bones in happiness in the country. I milked cows and houseworked and gathered eggs and berries and mushrooms and went errands the mile to the village, with my eyes and hands and feet filled with content. The trees and grass blessed me every moment, and the night sky covered me with love. I have never been in a place, not even [the] Lakes and Cornwall, that I loved so much. I felt bitter swords inside me when after three days I had to come back to the dirty bricks of London."

21 Olivia was referring to the experimental community health centre set up in the south London suburb of Peckham. The centre's work was described and explained in a book published in 1943 by Innes H. Pearse and Lucy H. Crockes, *The Peckham Experience: A Study in the Living Structure of Society* (London: Allen and Unwin). For an evaluation of its philosophy and practices, see Jane Lewis and Barbara Brookes, "A Reassessment of the Work of the Peckham Health Centre, 1926–1951," *Milbank Memorial Fund Quarterly*, 61, 2(1983): 307–50.

22 A *Declaration of the Rights of Man* (1940) was prepared under the chairmanship of Lord Sankey. It articulated eleven core values, including the "Right to Knowledge," the "Right to Work," "Duty to the Community," and "Protection of Minors."

Epilogue

1 In writing about Olivia Cockett's life after 1942, I am heavily dependent on the recollections and testimony of her nephew, Michael Cockett (born 1938), and her niece, Hilary Munday (born 1941). Both have been exceptionally helpful and forthcoming in answering questions and offering information and opinions, and I am very grateful to them, and to David Munday, Hilary's husband, for their opinions and co-operation. I have also benefited on several occasions from the perceptive comments and reflections of Olivia's great-niece, Danielle Blyfield (born 1963, daughter of Michael). The documentary sources that I have drawn on in composing this epilogue are mainly Olivia's letters and responses to questionnaires from the Mass-Observation Archive between 1989 and 1995, held in the Mass-Observation Archive at the University of Sussex (file no. H.2160); and various personal papers that Hilary Munday inherited from her aunt and that remain in her possession. Dorothy Sheridan,

head of Special Collections and director of the Mass-Observation Archive at
the University of Sussex, provided timely and generous assistance in the use
of the postwar papers held in the Mass-Observation Archive.

2 Public Record Office, Kew, Work 45/25, "Memoranda of Chief Licensing
Officers 1942–46," memorandum of May 17, 1946 regarding the reorganiza-
tion of HQ staff.

3 "Supplement to the *London Gazette* of Tuesday, December 29, 1964," 11.

Appendix

1 Charles Madge and Tom Harrisson, *Britain, by Mass-Observation* (London:
Penguin, 1939), 231 and 225.

2 Tom Harrisson and Charles Madge, *War Begins at Home, by Mass Observation*
(London: Chatto and Windus, 1940), 24.

3 *May the Twelfth: Mass-Observation's Day-Surveys 1937*, edited by Humphrey
Jennings and Charles Madge (London: Faber and Faber, 1937), v.

4 Charles Madge and Tom Harrisson, eds., *First Year's Work, 1937 38, by Mass-
Observation* (London: Lindsay Drummond, 1938), 66.

Illustrations